Ronald Reagan

Jules Tygiel

San Francisco State University

Ronald Reagan

and the Triumph of American Conservatism

Second Edition

THE LIBRARY OF AMERICAN BIOGRAPHY

Edited by Mark C. Carnes

New York   Boston   San Francisco
London   Toronto   Sydney   Tokyo   Singapore   Madrid
Mexico City   Munich   Paris   Cape Town   Hong Kong   Montreal

Executive Editor: Michael Boezi
Executive Marketing Manager: Sue Westmoreland
Production Coordinator: Virginia Riker
Text Design and Electronic Page Makeup: Alison Barth Burgoyne
Cover Designer/Manager: John Callahan
Cover Illustration/Photo: ©SuperStock, Inc.
Manufacturing Buyer: Roy L. Pickering, Jr.
Printer and Binder: Courier Corporation
Cover Printer: Coral Graphics

Library of Congress Cataloging-in-Publication Data

Tygiel, Jules.
    Ronald Reagan and the triumph of American conservatism / Jules
Tygiel. — 2nd ed.
        p. cm. — (The library of American biography)
    Includes bibliographical references and index.
    ISBN 0-536-12543-0
    1. Reagan, Ronald. 2. Presidents—United States—Biography.
3. United States—Politics and government—1981–1989. 4. Conservatism—United States. I. Title. II. Series: Library of American biography (New York, N.Y.)

E877.T94 2006
973.927092—dc22   2005033094

Visit us at www.ablongman.com

ISBN 0-536-12543-0

9 10 11 12—V013—15 14 13 12

Contents

Editor's Preface		vii
Author's Preface		ix
Introduction		xi
1	A Midwestern Boyhood	1
2	Surviving the Great Depression	15
3	The Making of a Hollywood Star	35
4	Fighting the Cold War	57
5	The Shift to Conservatism	81
6	Entering Politics	99
7	From Governor to President	119
8	"Stay the Course": The Reagan Presidency: 1981–1982	145
9	The Road to Reelection: The Reagan Presidency: 1983–1984	171
10	The Reagan Doctrine: The Reagan Presidency: 1985–1986	191
11	Scandals and Summits: The Reagan Presidency: 1987–1988	213
12	Legacy	235
Study and Discussion Questions		257
A Note on the Sources		263
Index		267

Editor's Preface

Few public figures have had a sunnier personality than Ronald Reagan. Minutes after being seriously wounded in an assassination attempt, Reagan said to his wife: "Honey, I forgot to duck." While being wheeled into the operating room, he quipped to the surgeons, "I hope you are all Republicans." It was one of the great strengths of his personality and thus his presidency.

Reagan's amiable personality made him popular with voters; he won his campaigns by huge margins. In this way he resembled Franklin D. Roosevelt, another president who translated his popularity into political power: They both took office in times of economic crisis and foreign threat; when they departed the presidency, the nation's economic woes had receded and its chief enemies had been vanquished.

FDR and Reagan, arguably, were the two most important presidents of the twentieth-century, but their legacies differed sharply. FDR laid the foundations for the postwar welfare state; it was a jerry-built affair, of which FDR was less architect than its chief contractor. Reagan's chief domestic initiative, on the other hand, dealt mostly with taxes and economics, while he vigorously attacked the regulatory state.

Jules Tygiel, author of this biography, explains how Reagan energized a near-moribund conservative movement and translated several simple concepts into a political revolution. Tygiel brings to the task a scholarly interest in the social and cultural history of twentieth-century California. In many ways, California seems to anticipate trends elsewhere in the nation; Reagan's rise in California prefigured his successful candidacies for the presidency.

Reagan's success, moreover, must be understood as a cultural as well as political phenomenon. Tygiel, again, is well-positioned to assess such matters. The author of majors work on baseball and American culture, Tygiel puts his skills as a cultural analyst to bear on Reagan. "Few institutions in American life reveal as much about the evolution of our society as baseball," Tygiel explains. "Similarly, perhaps no single career captures the scope and depth of change during the past century as much as that of Ronald Reagan, who, coincidentally, first gained public attention as a regional baseball broadcaster and by the time of his death in 2004 had become a national icon."

Tygiel's fine, concise biography is a superb introduction to an intriguing personality, powerful political leader, and enduring national icon.

Mark C. Carnes

Author's Preface

Since this book was derived exclusively from secondary sources, I do not have the usual lengthy list of archives, libraries, and librarians to acknowledge. On the other hand, colleagues, friends, and family did their usual yeoman service in reading this manuscript and offering suggestions. Tony D'Agostino, Bob Cherny, Peter Carroll, and Mike Kazin all read sections or the entirety of the manuscript, frequently saving me from myself. Luise Custer, with whom I wrangle through life, not only critiqued each chapter, but lovingly wrangled over the introduction with me until I got it right. At Longman, I am grateful to Jay O'Callaghan, who honored me with the invitation to contribute to the venerable Library of American Biography series, and Priscilla McGeehon, who approved the Reagan project. Roger Bromert, Southwestern Oklahoma State University, Leslie Heaphy, Kent State-Stark Campus, Jonathan Lee, San Antonio College, Michael V. Namorato, University of Mississippi, and David L. Snead, Liberty University, offered valuable commentary as readers for Longman.

The first edition of this book appeared the same week that Ronald Reagan died. This second edition includes sections on Reagan's passing and funeral and how these events renewed the debates in the nation over the former President's legacy Since the Library of American Biography series does not include footnotes or citations, readers may find a detailed annotation of my sources on my Web site: http://bss.sfsu.edu/~tygiel.

JULES TYGIEL

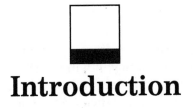

Introduction

On December 13, 1979, when Ronald Reagan announced his intention to run for president of the United States, he offered a brief biography. "I've seen America from the stadium press box as a sportscaster, as an actor, officer of my labor union, soldier, office holder, and as both Democrat and Republican," he proclaimed. "There have been four wars in my lifetime and I've seen our country face financial ruin in the Depression. I have also seen the great strength of this nation as it pulled itself up from that ruin to become the dominant force in the world." Over the next decade, Reagan would add substantially to this already impressive resumé. He was twice elected president of the United States, survived an assassination attempt, overhauled the nation's tax structure, restored for many Americans a sense of national pride, and presided over the end of the Cold War. Moreover, he established a near-moribund political conservatism as a viable, if not dominant, American ideology. Among American political figures in the twentieth century, only Franklin Delano Roosevelt, whose 1930s New Deal reforms reshaped the American scene for succeeding generations, matches or exceeds the influence of the movie star who became president.

The life of Ronald Reagan in many ways personifies the twentieth-century American experience. Born in 1911 and still alive at the century's end, Reagan, as biographer Garry Wills observes, "spans our lives culturally and chronologically." He was the son of a hard-drinking,

Irish-Catholic father and devout prohibitionist Protestant mother. His Midwestern youth in the 1910s and 1920s reflected the nation's cultural conflicts during those decades. As a young man, he faced the uncertainties and privations of the Great Depression and embraced the liberal political philosophies of Franklin Roosevelt's New Deal. Reagan appeared prominently in the twentieth-century media revolutions that reshaped the nation. During the formative years of the radio industry, Reagan became a well-known sportscaster in the Midwest. He boldly abandoned that regional celebrity to gamble on a career as an actor in Hollywood and emerged as one of the highest-paid film stars. When his movie career faltered in the 1950s, he advanced into the new world of television, establishing himself as one of America's most recognized personalities.

Throughout his life Reagan always evinced a strong interest in politics and public affairs. In the 1930s and through World War II, he adhered to his father's Democratic political beliefs and even dabbled with more radical ideas. During World War II, although Reagan was exempt from combat service because of poor eyesight, he served in the "Celluloid Commandos," an innovative propaganda wing of the war effort. At the war's end he grew increasingly active in the Screen Actors Guild. Amid the Cold War-inspired battles to drive communists out of the film industry, his politics gradually shifted to the right. In the late 1940s and early 1950s, Reagan became a symbol of anti-communism in Hollywood, a key figure in the politics of the blacklist during the McCarthy era.

Even as he pursued his acting career, Reagan's passions drifted more and more into politics. In the 1950s, as a television host and spokesperson for General Electric, a company whose appliances represented the promise of progress and consumerism, Reagan embodied American postwar affluence. He traveled throughout the nation speaking on behalf of General Electric, polishing his presentation style and political message. During these years an ardent conservatism comprised of strident anti-communism, defense of free enterprise, and broad critiques of government replaced the liberal politics of his earlier years. By the early 1960s, in a nation dominated by the liberalism of Presidents John F. Kennedy and Lyndon Johnson, Reagan had become a familiar figure on the far reaches of the unpopular and often-ridiculed political right.

Reagan attracted national attention in a speech in support of presidential candidate Barry Goldwater in the 1964 Republican campaign. Two years later he won the party's nomination for governor of California. His campaign became a landmark of modern politics. Reagan came to personify the backlash against civil rights, anti-war, and student protest, easily swamping the Democratic incumbent at the polls. In a decade mainly recalled for radical protests and countercultural challenges to authority, Reagan emerged as one of the prime political beneficiaries of the unrest and uncertainty. He clashed with radical militants on college campuses and in the African-American community, while preaching a doctrine of low taxes, less welfare, and smaller government. These issues, underpinned by a strident anti-communism, became the clarion calls of a resurgent conservative movement.

Reagan left the California governorship in 1975. For the remainder of the decade, in weekly radio shows and campaigns for the presidency in 1976 and 1980, he expressed the growing American frustration with a weakening economy and the general malaise that seemed to have gripped the nation in the aftermath of the Vietnam War and Watergate scandal. He embraced both the rising political influence of evangelical Christians, who had mobilized for political action in the Religious Right, and the burgeoning "tax revolt" among American voters. In his speeches, he fused these movements to the demands of a more traditional ideological economic conservatism. At the age of almost 70, when most Americans have retired, Reagan assumed the presidency, becoming the oldest man to ever hold that office.

In the 1980s Reagan no longer reflected the American experience—he defined it. He launched what supporters would call the Reagan Revolution, a revamping of American domestic and foreign policy. At home he proposed a new "Reaganomics" as the key to economic growth, pushing through major tax cuts and massive increases in defense spending, risking the consequences of rising deficits. In foreign affairs his administration adopted a more aggressive stance toward the Soviet Union than any of his Cold War predecessors, seeking not merely to contain the spread of communism, but to defeat it, and even to vanquish the Soviet Union itself.

In both the domestic and foreign spheres, political observers and historians still debate to what extent Reagan's policies actually caused the momentous events of his presidency and how beneficial the outcomes of his initiatives truly were. Critics note that the nation's economic health plummeted during Reagan's early years in office, causing widespread unemployment, dislocation, and suffering. To fund his tax cuts and defense buildup, the United States amassed unprecedented budget deficits. Corruption and abuses of power ran rampant in his administration and the broader society. Deregulation triggered wasteful speculation and scandals in the savings and loan industry, costing the nation's taxpayers upwards of a trillion dollars. Nonetheless, as his defenders argue, his policies successfully tamed the inflation that had weakened the economy in the 1970s, leading to economic growth and relative prosperity during the latter years of the Reagan regime.

Reagan's foreign policy also left a disputed legacy. The Reagan years witnessed historic breakthroughs in arms control negotiations and the developments that led to the demise of the Soviet Union and the end of the Cold War. But many people challenge the significance of Reagan's role in achieving these results. Furthermore, they question the Reagan Administration's use of covert activities, some of dubious legality, to advance its anti-communist goals in places like Nicaragua and Afghanistan and its support of brutally repressive and anti-democratic forces in many nations. These policies would come to haunt the United States in the succeeding decade and the post-September 11, 2001, world.

Historians similarly struggle to come to grips with Reagan's enigmatic personality. Given the diversity of his experiences and the contradictions inherent in his nature, capturing the essence of Ronald Reagan has never been easy. Supporters and critics alike marveled at how a man so limited in many obvious respects, so able to believe in illusions at odds with reality, could have achieved so much. In the years since Reagan rose to political prominence, historians, biographers, and other commentators have wrestled with the inconsistencies of his character. Many resort to paradoxical descriptions to explain him. Reporter Lou Cannon, who covered Reagan in Sacramento when he was governor and later in Washington, D.C., writes that Reagan had "the courage and the ignorance to ignore the collective wisdom of the experts and follow his own counsel when he was convinced he was on the right course." Conservative commentator Dinesh D'Souza begins his laudatory biography of Reagan with a chapter titled "The Wise Men and the Dummy," in which an outwardly simple Reagan proves more sage than the presumed authorities.

When Edmund Morris, a Pulitzer Prize-winning author, was named Reagan's authorized biographer, he gained unprecedented access to the president. After months of contact, he discovered that Reagan was "the most public yet most private of men," "a man of benign remoteness and no psychological curiosity," and a glacier, "possessed of no inner warmth, with no apparent interest save in its own growth." Unable to fathom Reagan's inner depths (or even discover if he had any), Morris resorted to the unusual biographical strategy of inserting himself, the author, as a fictional character into the narrative in an attempt to explain Reagan's illusive reality.

Another difficulty in understanding the unique career and persona of Ronald Reagan is that the dots in the lines of his life do not always connect. He was reared according to the tenets of his mother's strict Disciples of Christ faith, maintained a strong belief in God, and courted and won the support of Christian evangelicals. But he generally eschewed organized religion, attended church irregularly, and steered away from moral controversies that might undermine his broader political base. Although many people have tried to find roots for his political beliefs in the movies he starred in, this seems as helpful as using a divining rod, a hit-or-miss proposition that strikes dry holes more often than water. His crucial transition from leftist liberalism to arch-conservatism in the 1950s seems strikingly abrupt and difficult to reconcile. His rightward plunge precedes and anticipates that of the rest of the nation, reaching extremes that would have rendered him unelectable if left unrestrained. Yet he managed to transform himself into a candidate wildly popular with mainstream American voters.

To the end of his career Reagan portrayed and regarded himself as an outsider: an actor and citizen drawn into the political arena to restrain runaway government, reestablish the nation's founding values, and ward off the threat of communism. This was "his most remarkable self-deception," writes Cannon. For a quarter of a century and more, Reagan was not merely a practicing politician, but a masterful one, the nation's consummate practitioner of the art. He ran seriously for public office five times and emerged victorious on four of those occasions.

The true measure of Reagan's impact, however, is the extent to which Americans in the twenty-first century live in a world that he first envisioned and then, as much as any other individual, brought forth. For better or worse, the United States in the twenty-first century is a far more politically conservative, individualistic, and militarily dominant nation than it was when Ronald Reagan formally entered the political arena in 1966. His commanding, if at times quixotic, imprint looms over us all.

Ronald Reagan

1

A Midwestern Boyhoo

In late spring 1922, Ronald Reagan found a model
guide his life. Reagan had recently celebrated his 11
birthday. An avid reader, usually drawn to boyhood a
venture stories, young Ronald became enamored of an in
spirational novel written by Harold Bell Wright, a
author affiliated with the Disciples of Christ or Christian
Church attended by Reagan and his mother, Nelle. The
book was titled *That Printer of Udell's: A Story of the
Midwest* and it told the uplifting tale of Dick Falkner,
who rose from a childhood of poverty and the disgrace of
an alcoholic father to a life of respect and public service.

The prologue of *That Printer of Udell's* depicts Dick as
a boy at his mother's deathbed, his drunken father hope-
lessly sprawled on the floor of their cabin. The scene
quickly shifts to a midwestern town 16 years later, where
Dick, a young man, agnostic, trained as a printer, searches
for work. He finds employment with George Udell, a pub-
lisher, and becomes an accomplished craftsman. Although
not yet a true believer, Falkner begins to attend the Christian Church, where he impresses people with his good
looks, charm, and eloquence. As night manager of the
church reading room, Dick lures the young away from the
temptations of the saloon and urban underworld. Startled
when he discovers the body of a homeless man in the snow,
Falkner develops a plan to aid the city's impoverished

residents. He calls upon the wealthiest men in the city to construct a lumberyard, complete with a dormitory, where unemployed workers might work and reside until they could fend for themselves. As he pitches his plan to the townspeople, Falkner discovers a talent for oratory and basks in the applause of his listeners. The scheme succeeds, and Dick, having discovered the meaning of Christianity, joins the Disciples of Christ Church, marries the girl of his dreams, becomes a leading figure in the town, wins election to Congress, and, as the book ends, prepares to leave for Washington, D.C., to enter "a field of wider usefulness."

In later years Ronald Reagan would attribute his emergence as "a practical Christian" to *That Printer of Udell's*. Upon finishing the story of Dick Falkner, Ronald told his mother, "I want to be like that man." A few days later he announced that he wished to be baptized in the Disciples of Christ Church and persuaded his older brother, Neil, to join him. On June 21, 1922, the two boys, dressed in bathing suits, experienced immersion and baptism and became members of the newly built First Christian Church in Dixon, Illinois. Their father, Jack, a Catholic, was not in attendance. Neil would prove a less than apt Disciple, defying its restrictions on drinking and converting to his father's religion at the age of 18. Ronald, however, would retain the faith of his mother. And, in the tale of Dick Falkner, he had discovered a parable that would uncannily presage his own rise. In this world charm, commitment, and eloquence could raise a midwestern boy of modest means to professional success, a political career, and perhaps even the presidency of the United States.

Harold Bell Wright's morality tale captivated Reagan at age 11 not just for its overt inspirational value, but because of developments in Ronald's own life. He had recently celebrated his first anniversary of residence in Dixon, after a decade of itinerancy that had seen his family living in six different cities in six years. Setting down roots at long last

had injected an element of stability into the Reagans' life. But Ronald also had in the preceding months become more aware of his own family "curse," one that he shared with the fictional Falkner. One winter evening, Ronald arrived home to find his father lying drunk on the porch of their home. "I felt myself fill with grief for my father and at the same time I was feeling sorry for myself," Reagan later described the scene. "I bent over him, smelling the sharp odor from the speakeasy. I got a fistful of his overcoat. Opening the door, I managed to get him inside and drag him to bed." Ronald had already known of his father's "weakness," as he called it, but had never before been directly confronted with it.

The tension created by the struggle between his pious, Protestant mother and alcoholic, lapsed Catholic father mirrored the ethnic conflicts roiling the United States in the 1920s. The decade witnessed a sharp upsurge of fundamentalist Protestantism which, in its most extreme form, was manifested in the rise of the Ku Klux Klan and a sharp anti-Catholic bias. Debates over prohibition rent the nation. These divisions defined the Reagan household and shaped Ronald's childhood. His mother, born Nelle Wilson, had been reared on a farm in rural Illinois in a family that observed the Sabbath and abstained from drinking alcohol. The Wilsons moved to nearby Fulton, Illinois, when she was a teenager. Nelle, "a frustrated actress," according to her son, enjoyed dancing and performing, often giving readings at church. Sometime near her 20th birthday, she went to work at J.W. Broadhead's Dry Goods store, where she met Jack Reagan.

Jack's background diverged dramatically from Nelle's staid, respectable upbringing. Jack was born in Fulton, one of three children of Irish Catholic parents. When he was 6, his mother and father died of tuberculosis within six days of each other, and Jack's family determined he should live with an aunt and uncle in Bennett, Iowa. He dropped out of school at age 12 and went to work full-time in his uncle's general store, the first of a succession of jobs as a commercial clerk and salesman. At 16 he returned to Fulton and took a job at Broadhead's. During the ensuing years, both he and his brother, William, earned reputations as heavy drinkers. Despite their obvious differences, Jack charmed Nelle with his good looks, exuberance, and storytelling charm. They both enjoyed dancing. Although her father disapproved of Jack, Nelle and Jack, both 21 years of age, married in the local Catholic Church in November 1904.

In 1906, the Reagans moved 26 miles to Tampico, Illinois, where Jack took a job at H.C. Pitney's General Store, the leading emporium in the region, heading up the clothing and shoe department. Two years later, Neil, their first child, was born. At Jack's insistence, Neil was baptized a Catholic. After Neil's birth, however, Nelle became increasingly attracted to the teachings of the local Disciples of Christ Church, a perfectionist denomination with strong prohibitionist and anti-Catholic tendencies. The Disciples also forbade dancing, one of Nelle's favorite activities. On Easter Sunday, 1910, she accepted baptism as a Disciple. Shortly thereafter she became pregnant, and on February 5, 1911, after 24 hours of labor against the backdrop of a raging blizzard, Nelle gave birth to Ronald. Unlike Neil, Ronald would not be baptized at birth. The Disciples did not believe in infant baptism, and the more intensely devout Nelle refused to baptize her second son a Catholic.

The Reagans remained in Tampico until 1914. Nelle became increasingly involved in the church, attending prayer meetings on Wednesdays and Sundays and often visiting church members in need of care or assistance. Jack continued to work at Pitney's and also held a variety of local posts—councilman, assistant fire chief, and baseball team manager. Although he did not attend Catholic services, he served as finance chairman of St. Mary's ve the general store and a possible partnership. The World War I recession rendered this a dubious propo- . In September 1920 Pitney closed the store, and in mber the two men moved their families 25 miles heast to the larger community of Dixon, where they ned the Fashion Boot Shop, which Jack would manage , according to the plan, gradually purchase from Pitney. e Reagans had more or less settled down. They moved e more times within the confines of Dixon, but the mall industrial town of ten thousand remained their ome in the 1920s and 1930s.

Jack's alcoholism remained a problem. He was not an abusive drunk, nor did his drinking prevent him from performing his job. Nonetheless, his "weakness" caused numerous problems for the family. "Sometimes my father simply disappeared and didn't come home for days," related Ronald, "and sometimes when he did return, my brother and I would hear some pretty fiery arguments." Money that might otherwise be spent on family needs or invested toward the purchase of the Fashion Boot Shop went instead to buy intoxicating beverages. Prohibition became the law of the land in 1920, but speakeasies slaked the thirst of the working-class Dixon population, and liquor could also be acquired at Bootleggers' Knob along the Rock River. Nelle, a devoted prohibitionist, nonetheless forgave Jack his binges and urged her sons to be tolerant of their father's condition. According to Ronald, "My mother would pray constantly for him, she was on her knees several times a day." She remained optimistic that Jack would ultimately overcome his affliction.

Nelle received her main solace and salvation from religion. People who lived in Tampico and Dixon often described her as a saintly figure. "She was always there when anyone needed her," recalled a neighbor. She visited the residents at the state hospital, distributed Bibles to inmates at the local jail, and prayed at the bedside of those

Church and belonged to the Knigl
Tampico was a "dry" city moderated
periodically departed to Chicago on "k
his thirst. Both Nelle and Jack participat
group called the Opera House and starr
productions. Jack also appeared as a blacki

Life in Tampico seemed comfortable, if i
The Reagans lived in a relatively large rent
in 1913, Jack bought the family's first car, a l
Jack, realizing his limited prospects in the i
restless. In January 1915, shortly before Rona.
birthday, the family moved to Chicago. Jack jc
shoe department staff at the Fair Store, a massi
story complex that billed itself as the biggest depa
store in the world. Chicago, however, offered far too
temptations for a man with Jack's predilections. *
eight months, Jack's arrest for public drunkenness, a
dismissal from the Fair Store, forced the Reagans to pa
up and move to Galesburg, Illinois.

The stability of Tampico behind them, the Reagans
now became itinerants, moving regularly from one small
Illinois town to another, driven by Jack's ambitions or
drinking problems. In 1918 they moved to Monmouth, reportedly after Jack was fired for drunkenness in Galesburg.
In 1919 they returned to Tampico and J.C. Pitney's, where
Jack became store manager. During this odyssey, Ronald
and Neil attended four different schools in four years. The
family no longer lived in a house, but in a series of small
rented apartments. Some, like one in Tampico, had no in-
door toilet. In Monmouth, Galesburg, and Tampico, Jack
worked in the largest general store, increasingly specializing
in shoe sales. At one point he took a correspondence course
in the field, prompting the *Tampico Tornado* to herald him
as "a graduate of the American School of Practipedics."

Jack had returned to Tampico in 1919, after receiving
promises from his former boss, J.C. Pitney, of a flat to live

who fell ill. Nelle even developed a reputation as a faith healer. "It was the way she prayed, down on her knees, eyes raised up and speaking like she knew God personally, like she had lots of dealings with him before," explained one believer. At the church, she taught Sunday school and gave Bible readings in a rich, mellifluous voice. She also gave dramatic readings and wrote religious poems and plays, including a temperance drama performed at the church.

In the Reagan household, the two boys were torn between the poles represented by their parents. Neil was always his father's son—athletic, extroverted, mischievous, and often irresponsible. As a teen he also embraced his father's passion for alcohol. Though both boys had always attended church with their mother, and Neil had accepted baptism in the Christian Church along with Ronald, Neil ultimately opted for his father's faith. Ronald, on the other hand, favored his mother in most respects. He was less outgoing than Neil and more introspective. He loved to watch Nelle when she gave her dramatic readings and often appeared in the plays she wrote. At age 9 he recited renditions of "About Mother" and "The Sad Dollar and the Glad Dollar" at the church. At 11, he accompanied her to the Dixon State Hospital, where, according to the local newspaper, they "entertained the patients with a short and enjoyable program," Nelle playing the banjo and Ronald presenting two readings. Unlike Neil, Ronald's life revolved around the church, especially after Ben Cleaver became the minister. From the Disciples Ronald absorbed their optimistic outlook and belief in progress, as well as their view that the United States represented a "City on a Hill," a model community of God's grace that other peoples might emulate. Furthermore, Reverend Cleaver offered an alternative father figure for Ronald, who spent a great deal of time in Cleaver's home. In his teen years, Ronald began dating Cleaver's daughter, Margaret.

In Dixon everyone but their mother called the two boys by their nicknames. Friends dubbed Neil Moon, after the cartoon character Moon Mullins. Since Jack had always referred to the infant Ronald as his "fat little Dutchman," Ronald became Dutch. Both young Reagans loved sports. Neil, more broadly built, was the better athlete, but Ronald had the greater passion for athletics. Because of poor eyesight, he lacked the ability to hit or field a baseball. He threw himself instead into football, where he could more easily identify his opponents by the color of their shirts and thrust his scrawny body with abandon into the fray. He also took up swimming at the YMCA, an activity requiring no distance vision. Reagan instantly displayed a sharp aptitude for the sport.

Despite the disadvantage of frequently changing schools during his formative years, Ronald performed well in the classroom. Although two years younger than Neil, Ronald, who skipped a grade during the family's travels, was only a year behind him in school. While he could barely read the blackboard, even sitting in the front row, Ronald possessed a photographic memory for things he read and heard and used this gift to great effect in his studies. Neither Ronald nor his parents suspected the severity of his nearsightedness until a Sunday car trip, shortly after he turned 13. Unable to read the signs along the road, Ronald tried on his mother's glasses, revealing a new, more sharply focused world. Equipped with his own spectacles, albeit ugly, huge black-rimmed ones that he grew to hate, Ronald could now overcome the vision problems that had plagued him as a child. He also could better enjoy the movies that the family went to every Friday night and the Saturday matinees that he attended whenever he could raise the dime for admission.

In high school, Reagan excelled more in the realm of extracurricular activities than in the classroom. He maintained a low-B average, but participated in an unending stream of sports and clubs. He played on the varsity football and basketball teams, served as art editor for the *Dixonian*, the school annual, and became vice-president of the Boys' Hi-Y (a moral uplift group) and president of the senior class. Ronald also joined the Dramatic Club, where, with girlfriend Margaret Cleaver, he starred in *You and I* and other plays. He seemed a natural on the stage. "He possessed a sense of presence . . . a sense of reality. He fit into any kind of role you put him in," recalled the club's faculty adviser. Ronald and Margaret were the school's model couple—she the top student, he, arguably the most popular boy. Most people in the church and town assumed they would eventually marry.

During high school, Ronald also demonstrated his first inclinations as a writer. He wrote a series of sketches describing life in Dixon. In "School Spirit," written when he was 16, he sanctimoniously reprimanded those who failed to take the school song seriously. Another piece, "This Younger Generation," satirized unruly teenage antics at the Dixon Family Theater. His article titled "Gethsemane," about a talented football player who quit on his teammates, only to realize the error of his ways in an inspiring final game, appeared in the *Dixonian*. A poem called "Life" advised, "We make our life a struggle, when life should be a song." Reagan's high school writings were uplifting, yet conventional in their wisdom and conformist and unquestioning of traditional mores. He had begun, however, to acquire the ability to put his thoughts on paper, a talent that would serve him well in later years.

Jack Reagan appears to have given minimal support for any of Ronald's interests. While he might pal around with his sons at times, the discipline in the household came from Nelle. And although Neil was a high school football star and Ronald an athlete and actor, Jack rarely attended their extracurricular events. He spent most of his time managing the Fashion Boot Shop. The economic prosperity of the 1920s that roared in other parts of the nation barely growled in Dixon. The Midwest farm belt never really recovered from the post-World War recession of 1920–1921. Wheat prices remained low, forcing foreclosures and reducing the buying power of farmers in the surrounding regions. The Fashion Boot Shop, despite Jack's reputation, as described in the local paper as "an experienced shoe man and . . . graduate orthopedist [who] understands all foot troubles and the correct methods for all foot discomforts," proved profitable, but not lucrative. Keeping up with the innovations of the day, Jack brought in an X-ray machine for more accurate fittings. Nonetheless, he made little progress in making payments toward the purchase of the store, and the family's moves to progressively smaller lodgings illustrated their struggling economic status. For a time the boys slept on an enclosed porch attached to a small rented house. The Reagans were by no means impoverished, but once money was paid for basic expenses, Nelle's tithes to the church, and Jack's need for alcohol, little remained for luxuries of any sort.

Jack seems not to have engaged in the types of civic activities that he had partaken of during his younger years, but he retained a strong interest in politics, particularly those issues involving the culture wars of the era. Despite the Republican ascendancy in national and local politics, Jack remained a staunch Democrat and active party worker, opposed to Prohibition and appalled by the anti-Catholicism of the insurgent Ku Klux Klan. When the movie *Birth of a Nation* came to Dixon, Jack barred Neil and Ronald from attending because of its glorification of the Klan. On another occasion, Ronald remembered his father bypassing a hotel because it did not cater to Jews. When drunk, he might rail against the rapacity of big business. In the 1928 election, he campaigned ardently for Al Smith, the first serious Catholic contender for the presidency, a "wet" candidate pledged to the termination of

Prohibition. Banners touting Smith's candidacy flowed from the Reagan automobile. Nelle's preferences have gone unrecorded.

Like most boys of their era and social standing, Ronald and Neil worked at summer jobs to supplement the family income. They caddied at the country club and on another occasion enlisted as roustabouts when the Ringling Brothers Circus arrived. When he was 14, Ronald worked for a contractor, swinging a pick to clear a construction site. He found his greatest fulfillment and sense of identity, however, in his role as a lifeguard at Lowell Park, a position that he held for six years, starting at age 16.

Lowell Park stood along the Rock River, which ran through Dixon. Its hazardous currents posed a threat to unwary swimmers. Ed and Ruth Graybill, who owned the concession for the bathing area along the river, hired Ronald, a graduate of a Red Cross lifesaving course at the YMCA, to protect their patrons. The job was a demanding one, requiring a strong sense of responsibility. His day began at 10 A.M., when he picked up Mrs. Graybill and drove her van to gather supplies, including a 300-pound block of ice, for the food stand. At the river he broke up the ice into three 100-pound blocks before starting his work as lifeguard. Once on the stand, he had full responsibility for the safety of the swimmers. On the long days of the summer he would remain on duty until 10 P.M. For the twelve-hours-a-day, seven-days-a-week job, he received from $15 to 18 a week and all the food he could eat at the concession stand. In many years he supplemented this income by giving swimming lessons.

Ronald's performance as a lifeguard won him a measure of acclaim and celebrity throughout Dixon. Early on, his father had suggested that he carve a notch on a log for every rescue. As the years passed, people counted the notches in admiration. The local newspaper first took notice of his exploits on August 3, 1928, during his second summer on the job, under the headline, "Pulled From the Jaws of Death." The story depicted how Ronald had pulled a man out of the river after dark, after another potential rescuer had failed. The swimmer had ducked under the water once before Reagan reached him, pulled him to shore, applied artificial respiration, and revived him. The rescue, reported the newspaper, was Ronald's twenty-fifth in two years. In 1931, he again appeared on the front page on the occasion of his 51st rescue. Although most of the rescues were not as dramatic or perilous as the 1928 episode, during his six-year stint, working without any assistance, he recorded 77 notches on his log.

Being a lifeguard offered numerous satisfactions for the teen-aged Reagan. It enabled him to display his skills as a diver and swimmer, the only sports in which he truly excelled. In 1928 he set a record for the annual cross-river swim. Girls swarmed around him admiringly, and he became a local hero. As a lifeguard, he served his community and demonstrated the responsibility, maturity, and authority necessary for his transition to adulthood. Several of his writings focused around his job at the river, illustrating how it increasingly defined his self-image. In his high school yearbook, Ronald offered the "Meditations of a Lifeguard." Another article described a fictional "Bus Burke, Lifeguard." In a third piece, written in 1929, he reflected, "LIFE GUARD, the title held infinite possibilities of approach." Reagan relished his summers at Lowell Park. "You know why I had such fun at it?" he later confessed. "Because I was the only one up there on the guard stand. It was like a stage. Everyone had to look up at me." And Reagan clearly enjoyed the attention of this audience.

Ronald graduated from high school in 1928. Neil had left school after graduation and gone to work at the Medusa Cement Plant in Dixon. Ronald, however, encouraged by his mother, wanted to attend college. He set his sites on Eureka College, a Disciples of Christ institution

Dutch Reagan as a lifeguard, Lowell Park Beach in Dixon, Illinois, 1932. (Courtesy Ronald Reagan Library)

100 miles south of Dixon. His girlfriend, Margaret Cleaver, had also decided to attend Eureka, providing an added inducement. Thus, in September 1928, after his second summer of lifeguarding, Reagan departed Dixon. Other than the family's ill-fated sojourn in Chicago, this marked his furthest journey from his birthplace in Tampico. He returned to Dixon for summers and to visit his parents, but for all intents and purposes, his boyhood had ended.

In his autobiography, Reagan referred to these formative years as "one of those rare Huck Finn-Tom Sawyer idylls." Although the notion of an "idyll" reflects a fundamental misreading of Mark Twain's classic works, what Reagan meant to convey was a childhood of carefree innocence. That Reagan could draw this meaning from his own experiences illustrates how well he had navigated the shoals of the challenging Rock River posed by his own childhood. The Protestant-Catholic conflict that raged in the nation and in his own home had left him seemingly unscathed. The family's early itinerancy and economic struggles had produced not a sense of despair, but rather an ethic of ambition, hard work, and responsibility. From his father he had taken a love of sports and storytelling, but, unlike his brother, none of the baggage, neither habitual nor psychological, of his alcoholism. From his mother, he had acquired a deep sense of faith, propriety, service to others, the joy of performance, and a boundless optimism. These attributes would serve him in good stead as he embarked, as had Dick Falkner, into "a wider world of usefulness."

2

Surviving the Great Depression

Ronald Reagan arrived at Eureka College in September 1928. The Great Depression would not officially begin for another year, but the already declining economy in the rural Midwest dogged Reagan's college years from the outset. The nation's economic collapse would shape the contours of his higher educational experience, affecting Eureka College, Reagan's family, and his political outlook. Yet, by 1933, even as Franklin Roosevelt assumed the presidency and launched his New Deal, Reagan had already overcome unemployment, embarked on his profession in entertainment, and triumphed over economic adversity. By 1937, as Roosevelt began his second term, Reagan was en route to Hollywood and a career as a movie star. Reagan, like tens of millions of people, felt the pain of the Depression. But his suffering would be muted and relatively short lived, and his recovery, unlike the nation's, spectacular and rapid.

In many ways, Eureka College marked a logical extension of Reagan's early life. Situated in yet another small Illinois town, Eureka was a center of religious training under the auspices of the Disciples of Christ. The athletic teams went by the nicknames of the Preachers or, sometimes, the Christians. The Church rules forbade dancing. Children of ministers and those studying to be ministers paid no tuition. The school, a complex of nine ivy-covered buildings and several farms, hosted a total of 187 students.

Eureka was coeducational and, reflecting the Disciples of Christ abolitionist heritage, racially integrated. Reagan's entering class included at least six African-American students.

Relatively few Americans attended college in the 1920s and 1930s. Only eight percent of Reagan's Dixon High School graduating class pursued a higher education. Reagan himself, though determined to enroll, could not afford the cost of matriculating at Eureka. He had saved $400 from his work as a lifeguard and swimming instructor, but could expect no help from his parents. The always-modest business at the Fashion Boot Shop had tailed off considerably as the economy accelerated the store's decline. Reagan secured a half-tuition athletic scholarship (though the football coach, Ralph McKinzie, apparently had few illusions that the still relatively scrawny Ronald would play as a freshman) and agreed to wash dishes at one of the two female dormitories.

In 1928, Eureka, rarely financially stable in the best of times, had fallen into dire straits. Student tuition fees never fully matched the operating costs, and enrollments had begun a precipitous drop. Sixteen fewer freshmen appeared in 1928 than had the previous year. As the economy worsened throughout the academic year, other students dropped out, either unable to meet their expenses or required to return home to assist struggling families. The college increasingly laid off its workers and called upon the students to perform maintenance, operate the laundry, tend the grounds, and work on its farms. At times, professors went without pay and survived on credit from town merchants.

The economic climate combined with a restiveness among students influenced by the 1920s youth culture and internal faculty politics to make Reagan's first semester a tempestuous one. Eureka had long been divided between Dean Samuel Harrod, the charismatic chairman of the faculty, and Bert Wilson, the college's puritanical president.

Throughout the 1920s, Wilson had insisted on enforcing the church ban on dancing. Many students, however, defied his edict, secretly gathering in the gardens and dormitory rooms for post-class socials, or, more scandalously, going to the ballroom at the town Legion Hall, disapprovingly dubbed "Damnation Hall" by church officials. More significantly, Wilson determined in fall 1928 to slash costs by consolidating departments and cutting programs. Eureka's board of trustees approved his plan, but the faculty, led by Harrod, who apparently had his eyes on the presidency, balked at the changes. Students, already frustrated by Wilson's tight discipline, supported the faculty.

Upon arriving on campus, Reagan had become a pledge at Tau Kappa Epsilon (Teke) and taken a room at the Teke House. Unbeknown to him, his fraternity would soon be at the center of a rebellion. On November 20, the students, led by Teke president, Leslie Pierce, presented a petition to the board calling for Wilson's ouster. "The student body, the alumni and the faculty were not able to work harmoniously with the present administration and had not been in harmony, the past four years," protested the students. Wilson handed in his resignation, but not before implicitly questioning the moral fiber of his opponents. "The real question is," he intoned, "can Eureka, a small church college in a small town, survive at all in the face of the present trend of education and civilization?" The students, and the faculty who had instigated their movement, seemed to have won. Six days later, however, the trustees announced that they would not accept Wilson's resignation.

The students responded with a mass meeting on November 28. Speaker after speaker arose to denounce Wilson and the trustees and to call for a strike. Among the orators was Ronald Reagan, only nine weeks a freshman. In his autobiography, Reagan depicted himself as deliberately selected to be the final spokesman. His eloquence rallied the students, who "came to their feet with a roar" and voted by acclamation to strike. More likely, most biographers have concluded, Reagan was one of many speakers who addressed the crowd. If he actually presented last, it was due more to his junior status than by design, and his words simply reiterated those spoken before him. Nonetheless, for Reagan the experience was indeed, as he wrote, "heady wine."

The inconsistency that the future president of the United States, who would launch his own political career denouncing student radicals in the sixties, had engaged in protest himself did not escape Reagan. He presented his own generation as noble and disciplined fighters. "Not once did we neglect our studies," he claimed in 1965. "To do so would have been to contradict the whole spirit of what we were fighting for. The [strike] committee set up regular study hours and enforced them." Other students, however, remembered no such regimen. Indeed, some recalled that as a further act of rebellion, they held dances instead of attending classes.

The strike lasted for two weeks and garnered national attention. The trustees held firm that they would not remove Wilson under pressure. The resolution involved an intricate pantomime wherein the students, under the threat of suspensions of the strike leaders and a firing of faculty supporters, withdrew their demand for Wilson's ouster. The trustees thereupon accepted Wilson's resignation, placed Dean Harrod, whom they apparently blamed for the uprising, on probation, and instituted the program cuts that had sparked the rebellion. Reagan recollected this all as a great triumph, engineered by a "policy of polite resistance." The actual outcome, however, was far more ambiguous, a reflection of the college's struggle to maintain its viability in the face of the ongoing economic calamities facing the rural Midwest.

With the strike over, Eureka College returned to its normal routines. As in high school, Reagan found more fulfillment in outside activities than in his studies. He tried out for the football team but, despite his experience as a two-year starter at Dixon High School and his dogged dedication in practices, he remained on the bench throughout the season. He never appeared in a regular game and was omitted from the team picture because the program lacked enough jerseys to outfit all of the athletes. Reagan, who had played high school basketball, also thought that he might make the Eureka squad. But even at a small school like Eureka, he realized that he was overmatched. At the first practice, he later wrote, "I saw fellows doing things with a basketball that I just didn't believe." In response, he withdrew. Unfortunately, Eureka lacked a team in swimming, his best sport.

Frustrated in athletics, Reagan nonetheless had ample opportunities to expend his energies and interests. Through his journalism class, he covered football games for the school newspaper, *The Pegasus*. He became the yell leader for the basketball team. He was an avid participant in the Teke fraternity and also won admission to Alpha Epsilon Sigma, Eureka's dramatic club. He supported himself by washing dishes and continued his courtship of his high school sweetheart, Margaret Cleaver. Unlike Margaret, who again ranked near the top of the class, Ronald reportedly still put a minimum of effort into his schoolwork, relying on his photographic memory to get by.

Throughout his freshman year, Reagan could not have been encouraged by news from his family. In October 1928 Neil lost his job at the cement plant. Sometime during the early months of 1929 the Fashion Boot Shop failed. Jack Reagan briefly went to work at the Dixon Home for the Feeble-Minded, a job he found humiliating. He then secured employment as a salesman at one of Dixon's other shoe stores, a humbling fall for a man who had run his own shop for almost a decade. Nelle took in work as a seamstress to replenish the family finances. When Ronald came home for the summer in June 1928, he resumed his chores as lifeguard at Lowell Park, saving his money as best he could for his return to Eureka College.

During his sophomore year, Reagan experienced several changes that enhanced his college experience. He had urged his brother to join him at Eureka, and when Neil balked at the expense, Ronald arranged an athletic scholarship. Both Reagan boys played on the football squad. Ronald won a starting position as a guard, while Neil starred as an end. The relationship between the two brothers proved an odd one. Ronald, though two years younger than Neil, was, in effect, the older brother at Eureka. When Neil pledged Teke, he had to bow down to Ronald and serve him at the table. Since fraternity brothers got to paddle pledges, Ronald took his licks against Neil. Although Neil was by far the better student, at times receiving straight A's, Ronald clearly flourished more socially. The Catholic, hard-drinking Neil seemed out of place at the dry, Disciples college. He dropped off the football team during his sophomore year, and although he graduated in four years, never seemed as much a part of the Eureka scene as his more fully engaged brother.

Ronald, meanwhile, partook in a dizzying array of activities. At his urging, the college added a swimming team, on which he became the standout performer and, at times, the coach. He started as a lineman on the football team for three years. Reagan edited the yearbook, served on the Student Senate, and won elections to be the president of homecoming, the Booster Club, and ultimately, his senior class. He scored some of his greatest successes on the stage. Reagan appeared in seven productions and in April 1930 traveled to Northwestern University in Evanston for a drama tournament. The Eureka College contingent presented *Aria da Capo*, an avant-garde play by Edna St. Vincent Millay, with Reagan portraying Thyrsis, a shepherd boy. Eureka took third place in the competition, and

Reagan won recognition as one of the six best performers in the tournament. A Northwestern speech professor advised him to consider acting as a profession.

As in high school, Reagan continued to write stories. The protagonist in tales like "The Stadium" or "Moral Victory: A Football Story" was now more likely to be a football player than a lifeguard. "Rock Redux: A Tale of the Supernatural" represented a fictional reversal of the well-known Knute Rockne-George Gipp legend, which would play a major role in Reagan's film and political careers. In Ronald's rendition, Rock, the dying coach, tells Punk Evans, his star player, "If sometimes the boys are going down, tell them I'm on the bench asking for a score." In "The Return of Jerry Dale, Senior," Reagan borrows heavily from his own life to create a portrait of a college football hero. In reviewing Reagan's high school and college writings, biographer Edmund Morris writes, "Time and again in these stories, a tall, genial good-looking boy goes about his business (or lies comfortably, doing nothing) untouched by and unconcerned by the agitation of others. He is sexy without being sexual, kind yet calculating, decent, dutiful, gentle, and massively self-centered." Inherent in these writings, adds Morris, "is our hero's intense delight in being looked at. The stare of any eyes—male or female, young or old."

Not all of Reagan's pieces, however, reflected this self-absorption. Reagan had grown more interested in politics and world affairs. Like many college students in the interwar period, he dabbled with the notion of pacifism. Two pieces written in 1931, "Killed In Action: A Short Story" and "November 11, 1918" reflected his anti-war sentiments. Reagan even told his father that he would not fight on behalf of the United States.

An incident involving African-American football teammates also reflected Reagan's social perspective. Reared in central Illinois, Reagan had had minimal exposure to

African-Americans. About a dozen black families resided in Dixon, where they experienced a pattern of discrimination familiar to the Midwest. African-Americans faced no segregation at local stores, luncheonettes, or movie theaters and attended integrated schools, but found themselves barred from more elite institutions like the local hotel and country club. Reagan's Eureka football squad included two African-American players, W. Franklin Burghardt and Jim Rattan. When a hotel in LaSalle, Illinois, refused accommodations to the two blacks, Coach McKinzie pulled his entire team and suggested they would all sleep on the bus. Ronald offered instead to take the two men to stay at his home in nearby Dixon, where they found a ready welcome from Jack and Nelle. The episode reflected a pattern of thinking that would typify Reagan's racial perspective. He had an absence of prejudice where individual blacks were concerned, but a corollary streak of accommodationism to existing mores. McKinzie's solution, sacrificing the comfort of his team to make a political point, had a more egalitarian tone. Reagan's way out resolved the immediate problem in a humane manner, but skirted the underlying issues.

The primary matter confronting Reagan, his classmates, his family, and Eureka College, however, was the ever-deepening Depression. The stock market crash of October 1929 occurred early in Reagan's sophomore year. The already harsh economic climate facing the rural Midwest steadily worsened. In addition to his dishwashing chores, Reagan now began assisting in the college steam plant. In his junior year he gave swimming lessons. At home, Jack Reagan had acquired work as traveling salesman for the Red Wing Shoe Company, a position he maintained throughout most of 1930 and 1931. The job, based in Springfield, Illinois, frequently took Jack away from home. According to Morris, Jack acquired a girlfriend in Springfield, and he and Nelle stood poised on the brink of divorce. By late 1931, however, they had reunited in Dixon.

Reagan felt the full force of the Depression in his senior year. By this time, most Eureka students were receiving financial aid, and the college was strapped for funds. In October 1931 the school instituted the Eureka Plan, laying off all of the staff and requiring students to perform all necessary maintenance. Reagan applied to the college for a loan to carry him through for graduation. In the application he noted, "I have worked every vacation since entering college as life guard at Lowell Park and have worked during school earning my board each year." He requested $200 for his final year, although he noted that even this amount would leave him with a budget deficit of $37. The college granted him $115, leaving him a substantial gap to make up. To make matters worse, in December 1931, as the family gathered for Christmas (on Christmas Eve as Ronald melodramatically remembered it) Jack received a dismissal notice from Red Wing, leaving him unemployed. He remained out of work for five months. When Reagan graduated in June, he lacked the money to purchase a class ring.

As Ronald Reagan neared the close of his Eureka years, he seemed to have few plans for life after college. He had majored in sociology and minored in economics. His grades had been unimpressive. As a junior he had received D's in English History and the Life of Christ, 5 C's, a B⁻ and a B, though he fared better in his senior year. On his 1931 loan application he confessed, "I have no definite plans for the future outside of trying to get a position in some business, probably as a salesman." Nonetheless, Reagan did not lack for ambition or confidence. In his senior year, he bet his Teke fraternity brothers that within five years he would be making a $5,000 annual salary, a phenomenal sum during the Depression era.

In June 1932 Ronald Reagan graduated from Eureka College. His class consisted of only 45 survivors, as financial reality had forced many students who had entered in

1928 to drop out. Margaret Cleaver, still Reagan's sweet-heart, received honors for the highest grades. Reagan, as president of the senior class, addressed the graduates. With his higher education behind him, he returned to Dixon, moved back in with Jack and Nelle, and assumed the same job he had held before matriculating and throughout his college years. For the summer, at least, Reagan had work, returning as a lifeguard at Lowell Park, pulling errant swimmers out of the Rock River.

Given the depths of the Depression, Reagan had to feel fortunate to have even this temporary job. National unemployment rates had risen to 25 percent. Ironically, the dire condition of people in Illinois had already offered a lifeline to the Reagan family. Jack Reagan, after nearly six months of joblessness, had parlayed his years of laboring for the Democratic Party into a patronage position. He found employment as a work relief superintendent with the Illinois Emergency Relief Commission (IERC), a state agency formed to dole out assistance to the needy. Although established with a two-year mandate, the IERC, swamped by the poverty of its clientele, ran out of money within two months. A national relief act passed on July 31, 1932, however, gave the agency a new life, thereby prolonging Jack's employment and transferring him to the federal payroll.

Twenty-one-year-old Ronald passed the summer still unsure of his own future. He entered into discussions about his prospects with Sid Altschuler, a Kansas City businessman vacationing at Lowell Park. When Altschuler initially asked him about his plans after the summer, offering to help him find work, Reagan responded that he had no idea about what he might do. Altschuler urged him to think it over. When they next spoke, Ronald had an answer, one that he had doubtless harbored in the back of his mind all along. What he would like to be, he confessed, was a radio sports announcer. Altschuler responded that he had no connections in that field, but nonetheless encouraged Reagan to pursue his goal. "Take any kind of job, even sweeping floors, just to get in," advised Altschuler.

That Reagan would consider sportscasting as a career in 1932 demonstrated how imbedded in the national culture that calling had become in a relatively brief time. Commercialized radio had only begun in 1920. Sports did not become a staple of broadcasting until 1923 when Graham McNamee took the microphone to describe the 1923 World Series. During the next few years several major league baseball teams, particularly those in the Midwest, offered radio coverage of home games. Radio stations also brought championship prizefights into people's homes. College football teams started showcasing their games on the air as early as 1922. Throughout the 1920s McNamee, Ted Husing, and other pioneer radiomen invented the profession of sportscasting. "The announcers are stealing the glory which was once attached to the [sports]writer," commented one observer after a tour of the Midwest. Local sportscasters developed devoted followings and the craft of radio reporting became a familiar feature to millions of sports fans, including Ronald Reagan. Following football games at Eureka, Ronald, engaging in a fantasy that did not exist a decade earlier, would turn a broomstick into a microphone and recreate the game's play-by-play, mimicking the voices he had heard on the radio.

Having identified a profession, Reagan set out to make his adolescent reveries a reality. In September, after the Lowell Park swimming area closed for the year, he hitchhiked to Chicago and spent a day touring the city's radio stations, offering his services. He failed to secure even an interview, much less a job. A sympathetic receptionist counseled him to steer clear of the metropolis and focus his energies on the lesser stations in smaller midwestern cities. Reagan returned to Dixon, borrowed his father's car, and set out for Davenport, Iowa, across the state border, some 70 miles away.

Even in this minor market Reagan again experienced rejection after rejection. Finally, after being turned down at station WOC, a frustrated Reagan exploded, "How the hell do you get a job to be a sports announcer if you can't even get a job at a radio station?" WOC program director Peter MacArthur, needing someone to assist on that week's University of Iowa broadcast, asked Reagan if he knew anything about football. Reagan responded that he had played in both high school and college. MacArthur gave him an impromptu audition, putting him in a studio, and commanding, according to Reagan, "When that red light comes on, *you* start to imagining a football game." Reagan, with his remarkable memory and broomstick experience, presented a play-by-play of the final quarter of a Eureka College contest. MacArthur told him to report to Iowa City the following Saturday, October 1, 1932, to cover the Iowa-Bradley game. If he performed satisfactorily, he would be brought back for the season's final three contests.

The pay for the first assignment was only five dollars plus expenses, but Reagan leapt at the opportunity. Billing himself as Dutch Reagan, his showing at Iowa City earned him three more assignments at double the pay. The Davenport *Democrat and Leader* praised him lavishly, reporting, "Reagan, grand footballer and letter man, knew what it was all about. His crisp account of the muddy struggle sounded like a carefully written story . . . and his quick tongue seemed to be as fast as the plays."

Reagan had earned a total of $35, but he remained unemployed. He returned home to Dixon, where in November 1932 he enthusiastically cast his first-ever electoral ballot for Franklin D. Roosevelt (he had sported an FDR button on his bathing suit all summer), and awaited a summons from WOC offering more permanent work. The months between Roosevelt's election and his March 4, 1933, inauguration marked the darkest days of the Depression. The nation's economy seemed to grind to a halt as bank failures escalated and people anxiously awaited the transfer of power in Washington. Yet Reagan's break came during this gloomy period. In early 1933, after more than five months of effective unemployment, Reagan heard from MacArthur. He was to report to Davenport to become a WOC staff announcer on February 10, just five days after his twenty-second birthday, at a healthy salary of $100 a month. Since the impending New Deal would extend his father's employment, moving him from the IERC to a position with the Civil Works Authority (CWA), one of the early New Deal agencies, the desperate phase of the Great Depression had drawn to a close for the Reagan family.

Radio station WOC, where Reagan began his broadcasting career, bore the earmarks of many of the nation's pioneer radio outposts. In the 1920s numerous small businesses across the nation had seen radio as a way to publicize their operations. In Davenport, Colonel Bartlett Joshua (B.J.) Palmer, proprietor of the Palmer Chiropractic College, erected a 500-watt transmitter on the roof of his school and launched WOC (World of Chiropractic) in 1922. Two years later Palmer merged WOC with WHO in Des Moines, where he proceeded to construct a more modern station. WOC broadcast some of the nation's most popular radio shows to a wide swath of the Midwest. Despite this dramatic growth, it still functioned, to a large degree, as an extension of the Palmer Chiropractic College, promoting and publicizing Palmer's enterprise.

At WOC, Reagan served as an all-around announcer, playing records, reporting on news and weather, and introducing network programming. "This is WOC Davenport, where the West begins and the tall corn grows," he would intone. Within weeks of his hiring, however, the novice Reagan neglected to acknowledge a mortuary sponsoring an organ rendition of "Drink To Me Only with Thine Eyes," leading to his dismissal. When his replacement refused to work without a contract, Reagan, who had no such compunction, found himself temporarily slotted back in.

Program director MacArthur, needing someone to cover the Drake Relays, a major track and field event in April, dispatched Ronald to Des Moines. Although he knew little about the sport, Reagan read up on the history of the Drake Relays, the high points and previous winners, and the top performers in the current event. He produced a polished performance. When in May Palmer transferred MacArthur and other staffers to the more modern Des Moines station, MacArthur took Reagan along with him and made him the chief sports announcer, doubling his salary in the process. The station manager also convinced General Mills, producer of "Wheaties," to sponsor Reagan as the broadcaster of re-creations of Chicago Cubs and Chicago White Sox home games.

During the next four years Ronald Reagan became one of the most celebrated sportscasters in the Midwest. Best known for his work on major league baseball games, he also gave twice-daily sports reports and commentaries and wrote a regular sports column in the *Des Moines Dispatch*. "To millions of sports fans in at least seven or eight middlewestern states," reported the *Dispatch*, "Dutch Reagan is a daily source of baseball dope."

Baseball re-creations represented one of the new art forms of the radio era. Since local radio stations could not afford to send broadcasters to cover games live from the stadium, they instead placed their announcers in the home studio where they received barebones pitch-by-pitch reports via telegraph and transformed them into lively play-by-play accounts. In Des Moines Reagan sat at his microphone next to a turntable equipped with a record that simulated crowd applause and other stadium noises. He would receive slips of paper with coded information about the game from a telegraph operator in the next room and then add imaginary details about how the players swung or ran or the actions of the fans to flesh out the scene. He used a foot pedal to operate the phonograph with the background sound.

Of the three major sports, Reagan probably knew the least about baseball. Because of his myopia, he had rarely played the sport, and, when he began his re-creations, he had never attended a major league game. He traveled to Chicago to visit Wrigley Field and Comiskey Park to get a sense of the game on the field and the scenes at the ball-park. From these experiences he was able to portray a more realistic depiction of the action. Radio, Reagan later said, "was theater of the mind." Re-creations required quick thinking, rapid-fire talking, and improvisational and visualization skills. Reagan mastered these abilities readily and conveyed an infectious fan's enthusiasm. He also employed the type of truth-stretching storytelling he had long ago learned from his raconteur father. As historian Garry Wills has noted, "His games were often more exciting than the ones being played far away . . . He made up the game, then criticized the performance . . . of the players he called up in people's minds."

Sports announcing frequently blurred the line between reporting and promotion, reality and myth. As a commentator on his daily sports show and in his newspaper columns, Reagan relied heavily on moralistic, uplifting homilies, like the inspirational but fabricated legend of Knute Rockne invoking the dying words of superstar footballer George Gipp to inspire Notre Dame to victory. The performance often extended into Reagan's real life. "He had an inability to distinguish between fact and fantasy," recalled Margaret Cleaver, his longtime girlfriend.

Ronald Reagan became one of Des Moines' leading personalities. People came to the Iowa Fair Grounds to observe him as he recreated the games. He received hundreds of fan letters from his listeners. Reagan spoke about temperance to the local Boys Club and was invited to speak before other civic groups. He joined the Advertising Club, studying a parade of speakers at its gridiron lunches, for clues on public speaking. For a brief time he did voice-overs for Iowa newsreels. Photographs featuring his good looks appeared in newspapers and radio promotions. A gossip columnist reported, "He is over six-feet tall with the proverbial Greek-god physique: broad shouldered, slim-waisted and a face that would make Venus look twice." A friend later commented that Reagan, when in public, always seemed to be performing, as if to please an audience.

Not surprisingly, Reagan had an active social life. Early in his sojourn in Des Moines, Margaret Cleaver informed him that she was going to Europe, effectively ending their relationship. As an attractive, affluent, single young man, Reagan dated frequently. He also found a compatible social circle at Drake College, the local Disciples of Christ school. During these years Reagan became an avid horseman. A friend suggested that he could gain experience by becoming a reserve officer in the 14th Cavalry Regiment, stationed at nearby Fort Dodge. Reagan confessed that he "had no particular desire to become an officer," but, in exchange for once-a-week classes, he got to ride regularly. Reagan's poor eyesight should have disqualified him from becoming an officer, but the Army allowed officer candidates to train before passing their physicals. He therefore stretched out his training for two and half years, all the while developing his riding skills.

Politically, Reagan remained an ardent Roosevelt supporter, in no small measure because of the New Deal's effect on the Reagan family. In 1933 both Jack and Neil, recently graduated from Eureka (with Ronald paying part of his last year's tuition), worked for New Deal agencies. While Neil left after six months for a job Ronald secured for him as a radio announcer for WOC in Davenport, Jack had at long last found an element of economic stability, working his way up through the ranks of local New Deal agencies. In 1934 he won a promotion to county work relief superintendent with the CWA. Two years later he served as a superintendent for the Works Progress Administration. These government jobs, perhaps the most satisfying work experience of his life, restored Jack's self-esteem. Unfortunately, his resurrection proved short lived. A heart attack felled him in 1936 and he never fully recovered his health. From that point on, he and Nelle relied heavily on financial support from Ronald to sustain them.

By 1936, at the age of 25, Ronald Reagan had already reached the pinnacle of the opportunities afforded a celebrity in a regional market. He earned a substantial $3,900 a year, and a *Sporting News* poll named him the fourth most popular baseball announcer in a non-major league setting. When not broadcasting sports, he often interviewed visiting Hollywood personalities like Jimmy Cagney, whetting Reagan's ambition for a broader audience. Singer Joy Hodges, a Des Moines native now based in Los Angeles, appeared on the radio with Ronald and suggested that he might pursue a career in the movies. Reagan increasingly began to see his future in Hollywood.

During these years the Chicago Cubs trained on Catalina Island, a resort area off the coast of Southern California heavily frequented by people in the movie industry. Reagan approached his station manager at WHO with the idea he might accompany the Cubs to spring training to become more familiar with the team in preparation for the 1936 season. Reagan offered to use his own vacation time for the trip if the station would pay his expenses.

Reagan failed to make any significant contacts on his first trip to Southern California, but he enjoyed spending time with major league baseball players and used the experience to good effect upon his return home. One newspaper commented that Reagan's recreations were "even more colorful than last season because of his intimate

knowledge of the personalities of the players themselves."
WHO gladly sent Reagan for a return trip in 1937. This
time he determined to pursue his acting ambitions, so ne-
glecting his baseball duties that even Cubs manager Charlie
Grimm took vehement notice one day. Reagan mingled
with movie stars at the Avalon Casino on Catalina Island,
and *Variety*, the industry newspaper, noted his presence,
attesting to his own celebrity.

He approached Joy Hodges backstage at the Biltmore
Bowl in Los Angeles to ask her to help him get a screen test.
Hodges contacted her agent, George Ward of the Meiklejohn Agency, who met with Reagan and instantly appraised
him as the kind of "likeable clean-cut American" who often succeeded in the movies. Ward arranged a test at
Warner Brothers. Reagan spent a brief few minutes in front
of the cameras and then boarded a train for Des Moines.

Reagan had been home only a few days when on April 2,
1937, he received a telegram from Ward. "Warner's offer
contract seven years, one year's options, starting at $200
a week," read the wire. "What shall I do?" The proposition was not without risk. Hollywood contracts could be
terminated after a three-month probationary period, and
Warner's was not obliged to pick up the options. But
Reagan did not hesitate to surrender the security of his
announcer's position, nor did he reconsider when his
sponsor, General Mills, made a bid to keep him at WHO.
He immediately telegraphed back, "Sign before they
change their minds. Dutch Reagan."

Reagan spent an eventful last few weeks in the Midwest. He traveled to Chicago and spoke to the first convention of radio sports announcers. He continued to cover
Cubs and White Sox games and to write for the *Des
Moines Dispatch*. Having completed his course work with
the Army Reserve, Reagan finally submitted to the physical. He managed to somehow fake the eye test and on
April 29, 1937, became a second lieutenant in the Reserve

Corps. WHO threw him a goodbye party live on the radio, and the mayor of Des Moines appeared to bid him farewell.

On May 20, Ronald Reagan packed up his car and set off for Hollywood. In the nation, unemployment was again on the rise, and the people of the United States still had three years of economic travails remaining. But at age 26, Reagan could leave not only the Midwest, but also the Great Depression behind. His future now rested in California, the American promised land of the twentieth century.

3

The Making of a Hollywood Star

Ronald Reagan wasted no time in traveling from Des Moines to Los Angeles. He drove his fashionable Nash convertible more than 600 miles each day, completing the 1,900-mile trip in just three days.

Reagan was, of course, not the only person traveling westward to California in May 1937. Thousands of people, impoverished refugees from the great dust storms that had decimated the nation's midsection and added to the woes of the Depression, also migrated to the golden state at this time. Their exodus, in battered trucks and unstylish jalopies, offered a less dashing and romantic image than Reagan's sprint to the coast. But if Reagan passed any of these fellow California dreamers en route, he paid them no heed, never mentioning them in his recollections.

Reagan also was unaware of events transpiring in Hollywood that would have a profound effect on his future. The Screen Actors Guild (SAG), a labor union for film actors formed in 1933, had waged a four-year struggle to win recognition from the studios. In 1937 SAG petitioned the National Labor Relations Board, the recently created New Deal agency overseeing union efforts, and won certification to represent all actors in basic contract negotiations. SAG demanded a closed shop, requiring all actors to belong to the union, and threatened to strike if the studios failed to comply. On May 15, 1937, just days before

Reagan left for Hollywood, the studios surrendered, and in early June, shortly after Reagan's arrival, SAG signed its first contract with the movie industry.

Hollywood in the 1930s was dominated by a handful of large studios that signed aspiring actors to long-term contracts and dictatorially controlled their fates. Warner Brothers, which had lured Reagan to California, typified the industry. It was in every respect an industrial plant, a film factory dedicated to the mass production of movies. The Warner Brothers studio itself, where most production took place, occupied a vast expanse along the Los Angeles River, with 30 miles of streets, a hospital, a school, and its own security department that barred entry to unwanted visitors.

Within the studio walls, actors engaged in a fierce Darwinian struggle for survival. Like all studios, Warners signed large numbers of contract players, perhaps one in ten of whom might go on to become stars. Most actors, like Reagan, worked on short-term pacts that could be renewed or terminated every few months at the whim of the studio. Contracts usually guaranteed only 40 weeks or less of work, so performers could have long spells without an income. Warner Brothers dictated the roles that each of its employees would play. If an actor refused a role, he or she could be suspended without pay. While stars might risk the wrath of their employers and accept the suspension, newcomers and supporting players had far less independence. Workdays began early in the morning and often lasted late into the evening; actors frequently worked on several films at once. Studios also dictated promotional appearances away from the set.

During the Depression years Warner Brothers had the reputation as the most socially conscious of the major studios. Strong supporters of Franklin D. Roosevelt and the New Deal, Harry and Jack Warner drew many of their movie plots from the newspaper headlines, often focusing on social issues like urban and rural poverty. Movies, which had the power to sway public opinion, stated Harry Warner, "should have some moral lesson," and depict right and wrong "as the Bible says." But as Stephen Vaughn has written, "The more one looks into how Warner Brothers put its pictures together, the fainter is the trail of reform. . . . The question was how to create entertainment."

Furthermore, the Hollywood movie moguls did not exercise unlimited power. They operated under severe constraints in shaping their films. The Motion Picture Producers and Distributors of America (MPPDA), an industry watchdog created to ward off government interference and censorship, had established a Production Code in 1930 that dictated the limits of acceptable content. The code sought to impose a set of strict moral values. Movies must defend families, marriage, and the home, and omit or condemn any indications that extramarital sex might be condoned or normative. Nudity was forbidden. The cinema, according to one publication, should feature "good characters, the voice of morality, a lesson, regeneration of the transgressor, suffering and punishment." In 1934 the MPPDA created a Production Code Administration (PCA) to more effectively police the industry, and hired Joseph I. Breen of the Roman Catholic League of Decency to administer its efforts. The politically and morally conservative Breen reviewed film scripts before shooting could begin, protesting and often excising, in addition to moral lapses, excess violence and what Breen called any "false and unfair social and political philosophy."

Ronald Reagan entered this tightly controlled Hollywood world when he arrived at the Warner Brothers studio in June 1937. Warners had a clearly delineated two-tier system. Producer Hal Wallis supervised the A-movies, the high-budget, big-star vehicles that received top billing on theater marquees. Brian Foy produced the B-pictures, the lower-funded films that offered Saturday matinee fare and filled out the double features common in 1930s theaters. Most actors began working with Foy, hoping to work their way up to the A-movies. The studio itself reinforced this division. Stars ate in a lunchroom with studio executives. B-actors had a separate, less private facility.

Reagan found himself immediately dropped into a starring role, albeit in a B-film titled *Love Is On the Air*. Warners had cast him, appropriately, as a radio announcer fighting corruption in his small town. Shooting began on June 7, just days after his arrival at the studio, so Reagan had to learn his craft on the job. On the first day he discovered that he could not take a script and read it cold, injecting emotion into material he had not seen previously. Reagan took home the script and memorized it overnight, enabling him to act more naturally the following day. Reagan would follow this regimen in all of his films, earning a reputation for reliability that would serve him well. The power of the PCA was felt even in this minor trifle of a movie. Breen's objections led to the removal of several scenes deemed too violent for the American cinema.

Sometime during the shooting, Reagan also regained his given name. Throughout his childhood and radio days he had been known as Dutch Reagan, but studio officials rejected that appellation as unbefitting a potential movie star. Though many other famous actors received complete nominal makeovers (Archie Leach famously became Cary Grant), the publicity department decreed that the alliterative Ronald Reagan would resonate sufficiently among moviegoers.

No sooner had Reagan completed shooting *Love Is On the Air* than he found himself playing the title role in *Sergeant Murphy*, a B-movie about a cavalry soldier and his horse. In both of these early ventures Warners demonstrated a clear appreciation for Reagan's natural skills and talents. Not only was he cast in the familiar role of a radio announcer in the former, but studio publicity mixed fact and fancy to exaggeratedly promote Reagan as "an all-around athlete . . . broad-shouldered and with a slender waistline . . . proficient in almost every sport." Noting his cavalry commission, they described Reagan correctly as proficient with horses, but imaginatively as an "expert marksman as well." Publicity for *Sergeant Murphy* more accurately dubbed Reagan one of Hollywood's finest horsemen, who routinely did his own riding without the aid of stunt men.

Love Is On the Air opened on November 12, 1937, and Reagan received several sterling reviews for his performance. The *Hollywood Reporter* called him a "natural." The *New York Daily News* raved, "Young Reagan's debut takes on sensational proportions," adding that Ronald had "poise, a voice, personality, and a face that the camera loves." Warners, however, must have been less than impressed. While the studio renewed his contract after his first six-month option period, and again in June 1938, most of Reagan's subsequent roles consisted of brief appearances (often as an announcer) or as a minor supporting player. He had a small part in *Submarine D-1*, an A-picture, but his character never appeared in the screen version, consigned to the cutting room floor.

The most important of these roles for Reagan's career was a cameo spot as an announcer in *Hollywood Hotel*. The movie, starring Dick Powell, recreated the radio show of the same name on which Louella Parsons, the powerful syndicated gossip columnist of the Hearst newspapers, introduced and promoted celebrities and movie stars. Coincidentally, Parsons also hailed from Dixon, Illinois. The influential columnist, who had the power to make or break stars, took an immediate liking to and proprietary interest in Reagan, her fellow Dixonian. Favorable mentions in her column soon enhanced his credibility as a movie actor.

Although Reagan's career moved ahead slowly, the Hollywood lifestyle suited him. He dated many actresses and after only six months felt secure enough to move his parents out to a rented apartment (and later a two-bedroom house) in West Hollywood. Nelle joined the Hollywood–Beverly Christian Church and performed missionary work in hospitals and prisons. Ronald frequently joined her for services. Jack, still physically unable to hold a steady job, attained a $25-a-week position from Warner Brothers, handling Ronald's fan mail. Ronald, himself, covered most of their expenses. Brother Neil remained in Davenport, managing WOC, but within a few years would join the rest of the family in southern California.

Reagan appeared in a total of eight films in 1938. He found himself usually cast in one of two types of roles: the star's best friend in A-movies like *Brother Rat*, a popular comedy set in a military school, or the lead in B-movies like the melodramatic *Girls on Probation*. One of the B-movies, *Secret Service of the Air*, introduced Reagan to what would become a recurring role, that of Brass Bancroft, a heroic Secret Service agent, skilled as an aviator and fighter. In the first of these films, aimed at a children's matinee audience, Reagan, as Bancroft, broke up a counterfeiting and smuggling ring operation. Studio promos billed Reagan as "both in appearance and personality, the representative of all that is admirable in young American manhood. While he is tall and handsome, there is nothing of the pretty boy about him, for virility is his outstanding characteristic." Although Reagan feared flying, the publicists, again invoking his military reserve status, claimed he had frequently parachuted from airplanes.

Reviewers found Reagan, who displayed "charm and vitality" and "handles his fists well," fully suited to the role. The favorable reaction led to a follow-up, *Code of the Secret Service*. The quality of the sequel, however, fell below even the usually low B-movie standards. After promising they would not distribute it, Warners sent it out to small towns where it would escape the eyes of reviewers.

At this time, *Brother Rat*, the comedy about cadets at the Virginia Military Institute, ranked as the most successful of Reagan's movies. One of his co-stars in the movie was a 21-year-old veteran of more than two dozen B-productions, Jane Wyman. Wyman, usually cast as a loud, dim-witted blonde in these films, had already been married twice when she met Reagan. Still in the process of getting a divorce from her second husband during the filming of *Brother Rat*, she and Reagan did not connect. The two were reunited when Warners reassembled the cast for publicity photographs before the movie's release, and they began to date. Wyman, reared in a broken home and unsuccessful in marriage, felt a strong attraction to Reagan's easy-going solidity. "I was drawn to him at once," she later explained. "He was such a sunny person . . . I couldn't help wondering if some of his easy good nature could be an act." Reagan's devotion to his family also impressed her.

In late 1939, Warners decided to reunite the cast of *Brother Rat* for a sequel, *Brother Rat and a Baby*, throwing Reagan and Wyman into even closer contact. While Wyman seemed fully infatuated with Reagan, he seemed more indifferent to her charms. As the filming drew to a close, Wyman was hospitalized. Reagan rushed to see her in the hospital. By the time she was released, the pair was engaged to be married. The studio reported Wyman's ailment as a stomach disorder. Edmund Morris, however, implies in his biography of Reagan that Wyman had taken an overdose of pills to coerce Reagan into marrying her.

Whatever the true story, the Reagan-Wyman engagement quickly took on the trappings of a Hollywood fairy tale. Warner Brothers released the news to Louella Parsons, who elevated the courtship into an epic romance. "Two of Hollywood's nicest young people" had decided to tie the knot, wrote Parsons in her column on November 1, 1939. She arranged for Reagan and Wyman to appear on the tour

In these first 18 months in Hollywood, Reagan demoi strated both the strengths and limitations of his talent. H was a dependable worker who showed up on time, knev his lines, rarely required a stunt man, and did whatever th studio asked of him, either on the set or in publicity set tings. He performed best when playing himself—a likeable, All-American type, "boyish of face and gleaming of tooth," in the later words of *Time Magazine*. Unlike other actors, as biographer Anne Edwards has noted, Reagan never sought out acting lessons or joined a theater group that might help him to hone his craft. He seemed to fear unemployment more than he aspired to stardom. Only guaranteed income when he worked, as soon as Reagan finished one movie, he would implore B-producer Foy to find him another role. As a result he was often unavailable for more attractive parts that might have advanced his career.

Early in 1939, Warners gave Reagan a chance in his first prestige picture, *Dark Victory*. The film, a classic tearjerker, starred Bette Davis, Warners' leading female performer, as a dying socialite. Reagan played Alex Hamm, a well-to-do, often drunk playboy, who had fallen in love with the married Davis. Critics and subsequent commentators, including Reagan himself, agree that he turned in a hollow, unimpressive performance that banished him back to the domain of the B-movies. These films showed him to better effect. Reagan made two movies, *Hell's Kitchen* and *Angels Wash Their Faces*, in which he starred with the Dead End Kids, a contingent of youthful actors who in their early films addressed the problems of juvenile delinquency and urban decay as part of the Warners crusade for social relevance. He also returned for a third Brass Bancroft movie, *Smashing the Money Ring*. The Warner Brothers promotional campaign featured the creation of a "Junior Secret Service Club." Recruits received club membership cards signed by "Ronald Reagan, Chief."

of a traveling edition of *Hollywood Hotel*, with Reagan acting as the emcee. When the couple married at Wee Kirk o' the Heather, a church at the Forest Lawn cemetery on January 26, 1940, Parsons' husband gave the bride away. Parsons hosted two wedding receptions for the couple, one at her home and a second simulated event on the radio version of *Hollywood Hotel*. At the latter celebration, according to Garry Wills, radio performers "described the mythical hotel's opulent interior and named the milling stars, including some who weren't there."

The Reagan-Wyman nuptials occurred just three months after the outbreak of World War II in Europe. The war indirectly gave Reagan's career a sharp boost. Hollywood increasingly turned its attention to movies with military and patriotic themes, starring actors who physically embodied all-American themes and virtues. Youthful, handsome, and athletic, Reagan ideally suited the stereotype.

In September 1939, within days of the war's start, Reagan had begun shooting his fourth and final Brass Bancroft movie. Like all of the Brass Bancroft films, this was a strictly B-level affair, shot on a low budget in 12 days and aimed at the Saturday-matinee children's audience. When released in early 1940, the film was called *Murder in the Air*, but its working titles, *The Enemy Within* and *Uncle Sam Awakens*, reveal the studio's heightened war consciousness. Reagan, as Secret Service Agent Bancroft, no longer battled counterfeiters or smugglers, but spies. American scientists had developed "the most terrifying weapon ever invented," a "death ray projector" that used electronic beams to disable airplane engines from up to four miles away. This "Inertia Ray" would render the United States "invincible in war." Bancroft's job was to defend the secrets of the new weapon from enemy spies. The screenplay simultaneously hailed the death ray projector as "the most terrifying weapon ever invented" and "the greatest force for world peace ever discovered."

Nineteen-forty, however, marked Reagan's graduation from the B-movie ranks to more prestigious A-level films. During his first two and a half years in Hollywood, Reagan had never aggressively sought out any specific roles, gladly accepting whatever parts the studio offered. In January 1940, just days before his wedding, Reagan learned that Warners planned to film the life of Notre Dame football coach Knute Rockne. A centerpiece of the saga was the legend of George Gipp, a star player who on his deathbed had reportedly told Rockne to invoke his spirit when the team needed a boost. In a critical game Rockne conjured up the image of the dying Gipp in a locker room speech, inspiring Notre Dame to victory. The tale, a fanciful creation of sportswriter John B. Kennedy, had no validity. Gipp himself, rather than a quintessential all-American boy, was a gambler and carouser who skipped practices, squandered his talents, and earned at least one suspension from the university. But Reagan, like millions of other sports fans, passionately believed the myth. He had written a fictionalized version of the story while at college and recreated the saga as a radio announcer. He viewed himself as the ideal actor to play George Gipp.

Reagan approached producer Hal Wallis to plead his case, but Wallis initially turned him down. Reagan returned with a picture of himself in his Eureka football uniform and convinced Wallis to give him a screen test. Reagan not only won the role, but he sparkled in the film. He portrayed Gipp convincingly in the game sequences and movingly delivered the famous deathbed speech. "Someday when the team's up against it, breaks are beating the boys, ask them to go in there with all they've got. Win one for the Gipper," he implored actor Pat O'Brien, who played Rockne. Warner Brothers premiered the film in South Bend, Indiana, the home of Notre Dame. A quarter of a million people joined the festivities, greeting Reagan and O'Brien. Reagan, himself, broadcast fifteen minutes of that weekend's Notre Dame football game to a national audience over NBC. Warners, in tune with the patriotic tenor of the times, titled the film *Knute Rockne—All-American,* but it was Reagan, as Gipp, who most embodied the all-American theme. The movie proved his most successful to date. Reagan and his devotees embraced his image as "The Gipper" for the rest of his life.

Warners was so impressed with Reagan's work on *Knute Rockne* that as soon as he had completed the filming, they rushed him into his next venture, *Santa Fe Trail. Santa Fe Trail,* clearly pitched to a nationalistic audience, offered the type of historical reinterpretation that only Hollywood could invent. The movie (which had virtually nothing to do with the Santa Fe Trail) established an ahistorical pairing of Confederate officer Jeb Stuart (played by top box-office attraction, Errol Flynn) and Union General George Armstrong Custer (played by Reagan in a role designed for John Wayne) in "Bloody Kansas" in the pre-Civil War 1850s. When not competing for the hand of Olivia de Havilland, Flynn and Reagan confounded the twisted ambitions of militant abolitionist John Brown, portrayed as an irredeemably evil fanatic determined to divide the nation. PCA director Joseph Breen had warned Warners to downplay the issue of slavery, fearing that it might trigger an "adverse reaction" in the South. Indeed, the slaves depicted in the movie bemoan their acquired freedom. The strange mix made for poor history, but lively entertainment. Reagan once again portrayed little more than the likeable sidekick, but he did it in a big-budget, high-profile movie that greatly enhanced his visibility.

Knute Rockne debuted in September 1940, *Santa Fe Trail,* later that year. When Warner Brothers released an official roll of its stars at the close of the year, Reagan was listed just below the top echelon. The Audience Research Institute predicted that by 1943 Reagan would rank among the top ten box-office attractions. Thus, at the dawn of

1941, Reagan had achieved not just a substantial measure of stardom, but a clear place in the Hollywood firmament. He and Wyman, with a strong boost from Parsons, who repeatedly depicted them as the ideal Hollywood couple, became popular figures in the fan magazines. Their daughter, Maureen, was born on January 4, 1941, and the Reagans began building a home in the hills above Sunset Boulevard. Against the often-tawdry backdrop of scandal and decadence that often permeated the movie industry, the Reagans seemed to stand for the more wholesome Hollywood that the studios wished to project.

On the movie sets, Reagan had come to be known for his talkativeness and opinionated engagement. During the many breaks in the long working days, Reagan always sought out people to discuss world affairs, sports, or whatever topic had recently caught his fancy. He remained a dedicated reader, absorbing information from books, magazines, and several daily newspapers. He always had a fund of information, facts and statistics at his fingertips. "No one was quite sure he was accurate," observed one fellow actor, "but he sure as hell sounded accurate." He could entertain listeners with a joke or story he had read. Many found him an immense bore, someone who lectured at others, repeating things that he had read or heard, but without any original thoughts or analysis.

Others, however, enjoyed sparring with the garrulous young actor. Reagan's debate partners spanned the political spectrum. He became close friends with Dick Powell, a conservative Republican. Reagan and Powell "made many films together," recalled Powell's wife, actress June Allyson, "but arguing politics brought them together." Reagan also regularly exchanged ideas with conservative businessman Justin Dart, who frequented the Hollywood sound stages. Brother Neil, now in California, had also drifted to the political right.

On the far left, actor Eddie Albert and his wife Margo, a communist sympathizer if not party member, ranked among Reagan's closest friends. According to some reports, adamantly denied by Reagan, he considered joining the Communist Party, but was talked out of it by the Alberts and party members. For the most part Reagan maintained the political faith of his father, Jack. He remained a fervent, pro-Roosevelt New Dealer, and, as the wars in Europe and Asia grew fiercer, a firm proponent of FDR's policy of assisting Great Britain. Reagan resigned his membership in the Lakeside Country Club when he learned it would not accept Jews. He joined instead the Hillcrest Country Club, favored by most Jews in the film industry. Although many of Reagan's films had overtly political themes, there is no evidence from his memoirs that the films themselves influenced his beliefs.

Jack Reagan seemed to enjoy the life his son's success had brought him. Although he could not hold a steady job and the family still worried about his periodic binge drinking, Jack and Nelle had acquired a level of comfort and security that had always eluded them in Illinois. Jack accompanied Ronald to South Bend for the premier of *Knute Rockne—All-American* and remained engaged in Democratic politics. He felt a strong sense of betrayal when Neil began espousing conservative Republican beliefs. During the November 1940 presidential election, when Roosevelt sought a third term, Jack nervously followed election returns over the radio, unable to remain calmly seated. Six months later, on May 18, 1941, Jack died of natural causes. His death doubtless had a liberating effect on Ronald. He no longer had to fear his father's bouts with alcoholism, and he also would be able to explore other political options without experiencing his father's disapproval.

Shortly after his father's death, Reagan experienced his first serious involvement with the Screen Actors Guild. Initially Reagan had resisted union participation, resenting being forced to join by the closed shop. A lecture on the realities of labor-management relations in Hollywood by actress Helen Broderick, however, had convinced him of the necessity of the Guild. After his marriage to Wyman, an active SAG member who served on several union committees, Reagan began to attend meetings. In July 1941 SAG executive secretary Jack Dales asked Wyman if she would serve as an alternate delegate to the executive board. Wyman declined, but suggested that her husband would "make a better alternate than me." Reagan now added SAG and film industry concerns to his list of passionate interests.

Reagan continued to make his share of B-movies, but the door to the bigger budget films had now opened. When Flynn turned down the role of Jimmy Grant, an American pilot fighting the Germans in England's Royal Air Force (RAF) in *International Squadron*, Warners handed Reagan the part. In the film, Reagan, in effect, personified the American position in World War II in 1940–1941. As a cocky Yank, he lacks discipline or a sense of responsibility. When his actions cause the death of two of his fellow pilots, he experiences an instant maturation, becoming a dedicated fighter willing to sacrifice himself for the greater cause.

To introduce *International Squadron*, Warner Brothers teamed with Louella Parsons to produce a gala premiere in Dixon, Illinois, in September 1941. Dixon got to welcome not only its two most famous former residents, but a host of movie stars enlisted by Parsons including Bob Hope, Ann Sheridan, and Robert Montgomery. Reagan, accompanied by Nelle, not only enjoyed a gala homecoming, but the role of Jimmy Grant also garnered him some of his best reviews. The *New York Times* hailed his portrayal as a "slap-happy hell-diver" as "excellent," while the *New York Post* called his performance "tops in breezy, even style."

To accommodate the triumphant Dixon excursion, Warners had released Reagan from the set of his most prestigious and controversial movie project to date. His recent successes had encouraged producer Hal Wallis to give Reagan another chance at a serious drama, casting him as Drake McHugh in *Kings Row*. Reagan must have seemed a natural to play a happy-go-lucky, small-town midwesterner, but Kings Row, the name of the community, bore no resemblance to any town that Reagan had lived in. An associate producer summarized the best-selling novel by Henry Bellamann on which the film would be based as one in which "The hero finds out that his girl has been carrying on incestuous relations with her father, a sadistic doctor [who] amputates legs and disfigures people willingly," and the town is populated by "a host of moronic and otherwise mentally diseased characters, the background of a lunatic asylum [and] people dying from cancer and suicides." Most of this material, he concluded, "is for the most part either censurable or too gruesome or depressing to be used."

Joseph Breen of the PCA agreed. He suggested that Warners not even attempt to develop a screenplay. "All the illicit sex will have to be removed. . . . The mercy killing will have to be deleted; and the several suggestions of loose sex, chiefly in the attitude of Drake . . . will have to be entirely eliminated," advised Breen. Nonetheless, Warners, which had paid $35,000 for the rights to the novel, persisted in its efforts. The screenplay went through five drafts before Breen gave his hesitant approval.

The result is a melodrama that, while muddled in parts and toned down significantly, still offers an unsettling depiction of the hypocrisy and cruelty of small-town life. Reagan, although once again cast as the supporting actor rather than the lead, has more screen time than usual and delivers a spirited, winning performance as the loyal friend to tormented town prodigy Parris Mitchell (played by Robert Cummings). McHugh, a local playboy who finds himself defrauded of his inheritance and consigned to a working class life on the wrong side of the tracks (though with the consolation of a radiant Ann Sheridan as a girlfriend), injures his legs in an accident. The sadistic physician unnecessarily amputates both legs. In a climactic dramatic scene, Reagan awakens from the surgery and discovers that his legs are gone. He howls memorably in horror, "Where's the rest of me?"

Reagan considered *Kings Row* "the finest picture I've ever been in" and his own performance the best of his career. Contemporary critics offered mixed verdicts on both counts. The *New York Times* called the movie "One of the bulkiest blunders to come out of Hollywood in some time," and asserted that Reagan "made only occasional acquaintance with the character." Other critics found his performance "living, laughing natural," and "breezily at ease." "Reagan has never appeared to such excellent advantage," reported the *New Yorker*. Movie audiences also responded favorably, making *Kings Row* a box office success.

In the six months between the completion of filming *Kings Row* and the movie's release, however, Reagan's life, even more than others, experienced a striking shift of fortunes. Not only had Reagan's star status increased, his financial position now had also improved dramatically. Since Reagan's arrival in Hollywood in 1937, the William Meiklejohn Agency had represented him in negotiations with the studio. In the late 1930s, however, the Music Corporation of America (MCA), an aggressive agency with strong ties to organized crime, which had long held a virtual monopoly over the booking of the big bands in the nation, had invaded Hollywood with the intent of gaining a similar domination with actors as well. MCA bought out numerous smaller agencies, including Meiklejohn. Thus, by 1941 both Reagan and Wyman, like most of the major Warners stars, found themselves represented by MCA, and their master dealmaker, Lew Wasserman. Wasserman negotiated a new seven-year agreement for

Reagan with a salary starting at $1,650 per week, rising to $5,000 in its final year. Wasserman also garnered Wyman, who still seemed anchored in B-films, a greatly enhanced three-year pact. The combined value of the Reagan-Wyman contracts approached $750,000.

Reagan signed his lucrative deal on November 18, 1941. In January 1942 a Gallup poll placed him on its list of the top 100 Hollywood stars, tied for seventy-fourth place with Laurence Olivier. But American entry into World War II sharply curtailed Reagan's stellar trajectory. As a reserve officer in the cavalry, induction into the military had loomed over Reagan's head for almost a year. He had received orders to report as early as February 9, 1941, but Jack Warner himself had written to the Army requesting a deferment to allow Reagan to complete his film commitments. Reagan received a second induction notice on August 29. Warner Brothers responded with a letter listing the movies lined up for Reagan and asked that he be delegated into the "reserve pool," which would have effectively kept him out of the service. The Army refused this request, but gave Reagan a further deferment until January 1, 1942.

Even after the bombing of Pearl Harbor, Reagan did not rush willingly into the service. On January 1, Jack Warner again personally intervened, securing a postponement of Reagan's induction until April 9, 1942. During these months Reagan made two more movies, *Juke Girl*, in which he played a migrant Florida fruit worker framed for murder, and *Desperate Journey,* once again supporting Errol Flynn and, as in *International Squadron*, playing an American pilot in the RAF, this time on a bombing run over Nazi Germany. In March Warners floated Reagan's name as a possibility for one of the leads in *Casablanca,* a war-based suspense movie that would become one of Hollywood's most enduring classics.

On March 30, with Reagan's scheduled induction just nine days away, Jack Warner again requested a deferment for his employee, based on his work on "the patriotic film, *Desperate Journey.*" On April 2 the Army telegraphed back: "Regret to inform you that another deferment cannot be granted." Reagan was ordered to report on April 19.

Thus Ronald Reagan marched off to war at a particularly inauspicious time in his career. With *Kings Row* just opened and *Desperate Journey* awaiting release, Reagan stood on the brink of true stardom. His family had just moved into their new home in the Hollywood Hills, but now his generous new contract would be suspended for the duration of his enlistment.

Wartime fan magazines portrayed the Reagans as a symbol of the sacrifices made by military men and their wives, with Ronald off serving his country and Jane dutifully maintaining the family at home. Daughter Maureen was only a year old, and Reagan was the first film star with a child to be pressed into service. *Modern Screen* described "Ronnie [leaving] Jane and Hollywood for the Army." When he appeared with Wyman at a fundraiser, *Movie Life* depicted him as "on a short leave."

In reality, Reagan, ineligible for combat because of his abysmal vision, completed most of his service in Los Angeles, working in a special wartime branch of the movie industry. He spent several weeks in an initial posting as a second lieutenant with a cavalry unit in San Francisco. Then, thanks to the intercession of his once and future employer, Jack Warner, now an Air Force colonel, Reagan was transferred to the First Motion Picture Unit (FMPU) in Culver City, an adjunct of Hollywood. Located at the Hal Roach Studios (now dubbed Fort Roach), the FMPU, or "Celluloid Commandos," employed actors and other film craftsmen to make training films and documentaries. Reagan thus spent the remainder of his service tour making movies. Though formally stationed at Fort Roach, Reagan could regularly visit Jane and Maureen.

Nonetheless, Reagan's service to his country was not inconsequential. He appeared in several films and narrated many others used to train fighting men or stimulate popular patriotism. In his first assignment, *Rear Gunner*, Reagan played an Air Force lieutenant and offered the voiceover to a tale of a young airman trained to man the difficult gunnery position at the back of an aircraft. The short movie, originally designed for training purposes, was eventually distributed to theaters where it appeared alongside feature films. Reagan also starred in *For God and Country*, which not only honored Army chaplains, but also exemplified the wartime theme of brotherhood. Cast as a former star college quarterback turned Catholic priest, Reagan, along with his two fellow chaplains and best friends, a Protestant and a Jew, catered "to all men, regardless of classification, color, or creed." Chaplain Reagan, whose principles would not allow him to use a gun, dies trying to save an American Indian soldier. A third film, *Recognition of the Japanese Zero Fighter*, made for American pilots, cast Reagan as a P-40 flyer in the Pacific who mistakes an American plane for the enemy with near disastrous results. Reagan had a final brief role in *Land and Live in the Desert*, another training film.

After Fort Roach officials decided to cast unfamiliar faces rather than stars in training films, Reagan's work shifted to narration. In the most elaborate and potentially most significant of these projects Hollywood special effects men created a miniature reconstruction of Japan and simulated bombing runs. Reagan provided the voiceover instructing pilots in the art of high-altitude precision bombing, familiarizing them with their missions before the actual flights. Reagan's efforts might have played a significant role in the bombing of Japan, but the military abandoned the high-altitude strategy in favor of lower-level attacks, rendering these simulations instantly obsolete. He also narrated *Wings for This Man*, a documentary about the Tuskegee Airmen, the elite African-American pilot brigade.

Stationed in Los Angeles, Reagan, in uniform, also became a familiar figure at bond drives, fundraisers, and military events. In 1943, when Warner Brothers made a film version of Irving Berlin's Broadway hit, *This Is the Army*, Reagan appeared in the movie in a choice role as Jerry Jones, the spoiled son of a musical comedy star, now enlisted as a private, and the humorous target of the movie's most popular song, "This Is the Army, Mr. Jones." During the filming of *This Is the Army*, Reagan lived at home with his family. The movie also brought Reagan into contact with singer-dancer George Murphy, an ardent conservative and SAG activist, who, although only nine years Reagan's senior, improbably played his father in the film. The pair frequently debated political points during breaks in the shooting.

Within the military hierarchy Reagan consistently received outstanding performance evaluations. His reviewers described him as "excellent plus" and "superior," "an officer of exceptional ability, demonstrating unusual initiative." He was promoted to first lieutenant and then captain. In summer 1943 he became the post adjutant at Fort Roach, in charge of processing all orders. Shortly before the end of the war, he was recommended for promotion to major.

As the war drew to a close, Reagan had one more experience that would not only leave an imprint on his memory but distort it as well. An FMPU film unit had entered the Nazi concentration camp at Buchenwald and shot graphic footage of the devastation of the Holocaust. The film arrived at Fort Roach for editing and was shown to selected officers, including Reagan. The stacks of the dead and the emaciated bodies of the living had a devastating impact on Reagan. In later years he showed *Lest We Forget*, the film created from this footage, to each of his sons when they turned fourteen. As an older man, he came to believe that he himself had been present at the liberation of Buchenwald.

In reality, however, Reagan had never left Hollywood. As a civilian actor, his final film had been a war movie. As a "Celluloid Commando," his duty was, Garry Wills has noted, "to make more war movies." When the conflict ended, he had seen no combat, nor traveled any further from home than San Francisco. Yet, he had clearly played a praiseworthy role in "The Good War."

Ironically, his absence from Warner Brothers had only enhanced his popularity. Numerous photographs depicted him heroically in uniform. His wife, Jane Wyman, had toured the nation in 1944 on a 12-week war bond drive, reinforcing the image of a patriotic family. *Rear Gunner* had been distributed widely in theaters. *This Is the Army* proved a tremendous hit. In box office records for films released in 1942 and 1943, which included that film, Reagan ranked among the industry's top draws, finishing ahead of Jimmy Cagney, Bing Crosby, and Clark Gable. Lew Wasserman, his canny agent, seized this moment to renegotiate his contract with Warner Brothers, giving Reagan a new agreement that would pay him $3500 a week for seven years upon his return from the army. The pact, the first "million-dollar contract" in Hollywood history, made Reagan one of the highest paid actors in the industry.

Reagan received his discharge on July 11, 1945. Four months earlier, he and Jane had adopted a son, Michael. In his autobiography, he would later write somewhat grandiosely, "All I wanted to do—in common with several million other veterans—was to rest up awhile, make love to my wife (though as Wills observes, 'Where had he been that he couldn't make love to his wife?'), and come up refreshed to a better job in an ideal world." But, Reagan added in a postscript, he was to be "disappointed in all these post war ambitions."

4

Fighting the Cold War

Although he had never really been far from home, Ronald Reagan, like most returning veterans, found his world in late 1945 a far different place from what he had left in 1942. Not only had his family grown with the addition of a second child, but Reagan also discovered that Jane Wyman, his wife of five years, had changed as well. Wyman, a bright, talented, ambitious young actress, had found herself, even more than Reagan, suspended in the web of the studio system. Warner Brothers rarely elevated Wyman above B-movies, typecasting her in best-friend roles, her naturally brown hair dyed blonde, and her intelligence obscured by light comedic dialogue. Unlike Reagan, she had been unable to elude this trap before the war as Warners rebuffed her pleas to try a dramatic role. In 1944 she approached Warners and suggested that, if they were unwilling to give her a serious part, they loan her out to another studio that would. Warners agreed and director Billy Wilder at Paramount cast her in a small, but powerful role as a woman in love with an alcoholic in *The Lost Weekend*.

The movie won the Academy Award for Best Film of 1945 and transformed Hollywood's image of Wyman, clearing the way for more substantial roles. When Reagan moved back into his Hollywood home, Wyman was working on *The Yearling*, her first major opportunity as a lead actress in a dramatic film. She left the house at 5 A.M. and returned home in the evening, never quite leaving her role behind. "Jane would come through the door, thinking about her part and not even notice I was in the room," commented Reagan.

Reagan, on the other hand, found his services to be less than in demand. The lucrative contract he had signed notwithstanding, Warners did not seem to know how to cast him. Reagan envisioned himself as a western or action hero along the lines of Errol Flynn or John Wayne. Studio executives felt that he lacked the presence or skill to carry these parts. While Wyman worked on *The Yearling*, Reagan sat idle for several months, well paid but, in effect, unemployed. The hiatus enabled Reagan to indulge his true passion, his interest in national and world affairs. During these months Reagan decided to plunge into the public arena. "I would work with the tools I had," he later wrote, "my thoughts, my speaking abilities, my reputation as an actor. I would try to bring about the regeneration of the world."

Reagan's political sympathies, judged by the speeches he gave and the organizations he joined, lay to the left of the political spectrum. In 1943, he had joined the Hollywood Democratic Committee, a pro-Roosevelt organization, organized by members of the Communist Party who supported the United States-Soviet Union wartime alliance. In June 1945, the organization, now headed by James Roosevelt, the deceased president's son, changed its name to the more unwieldy Hollywood Independent Citizens Committee of the Arts, Sciences and Professions (HIC-CASP) and attracted both communist and non-communist liberals to its ranks. He also joined the American Veterans Committee (AVC), one of the most left-leaning of a variety of groups appealing to returning servicemen. He became chairman of the AVC Hollywood membership board. Under his leadership the local chapter grew to the second largest in the country.

Reagan's public pronouncements in 1945 and 1946 attested to his commitment to leftist groups and politics. Shortly after his discharge he narrated a documentary for the AVC calling for housing for veterans. On December 8, 1945, he gave a speech at a United America Day gathering in Santa Ana condemning attacks against Japanese-Americans. Four days later he addressed a mass HICCASP meeting at the Hollywood Legion Stadium. In February 1946 his name appeared in an advertisement published in the communist *People's Daily World* protesting U.S. support for Chiang Kai-shek in China's civil war and attacking British and Dutch colonialism in Asia.

Many people began to take notice of Reagan's political presence. A group of Democrats asked him to run for Congress in the 1946 elections. HICCASP invited him to serve on its executive board. The FBI, which had maintained a file on Reagan for several years, now listed him among Hollywood figures displaying "records of Communist activity and sympathies." Reagan's brother Neil, who claimed to be a freelance spy for the FBI, hiding in bushes and recording license plate numbers outside radical meetings, urged Ronald to cut his ties with HICCASP.

In both AVC and HICCASP Reagan discovered himself in the middle of a struggle between liberal and communist elements for control of the organization. Reagan had known communists before, but he had never been exposed to their tenacious organizational combativeness. Reagan expressed shock at communist tactics and strategies and by what he saw as their hostility to American institutions and principles. After attending the AVC state convention in April 1946, Reagan marveled at how a relatively small group of communists had dominated the meeting. In a letter to Charles Bolte, chairman of the AVC national planning committee, Reagan protested, "They even succeeded in having the words 'private enterprise' struck from the paragraph reaffirming our support of the

Statement of Principles!" Reagan added, "I will defend to the death the right of communists or anyone else to belong to the AVC but . . . I think it will add strength to the entire liberal cause if we publicly re-affirm our belief in our present *form* of government. And our belief that our present *ills* can be cured within the framework of democracy."

A similar situation arose within HICCASP in the summer of 1946. The organization had come under attack for its acceptance of communists as members. At Reagan's first meeting as a member of the executive board on July 2, 1946, Executive Director James Roosevelt proposed a resolution affirming the organization's support for democracy and private enterprise. When Reagan and other liberals spoke in support of the measure, the communists on the board, led by screenwriters John Howard Lawson and Dalton Trumbo, responded with vituperative indignation, calling the moderates "fascists" and "capitalist scum." Reagan joined a committee that included Roosevelt, Lawson, and Trumbo to draft a clearer policy statement for HICCASP. But he found the communists no more agreeable in this forum. Lawson, according to Reagan, rejected his suggestion that the statement be approved by the general membership because they lacked the political intelligence to vote. Within weeks most of the moderate leadership of HICCASP had resigned, leaving the communists in control.

These confrontations left an indelible mark on Reagan. On numerous occasions he would deride the communists' "usual tactics, trying to run a majority of an organization with a well-organized minority." In 1951, he wrote, "We know they operate with a 1% minority but depend on organization. At meetings they 'come early and stay late' and they get confused 'liberals' to front for them at all times." Nine years later he spoke about "the countless hours of meetings, the honest attempts at compromise, the trying to meet dishonesty, lies and cheating with conduct bound by rules of fair play." By the end of the summer of 1946,

Reagan, like many liberals, had developed a strong distaste and distrust for the Communist Party and its tactics.

In addition to his efforts on behalf of AVC and HICCASP, Reagan also became more deeply involved with SAG. Reagan had served as an alternate member of the executive board before the war. In February 1946 he rejoined the board of directors. Although SAG had its pockets of left-wing supporters, it tended to be a relatively conservative organization dominated by big-name stars, rather than those at the lower end of the Hollywood salary scale. Robert Montgomery, a staunch conservative, served as president in 1946. His predecessor, George Murphy, also had right-wing political sympathies. Indeed, in early 1946 Reagan was among the few liberals on the executive board.

While Reagan fought these political battles he attempted to get his career on track. Late in 1946 Warners offered him the lead in *Stallion Road*, a movie about a veterinarian infected with a fatal dose of anthrax in a role originally intended for Errol Flynn, and later offered to Humphrey Bogart. Based on a popular bestseller, the studio had hired famed novelist William Faulkner to write the screenplay and planned a lavish Technicolor production. By the time the project reached Reagan in early 1946, however, Warners had jettisoned the Faulkner script, and it soon downgraded the movie to a lower-budget black-and-white venture. His next assignment, *Night Unto Night,* a glum melodrama, again cast Reagan as an afflicted man of science, a suicidal epileptic, attempting to cure a widow of delusions of communications from her dead husband. Neither film met his desire for an action role or qualified as a prestige vehicle.

Stallion Road and *Night Unto Night* were shot in 1946 against the backdrop of a violent labor dispute that divided Hollywood, elevated the issue of communist infiltration of movie production, sorely challenged SAG leaders and members, and ultimately lifted Ronald Reagan to the forefront of both his union and the national debate over communism. The Hollywood labor wars of 1945–1946 revealed both labor and management at their worst. They revolved around what to most outsiders seemed an obscure jurisdictional dispute between the International Alliance of Theatrical Stage Employees and Motion Picture Operators (IATSE) and the Conference of Studio Unions (CSU) over who would represent carpenters working on movie sets. The outcome of this battle would determine the future of organized labor in the film industry.

IATSE, which had begun as a union of stagehands and projectionists, had gained control of most studio workers during the 1930s. The threat of a strike by projectionists, who could prevent movies from being shown throughout the nation, close ties to organized crime, and a reputation for strong-arm tactics had given IATSE leaders great leverage with the major studios. In the late 1930s, film studios annually paid hundreds of thousands of dollars in bribes to IATSE officials to ward off strikes and more radical organizing. The CSU, led by painter Herb Sorrell, arose in 1941 as an alternative to IATSE. More democratic and not prone to corruption, the CSU attracted those on the left and other workers who rejected IATSE leadership and collusion with employers. The conflict cut across a wide sweep of union locals within the industry.

Events in 1941 established the dynamic between the two unions. When IATSE attempted to take over SAG, the actors' union hired a detective whose revelations ultimately led to prison terms for two IATSE leaders on extortion charges. Sorrell's painters' union, meanwhile, led cartoonists at Walt Disney studios to a victory over the notoriously anti-union Disney, prompting a flood of workers to join the CSU. By the end of the war, the CSU had 10,000 members, making it a potent rival to IATSE, which still served 17,000 workers.

The two unions, both affiliates of the American Federation of Labor (AFL), frequently clashed over jurisdictional matters. In 1943 a local of set decorators sought to bolt IATSE and join the CSU. Hollywood producers, favoring the corruption-laden IATSE over the more threatening leftism of the CSU, refused to accept the CSU as a bargaining agent for the decorators. Both the National Labor Relations Board and the War Labor Board ruled in favor of the CSU, but the studios still insisted on dealing with IATSE. Frustrated in all their efforts at mediation, the set decorators went on strike on March 12, 1945. IATSE threatened that if the studios bowed to the CSU, "every projectionist in every theater in the United States would take a walk."

That Sorrell could have picked this moment to strike testifies to his inadequacies as a union leader. The studios had a backlog of 130 unreleased films that would enable them to weather a lengthy strike. Furthermore, the AFL and the Congress of Industrial Organizations (CIO) had agreed to a no-strike pledge for the duration of the war. Unions that violated this promise, like the United Mine Workers, had triggered a substantial anti-labor public backlash. Sorrell, despite the validity of his claims, thus alienated many potential supporters. The CSU also suffered under IATSE charges that Sorrell was a communist, part of a broader conspiracy to seize control of the movie industry. These allegations ignored the fact that the Communist Party, which supported the no-strike pledge, opposed the CSU walkout and that Sorrell himself, although espousing strong leftist sympathies, was most probably not a party member and never obeyed party dictates.

The strike dragged on through October, pockmarked by sporadic violence. IATSE, which still had ties to organized crime, had little hesitation in bringing in goons to bolster their cause. Sorrell, a former prize fighter, also believed in violent intimidation as a tactic. "I love to hear the cracking of bones on a scab's legs," he once exclaimed. The CSU decided to focus all of its efforts on a mass picketing campaign directed at Warner Brothers. On October 9, bands of pickets stopped cars outside the studio gates, preventing entry. Warners responded by sending out their private security forces and hired thugs, many provided through IATSE's gangster connections, to attack the picket lines. Eyewitness accounts described cars driven at the picketers at high speed, strikebreakers swinging chains, and tear gas bombs and fire hoses thrust into the crowd. Sorrell responded, "If they want to make it bloody, let's make it bloody." For the next few weeks, violent clashes continued. Finally, on October 29, the strike reached an ambiguous conclusion. The studios recognized a greatly weakened CSU as bargaining agent for the set decorators. A three-man panel was established to resolve future jurisdictional disputes between IATSE and the CSU.

SAG, although publicly neutral in this dispute, in effect sided with IATSE. Had SAG refused to cross the picket lines the CSU might have prevailed, but when faced by the decision of whether to continue working in March 1945, SAG members had overwhelmingly voted 3,298 to 96 to enter the studios. Reagan, himself, had played no role in these events. Still in the service when the confrontation erupted, and not yet at work during the October violence, he took no public position regarding the conflict. During 1946, however, Reagan became increasingly active in SAG affairs. He rejoined the executive committee and ran for vice-president in fall elections. When the IATSE-CSU war erupted anew, he strode to center stage and assumed a leading position in the roiling debates.

The peace between IATSE and the CSU proved short lived. At the close of 1945, the three-man panel appointed by the AFL issued a jurisdictional ruling dividing work done by carpenters between CSU and IATSE affiliates. Unfamiliar with the intricacies of studio work, the panel, soon to be sarcastically labeled the "Three Wise Men," had inadvertently given the studios the right to fire 350 CSU carpenters and replace them with IATSE men. In August 1946 the Three Wise Men clarified their ruling, making it more favorable to the CSU.

The producers and IATSE held a series of meetings in which they plotted to ignore this "clarification," provoke a CSU work stoppage, then crush not only the strike, but also the CSU itself. The studio employed IATSE men to build sets on movies and then offered jobs on these same sets to CSU members, knowing that the CSU would balk at this violation of its jurisdictional domain. When CSU carpenters and painters refused to work alongside IATSE men, the studios fired them, laying off 1,200 men. In September, thousands of CSU workers walked off the job in sympathy, triggering another lengthy, violent battle. IATSE and studio leaders charged that the CSU strike, which they had deliberately provoked, was part of a communist scheme to take over Hollywood.

The anti-communist theme played better in autumn 1946 than it had in spring 1945. A national postwar strike wave involving millions of workers had stimulated widespread anti-labor and anti-communist sentiment throughout the country. More significantly, with the end of World War II the alliance between the United States and the Soviet Union had quickly crumbled and the Cold War had begun. American communists hastened to defend Soviet policies and also grew more aggressive in their attempts to gain control over political groups that might advance their cause. Anti-communists redoubled their efforts to delegitimize the Communist Party and to purge party members and sympathizers from labor unions and other institutions. Opportunists like the studios and IATSE wielded the anti-communist issue as a weapon to remove any opponents with a liberal tinge.

SAG found itself thrust directly into this dispute. Guild leaders, including Reagan, attended at least one of the industry-IATSE strategy conclaves that led to the strike. Although a minority segment of SAG actors advocated observing CSU picket lines, most wished to continue working. The Guild formed a Strike Emergency Committee, with Reagan as one of its most active members. Reagan seems to have had minimal understanding of or sympathy for the jurisdictional issues at the heart of the strike or any concerns about the corrupt history of IATSE or the illicit alliance forged between IATSE and the studios to break the CSU. Fresh from his experiences in AVC and HICCASP, he grew convinced the CSU had become "a vehicle for Communist aims . . . to gain economic control of the motion picture industry in order to finance their activities and subvert the screen for their propaganda."

The events of September and October 1946 reinforced Reagan's convictions. On September 24 hundreds of pickets appeared at the major studios, including Warner Brothers, attempting to shut down operations. Sorrell, in his inimitably irresponsible fashion, warned, "There may be men hurt, there may be men killed before this is over, but we're in no mood to be pushed around anymore." The strike quickly grew violent. Strikers overturned automobiles and shattered windshields. Studio and IATSE strikebreakers and local police responded with violent attacks on the picketers that sent many to the hospital. At Warners, actors, including Reagan, then filming *Night Unto Night,* were brought in on buses and encouraged to lie down in the aisles to avoid injury.

SAG called an emergency membership meeting on October 2 at the Hollywood Legion Stadium to discuss the crisis. With SAG President Robert Montgomery out of town, Reagan was asked to chair the gathering. Several days before the mass conclave, he crashed a meeting of CSU supporters meeting at the home of actress Ida Lupino and attempted to convince them of the desirability of crossing the picket lines. He met with a generally hostile reception.

The next day, according to Reagan, he received a telephone call while on the set of *Night Unto Night*. A voice warned him, "There's a group being called to deal with you. They're going to fix you so you'll never act again." Reagan interpreted this to mean that unless he ceased his activities, acid would be thrown in his face. The source of the threat remains unclear, but studio police gave Reagan a handgun for protection, and he remained armed throughout the long, increasingly violent conflict.

At the October 2 meeting, attended by thousands of actors, including the industry's biggest stars, Reagan made his first public appearance as a union leader. He presented the case for SAG's continued "neutrality" in the strike and urged members to vote to support the executive board's position, proposing that the vote be conducted by mail to minimize intimidation. His able performance impressed and surprised many in his audience, marking his emergence as a key figure in the Guild. The membership ultimately voted 2748 to 509 to approve the continued crossing of the picket lines.

The following week, Reagan and several other stars traveled to Chicago to attend the AFL convention. The SAG officials theoretically sought yet another clarification of the decision by the Three Wise Men, to bring an end to the strife in Hollywood. Their real intent, however, was clearly to turn the AFL against the CSU. The SAG contingent threatened to send stars to speak in major cities and place the blame for the Hollywood violence on the AFL. Conflicting accounts emerged from their confrontation with the arbitration panel. Reagan would tell a SAG mass meeting that the three-man panel had admitted to succumbing to intimidation from the carpenters union in modifying their original ruling. The Wise Men unanimously denied Reagan's account under oath.

Back in California, the violence escalated. A bus scheduled to take actors, including Reagan, into the Warners lot was firebombed and burned. As Reagan increasingly assumed the role of an anti-CSU spokesperson, the studio assigned armed bodyguards for his protection. In November bombs exploded at the homes of non-strikers. The studios obtained injunctions banning mass picketing, and when the CSU ignored the restrictions, police arrested 700 picketers, effectively breaking the back of the strike. Although the strike officially continued well into 1947, by December 1946 the CSU, considered by some to be "the only honest and democratic trade-union movement in Hollywood," had been soundly defeated.

On December 19, 1946, Reagan addressed another mass meeting of the Screen Actors Guild. Liberals Katharine Hepburn and Edward G. Robinson criticized SAG for its failure to support the CSU, but Reagan, speaking for the Guild leadership, defended its policies and asked the assembled membership for a vote of confidence in the executive board. The actors overwhelmingly affirmed the request by a ten-to-one margin. Four months later, when Robert Montgomery stepped down as SAG president, the executive board appointed Reagan to fill his term. While many remained critical of Reagan for his role in the destruction of the CSU, the general SAG membership clearly did not share this view. In November 1947, they formally elected him to a full one-year term as president; they would re-elect him four more times, in each case by wide margins.

The Ronald Reagan who assumed the SAG presidency in March 1947 had a far different notion of how "to save the world" than the Army veteran of 1945. He still identified himself as a liberal Democrat, a supporter of FDR's legacy and President Harry Truman's policies. Like many other liberals, however, he had lost his tolerance for communists and rejected the possibility of political alliances with party members. "Tyranny is tyranny, and whether it comes from the right, left, or center, it is evil," he now proclaimed. His experiences in the AVC and HICCASP and the violence and intimidation of the CSU strike, which he simplistically attributed solely to Sorrell's supporters, had transformed his thinking. "You can't blame a man for aligning himself with an institution he thinks is humanitarian," he told a reporter. "But you can blame him if he deliberately remains with it after he knows it has fallen into the hands of the Reds."

One month after the SAG board named Reagan president, on April 10, 1947, he and Wyman received a visit from three FBI agents. The agency, which only one year earlier had considered him a communist sympathizer, now wanted to recruit him as an informant to identify communists within SAG. According to Reagan's own account, he initially asserted that he would not "go in for Red-baiting." The agents, however, knew exactly which lever to pull. "We thought that someone the Communists hate as much as they hate you might be willing to help us," they told Reagan. When Reagan expressed chagrin, they quoted a party official as asking, "What are we going to do about the sonofabitching Reagan?" The implication of yet another physical threat, whether true or not, convinced Reagan to cooperate. He identified "two cliques within the Guild that on all questions of policy follow the Communist Party line," and provided a list of names of those within SAG whom he suspected of supporting the "Communist infiltration of the motion picture industry." The agents encouraged him to submit the names of others in the future. In their files, they assigned him a number, designating him as informant T-10. Like Brass Bancroft, identified as agent 565 in *Murder In the Air*, Reagan could now serve the government in defense of the nation. He would meet with FBI men several more times over the next few years.

Jane Wyman seemed less enthusiastic about cooperating with the FBI. While Reagan had been expanding his political activism, Wyman had emerged as one of the hottest film stars. Her portrayal of Ma Baxter in *The Yearling* had won her an Academy Award nomination for Best Actress. Reagan, on the other hand, continued to experience career frustrations. *Night Unto Night* turned out so poorly that Warners executives decided not to release it. Warners next cast him as a soldier on leave in the comedy *Voice of the Turtle*. Although the movie gave Reagan his first role as a romantic lead in an A-film, Reagan resisted the assignment as inappropriate. He balked even more vociferously at his next job, *That Hagen Girl*, in which he would play opposite legendary child star Shirley Temple in her first adult role. The story line, in which Temple suspected that Reagan might be her illegitimate father, only to fall in love with her much older co-star at the close, offended Reagan. Only promises by Jack Warner to place him next in more of an action role convinced Reagan to participate. When released, *That Hagen Girl* fulfilled all of Reagan's misgivings and doomed Temple's future in the movies.

In June 1947, while filming *That Hagen Girl*, Reagan contracted acute viral pneumonia, running a fever as high as 104 degrees. Wyman, meanwhile, was pregnant with their third child. While Reagan recovered in the hospital, losing 17 pounds in the process, Wyman suddenly went into labor three months prematurely. She gave birth to a girl who survived for one day before dying. With Reagan still hospitalized and severely ill, Wyman had to suffer the loss alone.

The tragedy widened the developing gulf between the couple. In the aftermath of their child's death, Reagan and Wyman both subsumed themselves in their careers. Reagan returned to work on *That Hagen Girl*, the production of which had been delayed by his illness, and plunged more deeply into his work as SAG president. Wyman began preparing for her role as *Johnny Belinda*, a deaf mute rape victim. She decided that she could better understand the world of the deaf by placing wax in her ears, both on the set and at home. Whether consciously or unconsciously, Wyman could thus totally shut off Reagan's incessant talking about union and national politics, which no longer held her interest. Their children, Maureen and Michael, seemed an afterthought. Reagan was a distant father; Wyman, obsessed with each of her roles, a mercurial mother. Reagan would later comment that Wyman "never learned to separate her work from her personal life." A nanny cared for the children during the week, and Reagan's mother, Nelle, often took them on weekends. "We missed having a normal relationship with [our parents]," recalled Michael, "because we saw each of them a couple of days a month."

Within SAG, the major issue of contention swirled around communism. Congress had recently passed the anti-union Taft-Hartley Act that required all labor leaders to sign declarations attesting that they were not communists. Some liberals in SAG opposed any cooperation with the law. On September 12, 1947, when a SAG board member proposed a loyalty oath for all Guild members, Reagan attempted to mediate the dispute. He proposed that rather than a mandatory pledge, members could sign a voluntary statement, "pledging true faith and allegiance to the United States of America," and repudiating "the teachings and program" of Stalinism and "every other form of dictatorship." Reagan seems honestly not to have understood that the refusal to sign this "voluntary" statement would just as effectively label people as communist sympathizers as an ironclad loyalty oath. The board approved Reagan's policy and also called on union officials to sign the statements required by the Taft-Hartley Act. SAG treasurer Anne Revere, an Academy Award-winning actress, refused to sign the affidavit and resigned her office, though she was allowed to remain on the board.

Six weeks later the House Select Committee on Un-American Activities (HUAC) held hearings in Washington, D.C., to investigate the alleged communist conspiracy to infiltrate the film industry. HUAC called both "friendly" witnesses, who appeared willingly and often were asked to name people whom they believed to be communists, and "unfriendly" witnesses, who appeared under subpoena and were asked to attest to whether or not they had ever belonged to the Communist Party. The hearings, designed more to generate publicity than to identify subversives, became a media circus. Hollywood liberals like Humphrey Bogart, Lauren Bacall, and John Garfield formed a Hollywood Committee for the First Amendment and attended the ceremonies to protest what they saw as "Hitlerian tactics" on the part of HUAC. Reagan and his two predecessors as SAG president, Robert Montgomery and George Murphy, appeared before the committee as "friendly" witnesses, though none were asked to "name names" of communists within the Guild. Their statements seemed designed to assure the assembled congressmen that SAG and the movie industry could handle the problem without government intervention.

Reagan testified that a small dissident clique within SAG had been suspected of following the dishonest "tactics that we associate with the Communist Party," but that he had no knowledge as to whether or not they were party members. He reassured HUAC members that "we have done a pretty good job of keeping those people's activities curtailed," exposing their lies, opposing their propaganda, and making "democracy work" by keeping other members informed as to their activities. He did not believe that "the communists have ever at any time been able to use the motion-picture screen as a sounding board for their philosophy or ideology." Reagan opposed outlawing "any political party . . . on the basis of political ideology," unless it could be proven that "an organization is an agent of a . . . foreign power." He hoped that the United States would never "become urged, either by fear or resentment of this group, to compromise with any of our democratic principles."

Reagan's message, which on the surface appeared to be a call for civil liberties and limited government, received widespread praise from anti-communist liberals. James Loeb, the executive secretary of the Americans for Democratic Action, called it "by all odds, the most honest and forthright from a decent liberal point of view." Reagan had not been asked to name names publicly and thus escaped the opprobrium that fell on those who informed on their fellow actors. (Reagan, however, had already clandestinely identified communists for the FBI.) Not all witnesses before HUAC fared as well. Ten members of the Screen Writers Guild, including Reagan's old nemeses John Howard Lawson and Dalton Trumbo, refused to testify before the committee. The Hollywood Ten, as the group became known, asserted not that they had the right to be communists and profess revolutionary principles, but they should not be compelled to reveal whether or not they were party members. HUAC declared the men in contempt and threatened them with jail sentences. Thus the zealots of the anti-communist right miraculously transformed authoritarian communists like Lawson into martyrs for the cause of free speech.

The leaders of the movie industry seized this opportunity to purge communists and liberals, most of whom had supported the CSU in its recent struggles, from its ranks. On November 24, 1947, the studios issued the Waldorf Declaration, suspending the Hollywood Ten without pay and stating that they would no longer employ communists or those advocating the overthrow of the government. Reagan, despite his growing anti-communism, expressed concerns about this position. At the December 3 meeting of the Association of Motion Picture Producers to clarify the Waldorf Declaration, Reagan questioned how the industry would determine who was actually a communist. When Louis B. Mayer answered that each studio would make the decision, Reagan objected that this would create a blacklist that might include those favoring liberal causes, but not communist sympathies.

At the next SAG board meeting, Reagan introduced a resolution criticizing the Waldorf Declaration. Although the Guild should reject both the theory and tactics of the Communist Party, proposed Reagan, producers could not discriminate against their employees on the basis of political beliefs. SAG should not deny memberships to communists, although communists would be barred from leadership positions by the Taft-Hartley Act. Reagan doubtless saw this as a compromise position, but board members overwhelmingly rejected it as too soft on communism. A second resolution less critical of the industry heads and promising cooperation with their anti-communist efforts passed the board with Reagan's support.

Reagan's shift into the anti-communist ranks did not yet constitute a shift to the political right. Many other liberals had also signed on to the anti-communist crusade. In the 1948 elections Reagan campaigned ardently for President Truman and other Democratic candidates, rejecting the more leftist challenge of Henry Wallace and the Republicanism of Thomas Dewey. Reagan made a national radio address on behalf of Truman and Minnesota senatorial candidate Hubert Humphrey. The speech, which attacked big business for causing inflation, revealed not only Reagan's continuing liberalism, but also the populist rhetorical style that he would employ throughout his career. "You may know me as a motion picture actor," he explained, "but tonight I am just a citizen concerned about the national election next month." Reagan used statistics to reveal that corporate profits had far outstripped wages, then presented an extreme story clipped from the newspaper about a skilled worker named Carpenter who, finding his retirement savings eaten up by "Republican inflation," had been forced to return to work. Reagan deftly delivered the telling punch line: "Mr. Carpenter is 91 years old."

As Reagan waged these political battles, conflicts on his personal domestic front had reached a denouement. In December 1947, he and Jane Wyman separated. A brief attempt at reconciliation failed, and in June 1948 Wyman filed for divorce. A disappointed Louella Parsons wrote, "No marital separation since I broke the story that Mary Pickford, America's sweetheart, was leaving Douglas Fairbanks, has had the effect of the parting of the Reagans." Wyman, having to justify her claims of "mental cruelty" as the legal grounds for her petition, cited "continual arguments on his political views." Reagan, though doubtless aware that he and Jane had drifted apart in no small part because of his relentless union activities and resulting inattention to his family, seemed genuinely surprised by the divorce, describing it as "something I never expected to happen to me." Jane received custody of Maureen and Michael.

The divorce occurred just as the opposing trajectories of their respective careers became more apparent. The 1948 release of *Johnny Belinda*, for which Wyman would receive the Academy Award for Best Actress, confirmed her place as one of the biggest stars in Hollywood, just as the debut of *That Hagen Girl* reaffirmed Reagan's declining fortunes. Warners had cast Reagan and Wyman to appear together in *John Loves Mary*, an adaptation of a popular postwar stage play about a returning soldier, but with their split, Reagan found himself playing opposite newcomer Patricia Neal instead. Another light film, *The Girl From Jones Beach*, followed. Warners next offered him the lead role in *The Hasty Heart*, yet another film about World War II veterans. Reagan rebelled and threatened to take a suspension from his contract rather than accept the part. Only the intercession of agent Lew Wasserman, who pledged to renegotiate his contract to give Reagan more freedom in selecting his roles and a promise from Jack Warner that Reagan would be considered for the lead in *Ghost Mountain*, a western property that Reagan himself had suggested to the studio, convinced Reagan to do *The Hasty Heart*.

The Hasty Heart proved a more rewarding experience than Reagan expected. Filmed in England, it marked Reagan's first trip outside the United States. The film itself was one of the most prestigious and successful that Reagan had appeared in, though most of the accolades would eventually go to his English co-star Richard Todd. Reagan also took note of conditions in Great Britain during his five-month stay and quickly became disillusioned with the welfare state. "I shed the last ideas I ever had about government ownership of anything," he later claimed.

Reagan returned to America in April 1949 in time to learn that Warners had offered the lead in *Ghost Mountain* to Errol Flynn. Reagan wired Jack Warner in protest. "I've always been good and done everything you've asked—even *That Hagen Girl*," wrote the disillusioned Reagan. Wasserman stepped in and renegotiated Reagan's contract with Warner Brothers. Warners, like other studios, was moving away from the contract system that had characterized the industry in the 1930s and 1940s. They released Reagan from his exclusive obligations, offering to pay half of his original salary for just one picture a year for the remainder of his contract. Reagan would be free to negotiate parts with other studios. Wasserman then turned around and made a five-picture deal with Universal that would pay Reagan $75,000 a film. Reagan would also have the right to sell his services to other studios.

The new arrangement freed Reagan from his restricted commitment to Warners, but it did not end his frustrations. Reagan objected in a published interview that he received such bad parts that "I could telephone my lines in and it wouldn't make a difference." When Warners cast him as an attorney in *Storm Warning*, he commented, "Here I am playing lawyers and dying to play in westerns.

If Warner Brothers ever got around to putting me in a western, they'd cast me as a lawyer from the East." Indeed, Reagan made 41 films for Warners over a 15-year period. Only one, *Santa Fe Trail*, was a western.

Meanwhile Reagan continued to flourish in his role as SAG president. He led the negotiations for a new contract in 1948, winning admiration from his colleagues. Jack Dales, SAG's executive director, later spoke glowingly of Reagan's abilities. "Depending on the situation he was two men," revealed Dales, "aggressive fighter across the table, then in conferences among ourselves in our caucuses . . . most realistic." Reagan also began to play a major role with the newly created Motion Picture Industrial Council (MPIC). The studios had formed MPIC as a public relations arm to counter charges of communist subversion and other criticisms of Hollywood. In July 1949 MPIC named Reagan its chairman, and he began making speeches on behalf of the movie industry. Reagan sought to dispel the image of Hollywood as a den of immorality. The movie industry, he proclaimed, was populated by "hard-working, church-going, family men and women." Hollywood marriages, he would add, conveniently ignoring his own recent divorce, had a high rate of success.

MPIC, however, remained primarily a vehicle to advance the growing Hollywood blacklist. In 1947 Reagan had still publicly opposed the dismissal of people for their political beliefs and in later years he would deny the existence of a blacklist. By the early 1950s, however, he had, through MPIC and his role as SAG president, become complicit in the practice. Communists, he had now concluded with ample justification, owed their "allegiance to Russia" and were "traitors practicing treason." Reagan saw his own task as assisting actors and others falsely accused of communism or former communists who now were truly penitent and could be rehabilitated within the Hollywood community. Former communists who had changed their minds, he wrote in 1950, "should be willing to . . . admit 'I was wrong'" and give information to government agencies fighting communism. When Edward Dmytryk, one of the Hollywood Ten, sought to return to the fold, he met with an MPIC "rehabilitation committee," led by Reagan. MPIC heralded Dmytryk's repentance in an advertisement signed by Reagan and others. The ad, headlined "You Can Be Free Men Again," certified that Dmytryk had sincerely, not opportunistically, renounced communism and should thus be reinstated.

When HUAC resumed its investigation of Hollywood in 1951, Reagan expressed no sympathy for those who refused to cooperate. For HUAC, rehabilitation meant the humiliation of identifying communists at public hearings. In March 1951 they subpoenaed Academy Award-winning actress Gale Sondergaard to testify. Sondergaard, in a letter published in *Variety*, the industry newspaper, announced her intention to refuse to name names by taking the Fifth Amendment. She called upon SAG to "make a public declaration that it would not tolerate any industry blacklist against any of its members." Reagan called an emergency session of the SAG board and urged the rejection of Sondergaard's request. The board responded with a letter expressing opposition to "any secret blacklist," but nonetheless endorsing the exposure of "all participants in the international Communist Party conspiracy" as enemies of the United States. "If any actor by his own actions outside of union activities has so offended public opinion that he has made himself unsaleable at the box office," they asserted, affirming the very rationale of the blacklist, "the Guild cannot and would not want to force any employers to hire him." Two months later, Anne Revere, a longtime board member and another Academy Award winner, informed the SAG leadership that she too had been asked to testify before HUAC and asked for help. Reagan advised her, "It's so simple. All you've got to do is name a couple of names that have already been named." Revere resigned from the board and, like Sondergaard, took the Fifth Amendment.

Actor Sterling Hayden, a former communist, took the alternative path. He appeared before HUAC and informed on his former colleagues. He also credited Reagan for blocking the communist threat in SAG. Hayden described Reagan as "very vocal and clear-thinking." Reagan was, extolled the repentant Hayden, "a one-man battalion against this thing." Hayden made 23 movies between 1951 and 1955 and worked steadily in Hollywood until his death in 1986. Nearly two decades passed before either Revere or Sondergaard made another film.

The Shift to Conservatism

As the president of the Screen Actors Guild, Ronald Reagan had achieved a kind of stardom and prominence that had largely eluded him in the movies. For his birthday in February 1950, the Friar's Club saluted him at a gala affair at the Beverly Hills Hotel. Six hundred of Hollywood's leading figures heard speeches lauding Reagan for the "dignity and stature" he had brought to the motion picture business. Friar spokesman George Jessel proclaimed, "Hollywood and the industry love him."

Reagan's quest for greater respectability within the movies, however, remained unfulfilled. Since the end of World War II Reagan had repeatedly called for roles in films that included "adventure and excitement." Westerns especially appealed to him. "I think the heritage of our country is based a great deal on those early days of violence here in the West," he explained. "They might even be athletic pictures, football or baseball or whatever, to show the principles America lives by; the pioneer spirit, the sportsmanship, the health and courage." By winning freedom from his contract with Warner Brothers, Reagan hoped to land more of these roles. But his first two pictures with Universal Studios were light comedies. In *Bedtime for Bonzo* Reagan good-naturedly played the lead opposite a scene-stealing chimpanzee. He turned down two other roles that Universal offered him. In 1951 Reagan accepted a smaller-

Ronald Reagan taking a break from his duties as host of General Electric Theater. (Courtesy Ronald Reagan Library)

than-usual fee to appear for Paramount studios in *The Last Outpost*, his first leading role as a western star. The movie confirmed what the studios had long suspected; Reagan lacked the ability to carry an action movie.

Late in 1951 Reagan made his last film for Warner Brothers. Ironically, it featured him in the type of role he had always craved. Reagan played baseball great Grover Cleveland Alexander in *The Winning Team*. As in his early days as a radio broadcaster, he got to mingle with the major league baseball players cast in the movie. During the filming Reagan learned that Universal had canceled the remainder of his five-film contract. When *The Winning Team* finished shooting on January 28, 1952, it also ended Reagan's 15-year relationship with Warners. He would be out of work for the next fourteen months.

Reagan felt that retribution for his union activities had contributed to his fall from grace, but several other factors probably had a greater influence. Having reached the age of 40, Reagan had passed the stage where good looks and youth alone could carry him into starring roles. Some actors weathered this transition readily, but Reagan, who had never developed his acting skills, could not command the greater depth that roles for older actors required. Had he been satisfied to play the comedy parts that best suited his personality, he might have prolonged his film career, but Reagan longed for and demanded action roles. In addition, the industry itself had changed. The end of the contract system benefited big-name stars, who could command high salaries in studio bidding wars. Lesser players like Reagan, on the other hand, lost the security of their long-term contracts. Finally, the rise of television had cut sharply into movie attendance, curtailing film production and reducing the number of roles available.

The lapse into unemployment came at an inauspicious time for Reagan. Since his divorce from Jane Wyman he had dated and bedded many of Hollywood's most attractive women. Increasingly in the early 1950s, however, he could be found in the company of Nancy Davis. Davis, the daughter of stage actress Edie Luckett and stepdaughter of prominent Chicago neurosurgeon Loyal Davis, had appeared in Hollywood in 1948 and had a mercurial flirtation with stardom. Her mother's connections had won her a screen test at MGM, and she began her career in an A-film, *East Side, West Side*. The following year she scored the lead in *The Next Voice You Hear*. But Davis lacked the combination of looks, talent, and ambition needed to be a star. In September 1951, after seven movies, MGM declined to pick up the option on her contract.

In studio publicity Davis identified her foremost goal as achieving "a successful happy marriage." From the first time she met Reagan in 1949, he became the target of her attentions. She became active in SAG and worked her way onto the executive board. In February 1952, a few weeks after Reagan ended his work at Warners and had been terminated by Universal, they learned that Davis was pregnant. The couple hastily arranged a wedding for March 4, 1952. Seven and half months later, their daughter Patti was born.

With Reagan not working on any movies, his duties as SAG president occupied most of his time. Television had become the foremost concern confronting the union. Many in the film industry saw the new medium, much of which was initially centered in New York, as a threat to their livelihoods. In 1951 Reagan had admonished SAG members, "I don't want to see any of you going over to the enemy," meaning television. A critical issue revolved around how actors would be paid for television shows, which might be aired more than one time, and for movies made for theaters but later shown on television. SAG sought residual payments for its members, compensation for each repeat television usage. The studios adamantly resisted such a plan.

Meanwhile, MCA, the aggressive talent agency that represented Reagan and many other movie actors, saw television as an entryway to greater industry dominance. MCA formed Revue Productions, a new branch that would create television programming. SAG bylaws, however, had long prevented agents from also acting as producers, fearing that this would create a conflict of interest. Now, in 1952, Lew Wasserman of MCA approached Reagan and the board and asked for a blanket waiver allowing MCA to continue to represent actors, while allowing its Revue subsidiary to produce shows. On rare occasions, SAG had given agents temporary waivers, allowing them to engage in a particular production, but the notion of a general suspension of the rules was unprecedented.

MCA offered two inducements for this substantial concession. Hollywood film studios had been reluctant to risk their assets on television production. MCA promised that Revue would be based in California, providing needed work to many actors. Furthermore MCA offered to become the first studio to pay residuals, providing greater compensation for performers.

By any definition of conflict of interest, Reagan should have stepped aside from these deliberations. Wasserman, Reagan's longtime agent, had negotiated lucrative contracts for him in the past and still held the key to Reagan's floundering career in his hands. Reagan, however, never had a clear sense of propriety in these matters. He saw no inherent clash in his status as an MCA client and his role as SAG president. In July 1952 the board unanimously approved and Reagan signed a waiver that allowed MCA's Revue auxiliary to produce television programs. The details of the pact remained confidential, preventing studios from learning that MCA had broken the line on residuals and others from suspecting that SAG had granted the waiver in exchange for financial considerations.

In later years Reagan would vehemently deny that any such quid pro quo had existed, insisting that the sole determinant was the creation of more jobs. Television production, however, would doubtless have drifted to California without the agreement. The true benefit for the union lay in the precedent of residuals, a practice that eventually expanded and greatly enriched not just actors, but writers, directors, and others who worked in television.

Whatever gains the actors made paled in comparison to the windfall that accrued to MCA. MCA could now offer its clients steady work in Revue Productions. Since SAG granted a blanket waiver to no other agencies, actors began abandoning their representatives and flocking to MCA. MCA came to dominate television production. Within ten years it had also acquired Decca Records and Universal Studios. MCA became known as "The Octopus," its tentacles described as "reaching out to all phases and grasping everything in show business," and Lew Wasserman became the most powerful man in Hollywood. The 1952 waiver formed the basis for this burgeoning entertainment empire.

No apparent benefits immediately accrued to Reagan for this largesse. In November 1952, he stepped down as president of SAG. He had served for almost six years, longer than any other person in that role. In 1953 he began to appear in the types of westerns and action movies he had long desired. None of them did well. His salary dropped to $30,000, less than half his peak of just a few years earlier. After he made *Tennessee's Partner* for RKO in 1954, he received no offers for two years. Nancy Davis made just one movie, the science fiction thriller *Donovan's Brain,* during this period.

Reagan increasingly supplemented his income with fees for speaking engagements, or the "mashed potato circuit" as he liked to call it. He appeared before Kiwanis Clubs, at colleges, and for other groups who wished to bask in his celebrity. Nonetheless, financial pressures had begun to mount. In 1951 he had bought a 290-acre horse ranch in Malibu Canyon that had yet to turn a profit. By 1952 he was deeply in debt. Reagan blamed much of his financial travails on the nation's tax structure. The progressive income tax of the postwar era claimed as much as 91 percent of the top earnings of the nation's wealthiest individuals. At the peak of his movie career, Reagan fell into this category. "True, I'd been making handsome money ever since World War II, but that handsome money lost a lot of its beauty and substance going through the 91 percent tax bracket," he later explained. Attacks on taxation began to appear in his speeches as early as 1951 when he complained that the "discriminatory taxes" targeted at Hollywood represented an "insidious . . . inroad" aimed "at our democratic institutions." At one point he proposed that actors, many of whom had relatively short periods in which they earned high incomes, should be accorded a depreciation allowance similar to that granted to oil producers.

In 1954 MCA approached him with a lucrative offer to appear in Las Vegas. The growing desert resort sought big-name performers to attract gamblers to its hotels. Reagan refused to appear when the El Rancho Hotel wanted him to host a show with a stripper on the bill, but, desperate for money, he accepted a two-week slot at the Last Frontier, as master of ceremonies for a 50-minute revue featuring the Continentals, a slapstick comedy group. The act went over well enough, but one critic pointedly questioned whether Reagan's debut meant that Las Vegas would "have to suffer a retreating army of fading Hollywood stars." The hotel offered to extend the booking, but Reagan, despite financial needs, demurred. "Never again will I sell myself so short," he informed his agent.

Both Reagan and Davis still remained on the board of the Screen Actors Guild. In spring 1954 SAG renegotiated its formal contract with the organization representing talent agents. The new agreement allowed agents to receive limited waivers to produce television shows and movies. MCA, on the other hand, requested a continuation of their arrangement permitting unlimited production. The board, including Reagan, Davis, and four other MCA clients, voted to approve this concession for MCA and MCA alone.

During this time, Reagan was filming *Cattle Queen of Montana,* another forgettable western. In the summer of 1954 MCA approached him with an unusual proposition. General Electric (G.E.) and its advertising agency had asked Revue to create *G.E. Theater,* a weekly half-hour television program in which well-known actors could appear in dramatic or comedic settings of their own choosing, often playing against their usual image. Thus comedian Jack Benny could appear as a hard-boiled detective; a dramatic actor might appear in a comedy. The show needed a master of ceremonies to provide continuity, introducing and closing each segment, and occasionally playing roles in the shows. G.E. also hoped that this individual might become a spokesperson for the company, touring its production plants and addressing local managers and employees. Reagan, with his experience as an announcer, actor, and public speaker, fit the bill perfectly. The job promised him an annual income of $125,000, dissipating whatever remaining reservations Reagan might have had about television. Reagan readily recognized the offer for what it was, "the cavalry [coming] to the rescue" of his beleaguered career.

Reagan debuted as the host of *G.E. Theater* on September 26, 1954, also appearing in the evening's episode. Two weeks later he starred in a feature titled "Long Way 'Round" as a man approaching a nervous breakdown. Nancy Davis played opposite him as his leading lady. *G.E. Theater*, slotted in a favorable spot on Sunday nights following the popular *Ed Sullivan Show* on CBS, became an immediate hit, ranking among the top ten shows of the season. Reagan starred in three more segments during the first year. In most of the shows, however, Reagan appeared only for a few minutes at the beginning and the end. He nonetheless appreciated the unprecedented exposure that the new television medium offered. "I am seen by more people in one week than I am in the movie theaters," he marveled.

G.E. Theater saved Reagan from a financial and career standpoint, but it was the subsidiary obligations of the contract, requiring Reagan to tour General Electric's 185 plants throughout the nation, that transformed his life. His contract required Reagan to spend 16 weeks a year visiting G.E. facilities. His main job was to mingle with the managers and boost the morale of the workers. G.E. employees had the opportunity to rub elbows with a famous star, listen to Reagan's tales of Hollywood and endless supply of jokes, and absorb his pep talks extolling the virtues of America, free enterprise, and the corporation itself. The personable Reagan enjoyed his interactions with people, most of whom appreciated his friendly, down-to-earth manner. G.E. increasingly dispatched him to speak to business and civic groups in each community as well. Reagan estimated that by 1956 he was presenting as many as 14 speeches a day. By 1958 he had become, according to one poll, one of the most familiar faces in America.

The combination of his weekly television appearances and widespread speeches made Reagan the embodiment of General Electric. His identification with the company extended into the domestic arena. In 1955 G.E. totally equipped his home in Pacific Palisades with new electrical appliances as a showcase for its wares. He and Nancy demonstrated their home of the future in a 3-minute G.E. advertisement. The company's motto, "Progress is our most important product," reaffirmed Reagan's natural optimism and faith in the powers of technology.

General Electric, by all accounts, did not dictate what Reagan had to say as long as he remained within the broad framework of corporate interests. Reagan wrote his speeches himself. He still avidly read newspapers and magazines like *Reader's Digest,* collecting facts, statistics, anecdotes, and jokes that he could present to his audience. He learned how to read his listeners, improving his timing and delivery, and weighing which tales and examples had the greatest impact. Reagan developed a philosophy of public speaking. "You have to keep pounding away with your message," he later explained, "because that's the only way it will sink into the collective consciousness. I'm a big believer in stump speeches—speeches you can give over and over again with slight variations. Because if you have something you believe in deeply, it's worth repeating time and again until you achieve it."

His earliest presentations reflected the concerns that he had developed during the postwar years: a blend of patriotism and anti-communism, a critique of the income tax, and a paean to free enterprise. As early as 1952, he began to present his own variation of the venerable Puritan image of America as a "City On a Hill," "a place in the divine scheme of things that was set aside as a promised land . . . God in shedding his grace on this country has always in his divine scheme of things kept an eye on our land and guided it as a promised land for those people who love freedom." Increasingly, however, Reagan's talks took a sharp turn to the political right with pointed attacks on government and sharp critiques of the New Deal programs he had once heartily endorsed.

During the early years with G.E. Reagan completed his migration from liberalism to conservatism. In part this stemmed naturally from his ardent anti-communism, but many who shared this philosophy nonetheless maintained their liberalism. Reagan still identified himself as a Democrat in 1954. He had urged Dwight Eisenhower to run for president on the Democratic ticket in 1952, then had supported the general as a "Democrat for Eisenhower" when he ran for the presidency. Traveling for G.E. reinforced Reagan's incipient conservative tendencies. Reagan later claimed that as he met with people throughout the nation he heard repeated tales of hardships caused by taxes and government regulations that shaped his thinking. Other factors also encouraged his rightward drift. Because of his fear of flying, Reagan made all of his trips by train, accompanied during the first two years by publicity man Earl B. Dunckel. Dunckel, a self-described arch-conservative, hammered away at the always easily engaged Reagan during these long excursions, railing about the evils of government. Reagan's father-in-law, Loyal Davis, a longtime contributor to right-wing causes, reinforced these messages. Within the G.E. corporate culture and among the business groups he addressed, Reagan found himself in a conservative environment. These audiences responded most enthusiastically to his attacks on taxes and wasteful government spending and regulations.

By the late 1950s Reagan had developed both the speaking style and much of the content that would characterize the remainder of his political career. He collected and presented a dazzling string of facts, quotations, statistics, and anecdotes that endorsed his anti-government message. Reagan never questioned that the "facts" he had come across might be false, the quotations misattributed, or the stories unrepresentative. He presented them as, and believed them to be, the unvarnished truth. One dubious, unverifiable factoid that he had chanced upon was the assertion that no civilization had survived when it taxed more than a third of the national income. Reagan over the years tracked the rise of this figure in the United States until it had exceeded the critical line, with the dire implications evident. He repeatedly attacked the progressive income tax as "spawned more than a hundred years ago by Karl Marx, who listed it as the prime essential of a socialist state." Reagan described plans for socialized medicine as "one of the traditional methods of imposing statism or Socialism on a people," criticizing even Veterans Administration hospitals as a government giveaway.

Reagan grew increasingly shrill in his attacks on the Soviet Union and the failure of the U.S. government to recognize the true stakes in the Cold War. "Whether we admit it or not, we are in a war. The war was declared a century ago by Karl Marx and re-affirmed by Lenin when he said that Communism and Capitalism cannot exist side by side," warned Reagan. He paraphrased Abraham Lincoln, asserting, "Today we are engaged in a great war to determine whether the world can exist half-slave or half-free."

Reagan's speeches were so crammed with information that they comprised a seemingly irrefutable case against the excesses of government and the need to restrain its growth. Though the implications about the international and domestic threats to American freedom were ominous, even apocalyptic, Reagan's infectious enthusiasm and optimism suffused his artful presentations. He converted his message into one of potential salvation and hope. Reagan presented these orations under different titles like "Losing Our Freedom On the Installment Plan," "What's At Stake," and "Encroaching Control." With their recurrent themes and frequently recycled examples, however, they all came to be commonly regarded by his partisans as "The Speech."

Reagan's speaking tours, his responsibilities with General Electric, and a lack of demand for his services had brought an effective end to his movie career. In 1955 he appeared in *Tennessee's Partner*, a western where he was once again relegated to playing a sidekick (named Cowpoke) to star John Payne. In 1957 he co-starred with his wife in *Hellcats of the Navy*, a World War II movie so bad that it effectively rang down the curtain on both of their movie careers. Nancy also acted in a few segments of *G.E. Theater,* usually playing opposite her husband, but for the most part she seemed content to stay at home rearing their children.

In May 1958, Ronald and Nancy Reagan had their second child, Ron, Jr. Although Reagan often extolled the virtues of family in his speeches, his own family had its peculiarities. A clear love and devotion existed between Ronald and Nancy, but their intense connection tended to isolate the children. Maureen and Michael, Reagan's children with Jane Wyman, saw little of their father, spending most of their childhood in boarding schools and summer camps. Ron's older sister, Patti, did not know that she had a stepbrother and sister until Michael came to live with the Reagans when Patti was seven years old. When challenged as to why he had withheld the information, Reagan responded, "Well, we just haven't gotten around to it yet." The children found Reagan likable, but distant; Nancy controlling and frightening. When Reagan came to speak at Michael's high school graduation, he seemingly did not recognize his son. Patti also recalled coming into a room where her father was working and have him "look up from his note cards as though he wasn't sure who I was."

Throughout these years both Ronald and Nancy remained on the SAG board. In late 1959 a new crisis, precipitated once again by the union's relationship with MCA, arose. MCA had purchased the rights to hundreds of movies made by Paramount Studios to be shown on television. The conglomerate earned $50 million in just two years from this transaction. SAG demanded that MCA and the other studios pay residuals to the actors in films upon broadcast. The studios, hoping to make a clear profit on these old movies, refused. In addition, the Guild hoped to set up a welfare and pension fund for actors. SAG braced for a showdown with the producers and requested that Reagan, seven years removed from the presidency, come back to lead the union. Some hoped that his close relationship with MCA would smooth the negotiations. "We wanted a strong leader," asserted SAG director Jack Dales, "and everyone turned back to Ronnie Reagan." Reagan, busy with his obligations to G.E., hesitated to accept until Lew Wasserman of MCA, far from an impartial party to the dispute, urged him to take the job.

In reality, Reagan was ineligible to serve as SAG president. He had recently renegotiated his contract with General Electric, giving him a one-quarter interest in the show's release rights, making him, in effect, a producer. The Guild had a longstanding policy against producers serving on the board. Indeed, Reagan had originally become president in 1947 when Robert Montgomery had stepped down in order to produce one of his own films. When challenged about this, Reagan and the Guild flatly lied. "He has no ownership interest, percentage participation or otherwise in the G.E. Theater. He is not a producer of the series," stated the Guild.

Reagan returned to the SAG presidency in November 1959. The residuals issue, however, proved intractable. On March 7 SAG went on strike. MCA and several smaller studios immediately settled with the union, but the industry giants took a firm stand. The strike lasted for six weeks, during most of which there was no progress toward a resolution. With the unemployed actors getting desperate, Reagan and SAG struck a deal with the studios. SAG surrendered all residual rights to films made before 1960 in exchange for the creation of a pension plan. The studios contributed $2.26 million (less than they had offered at the start of the strike) to start the plan and promised to contribute a small percentage of the sales of movies to television to fund it.

Reagan addressed the SAG membership on April 18, 1960, asserting that this was the best settlement possible. The actors, already drained by the lengthy strike, accepted this explanation. They voted overwhelmingly, 6,399 to 259, to approve the pact. Many actors, especially Reagan's contemporaries from the 1930s and 1940s, whose residual rights had been sacrificed, considered the 1960 contract "the great giveaway." "The pictures were sold down the river for a certain amount of money and it was nothing," complained Bob Hope, Reagan's close friend.

With the strike over, Reagan resigned his presidency and announced that he had indeed become a producer on *G.E. Theater*, "with an interest in the profits." His new contract notwithstanding, Reagan's relationship with General Electric had begun to unravel. In 1959 Reagan had added attacks on the Tennessee Valley Authority (TVA), a federal flood control and energy program dating from the New Deal, to his speeches. TVA was a major purchaser of G.E. equipment. When Reagan learned that his speeches had offended corporate leaders, he agreed to withdraw the references. But it had grown apparent to

G.E. that Reagan's growing politicization could prove an embarrassment. Perhaps more significantly, the ratings for *G.E. Theater* had begun to slip. NBC had programmed *Bonanza*, an immensely popular western series filmed in color, opposite the still black-and-white Reagan show. *G.E. Theater*, long a fixture in the top ten, dropped to twenty-third in the ratings.

Reagan's ever more extreme political utterances made him a growing liability. During the 1960 presidential election, Reagan campaigned doggedly for Republican candidate Richard Nixon, making more than 200 speeches on his behalf. Reagan had wanted to formally change his party registration to Republican, but at Nixon's urging he remained a Democrat, fronting for a largely bogus "Democrats for Nixon" organization. When Nixon lost to John F. Kennedy, Reagan turned his vitriol on the Kennedy administration. "Under the tousled boyish haircut," Reagan wrote of Kennedy, "he is still Karl Marx." In early 1962 he accused Kennedy and his aide Arthur Schlesinger, Jr. of leading the nation into social "slavery."

Meanwhile, Reagan's past activities as head of the Screen Actors Guild and the granting of a blanket waiver to MCA had come back to haunt him. The U.S. Justice Department had launched an antitrust investigation into growing MCA dominance of Hollywood. An internal justice department memo contended that the exclusive waiver had "vaulted MCA to the head of the television industry with advantages that its competitors could never hope to equal . . . The central fact of MCA's whole rise to power . . . was undoubtedly the SAG blanket waiver." Investigators believed that Reagan had participated in a "conspiracy between MCA and SAG." The FBI examined the tax returns for Reagan, his wife, and other members of the SAG board in the early 1950s, but apparently uncovered no evidence that they had received personal favors for their acquiescence.

On February 5, 1962, Reagan was called to testify before a grand jury considering the MCA-SAG relationship. He offered evasive answers to most of the questions. He admitted that his involvement in the negotiations constituted "a possibility of some conflict of interest" and stated falsely that he had been in Glacier National Park making a movie during the 1952 negotiations. He argued inaccurately that these waivers were commonplace, failing to give examples of other waivers. He denied that MCA had received concessions in exchange for residuals, only to retract that assertion when confronted by an MCA document proving the tradeoff. Reagan repeatedly testified that he could not recall specific details of SAG's dealings with MCA.

In July 1962 the Justice Department issued a civil indictment of MCA for violations of the Sherman Anti-Trust Act, naming SAG as a co-conspirator. MCA avoided further investigation, and possible embarrassment for Reagan, by agreeing to sever its original talent agency, now a relatively small part of its operations, from its production activities. For Reagan, however, the damage had been done. The combination of his potential implication in a federal suit, his political outspokenness, and declining ratings led General Electric to pull the plug on *G.E. Theater*. In March 1962, a few weeks after his grand jury testimony, G.E. unexpectedly announced its withdrawal from the sponsorship of *G.E. Theater*. According to one account, Reagan flew to New York and begged an official to reinstate the show. "What can I do?" he exclaimed. "I can't act any more. I can't do anything else. How can I support my family?" *G.E. Theater* aired for the last time in September 1962.

Reagan suffered another humiliating professional rebuke when MCA dropped him as a client. Wasserman claimed that he could find no more takers for Reagan's services. Reagan felt that the powerful Wasserman, a leading

Democratic fundraiser, had punished him for his political activities. Reagan signed on with William Meiklejohn, his original agent. Meikeljohn lined up a few television appearances with Reagan guest-starring on episodes of *Wagon Train* and *Kraft Suspense Theater* in 1963. Reagan also made a brief return to the movies. Revue Productions hired him to play a brutal gangster in a made-for-television version of Ernest Hemingway's short story, *The Killers.* Throughout his long career, Reagan had never before played a villain. The violence in the film, including a scene of Reagan slapping co-star Angie Dickinson, rendered it too intense for television. It was released in theaters in 1964.

Reagan's succor came from an unexpected source. His brother, Neil, had become an advertising executive for Boraxo, a soap product that sponsored *Death Valley Days,* a western anthology series. The show had long been introduced by an aging actor portraying "the Old Ranger," who now needed to be replaced. Neil suggested Ronald as the new host, essentially a reprise of his *G.E. Theater* role, only now Reagan would appear in the garb of his beloved Old West.

As Reagan struggled to earn a living, he continued his political activities, moving ever more to the right, endorsing a series of more and more radical issues and personalities. He appeared at rallies with Frederick Schwarz of the militant Christian Anti-Communist Crusade. He spoke at a fundraising dinner for Congressman John Rousselot, a member of the John Birch Society, an extremist organization prone to extravagant conspiracy theories. Reagan also accepted public service awards from Governors Ross Barnett of Mississippi and Orville Faubus of Arkansas, renowned for their support of racial segregation. As the election year of 1964 approached, Reagan seemed to be drifting further and further out of the political mainstream, regarded by many observers as a shrill spokesman for the furthest reaches of the far right political spectrum. Reagan himself, however, sensed something different. "I am convinced," he had written as early as 1959, "there is a groundswell of economic conservatism building up." This wave, he predicted, "could reverse the entire tide of present day 'statism.'"

6

Entering Politics

The 1964 presidential campaign had not gone well for conservative Republicans. In nominating Arizona Senator Barry Goldwater they had, to be sure, wrested control of the party apparatus from its moderate eastern wing. But as the election approached, poll after poll showed Goldwater headed toward a crushing defeat at the hands of incumbent President Lyndon B. Johnson.

Ronald Reagan had served dutifully as the state co-chairman of the California Committee for Goldwater, speaking up and down the state on the candidate's behalf. Many felt that Reagan conveyed the conservative message far more convincingly than the more taciturn Goldwater. In October, Republican activists and major donors Henry Salvatori and Holmes Tuttle decided to tape Reagan giving a version of his stock speech for broadcast to the nation on behalf of the campaign. Reagan readily agreed to the proposal, insisting only that rather than delivering his talk in an empty studio, he present it before an audience of enthusiastic conservatives. Goldwater's campaign managers balked at the plan, fearing that an appearance by Reagan would reinforce Goldwater's image as an extremist. The candidate himself, however, watched the tape and endorsed its airing.

On October 27, 1964, the Republican Party bought half an hour of prime time television on NBC. Reagan's talk, titled "A Time for Choosing," made the case, not so much for Goldwater, as for conservatism. Reagan presented himself as a former Democrat, offering not a scripted tract, but his own words and ideas. "The issue in this election," Reagan told his listeners, "[is] whether we believe in our capacity for self-government or whether we abandon the American Revolution and confess that a little intellectual elite in a far-distant capital can plan our lives for us better than we can plan them ourselves." Reagan employed statistics, examples, and anecdotes to demonstrate the foibles and excesses of government—the failure to balance budgets, the ironies of farm surpluses, the waste of welfare spending. A proposed plan to address school dropouts, he claimed, would cost $4,700 for each beneficiary. "We can send them to Harvard for $2,700," he archly observed. In the realm of foreign affairs, he warned, "we are at war with the most dangerous enemy that has ever faced mankind," and equated liberal policies of "accommodation" with the Soviet Union with pre-World War II "appeasement." He mentioned Barry Goldwater relatively infrequently, but defended him as a man of integrity, courage, and compassion. "You and I have a rendezvous with destiny," he concluded, shamelessly borrowing a phrase from liberal icon Franklin D. Roosevelt. "We will preserve for our children this, the last best hope of man on earth, or we will sentence them to take the last step into a thousand years of darkness."

Reagan's apocalyptic vision and his attack on big government probably swayed few voters. One week later, Goldwater suffered a staggering defeat. But "A Time for Choosing" energized conservatives. Donations began to pour into the Goldwater campaign. Republicans repeatedly replayed the speech on local stations. One commentator called it "the most successful national political debut since William Jennings Bryan electrified the 1896 Democratic convention." Conservative leaders began to envision Reagan as a potential presidential contender in 1968, or, at the very least, a California gubernatorial candidate in 1966. Overnight, Reagan became a political figure to be reckoned with, the standard bearer for the conservative cause.

In the wake of the 1964 elections, however, that cause seemed to have a dim future, regardless of who its spokesperson might be. Not only had Johnson swamped Goldwater, Democrats also won overwhelming majorities in both houses of Congress. The thorough rejection of the Goldwater campaign seemed to have relegated conservatism back to the nether lands of the American political scene that it had occupied since the days of the New Deal. "The humiliation of their defeat was so complete," reported *Time Magazine,* "they will not have another shot at party domination for some time to come."

Conservatives in America at this time fell primarily into two groups: traditionalists, those social and cultural conservatives who felt that the modern, liberal world had abandoned the natural Christian moral order; and economic conservatives, who believed in laissez-faire capitalism as the essence of American freedom. Although substantial differences separated the two factions, they shared several common assumptions. Liberals since the early twentieth-century progressive era had based their policies on a faith in the perfectability of mankind, a belief that corrective actions and less corrosive environments could remedy social ills. They also preached, particularly in the years since the Great Depression, an egalitarian creed that emphasized both social leveling, as embodied in the graduated income tax and welfare state, and attacks on discrimination of any type. The inability of local governments and communities to counter the power and abuses of modern corporations and the failures of churches, charities, and traditional networks of social support to care for the needy during the Great Depression had necessitated the expansion of the federal government. Conservatives adamantly rejected these assumptions.

Conservatives believed in eternal truths, established, as Goldwater wrote in *The Conscience of a Conservative*, by "the laws of God and nature." There existed an "objective moral order," based on individual responsibility, that the community must enforce to avoid chaos. Far from perfectable, argued conservatives, human nature was flawed; evil existed alongside good. The liberal emphasis on rationalism, moral relativism, and egalitarianism, underscored by a de-emphasis of religious faith, ignored these fundamental truths and led to permissiveness and moral decay.

In 1960 conservative intellectual James Burnham had composed a litmus test to distinguish liberals and conservatives. Burnham offered a series of 33 true-false propositions along the following lines: "All forms of racial segregation and discrimination are wrong"; "Any interference with speech and free assembly is wrong"; "Everyone has the right to equal pay for equal work." Liberals, wrote Burnham, would answer True to each of these assertions. A "consistent Conservative" would probably mark a majority, and "possibly even all of them," False.

To conservatives of all types, the expansion of government at the core of the liberal state both undercut the natural moral order and violated the precepts of a Constitution designed to limit governmental power. The liberal tendency to attach sociological reasons for societal ills absolved people of individual responsibility for their actions. The use of government to remedy these problems compounded the dilemma. Welfare needs were, a southern California woman wrote in 1962, "the responsibility of churches, neighbors, families, charities, insurance programs . . . acting in a voluntary way." As Reagan would later state, the nation's problems "all stem from a single source: the belief that government, particularly the federal government, has the answer to our ills and that is to transfer power from the private to the public sector, and . . . from state and local governments to the ultimate power center in Washington." For all conservatives, states' rights remained, in Goldwater's words, "the cornerstone of the republic, our chief bulwark against the encroachment of individual freedom by Big Government."

To economic conservatives whose arguments had a strong libertarian strain, the expansion of government also violated the precepts of laissez-faire capitalism necessary for both true freedom and economic growth. Private property rights reigned transcendent in the libertarian universe. The government should not be able to redistribute wealth by confiscating property through taxation or welfare policies, nor could it override one's absolute property rights in order to eliminate discriminatory practices. State regulation of the economy both violated these precepts and prevented the more beneficial natural workings of the free market, ultimately stifling competition and economic growth. Conservatives thus abhorred any forms of what they decried as "collectivism" or "centralizing."

Communism represented the most extreme variant of these trends, and both traditional and economic conservatives were uncompromisingly anti-communist. Liberals, they believed, failed to fully understand the international communist threat. Liberal domestic policy, sometimes unwittingly, sometimes deliberately, advanced the communist agenda at home. Liberal foreign policy, which naively sought to contain communism within its current boundaries rather than defeat it, betrayed those peoples forced to live under the veil of totalitarianism and laid the groundwork for the ultimate defeat of freedom. Unlike an earlier generation of conservatives who had advocated an isolationist foreign policy, Cold War conservatives called for an aggressive campaign against the Soviet Union and its satellite states. They nonetheless rejected, as did earlier isolationists, entangling foreign alliances, international agencies like the United Nations, or foreign aid to influence the allegiance of nations. Most conservatives called instead for a unilateral American policy that included what Burnham advanced as a "theory of preventative war," to defeat communism in the world.

Like all ideologies, modern conservatism possessed numerous internal inconsistencies. The unfettered capitalism extolled by economic conservatives had largely created the modern world excoriated by Christian traditionalists. While conservatives, like the nation's founders, remained keenly attuned to the threats to liberty posed by an expanded government, they turned a blind eye to incursions on individual freedoms perpetrated by ever more powerful national and multinational corporations. In their enthusiasm for the workings of the free market, conservatives ignored the dramatic role that federal spending on defense, highways, and research had played in the postwar prosperity. Nor were conservatives consistent in their attitudes toward government. Traditionalists, in particular, called upon government to regulate the morality and behavior deemed necessary to sustain the social order, an outlook which often conflicted with the more libertarian impulses of many economically driven thinkers.

The conservative emphasis on individualism and voluntarism left little room for concern for those who, because of personal misfortune or societal discrimination, had not shared in the general American affluence. Conservatism lacked, as a future conservative president would implicitly acknowledge, compassion. Conservatives had historically opposed even the most basic forms of government assistance like pensions for the elderly or aid for people with disabilities. Since the conservative worldview was based primarily on its conceptions of a white, Christian nation, there was neither sympathy nor concern for the plight of African-Americans trapped in the clutches of Jim Crow segregation or other minorities facing discrimination. Indeed, the conservative movement, in particular the traditionalist wing, drew many of its supporters from southerners and religious fundamentalists, who in the past had formed the backbone of the Ku Klux Klan and other anti-Catholic, anti-Semitic, and racist organizations.

As late as 1957, the *National Review,* the leading journal of conservative thought, could defend southern resistance to civil rights demonstrations by asserting that "The white community . . . for the time being . . . is the advanced race." By the early 1960s, however, mainstream conservatism, in its quest for greater acceptability, had abandoned attacks on Jews and Catholics and tempered its most extreme anti-black pronouncements. In many instances conservatives acknowledged the need to eliminate Jim Crow segregation in the South. But if conservative leaders paid lip service to integration they rejected all proposed remedies to the status quo. The civil rights movement, argued conservatives, violated the basic principles of order necessary for a stable society. Civil disobedience that challenged Jim Crow laws in the South, argued one California conservative, challenged "the nation's traditional precept of respect for law. . . . It is the moral and social obligation of the responsible citizen to support and obey a law regardless of his personal feelings." Federal civil rights laws desecrated the tenets of states' rights and personal liberties. "There is a limit to how far we can go without upsetting the constitutional rights to freedom of association," explained Goldwater. "I believe deeply in integration, but I believe that it must be brought about in accordance with our Constitution and fundamental concepts of freedom." In 1964 Goldwater opposed the landmark Civil Rights Act that became the basis for the defeat of Jim Crow laws in the South.

Rejecting civil disobedience and federal intervention, conservatives could offer scant solutions to the amelioration of the nation's racial problems. When they did address the problem, conservatives invoked the powers of the free market to bind the nation's wounds. Reagan, who bristled at charges that he held racially biased beliefs, called for "voluntary action on the part of individuals" to staunch "the cancer of racial discrimination." But the free market and "voluntary actions" had created the poisoned environment in the first place. Reagan himself made no efforts to include minorities in his appointments, a product, according to aide Lyn Nofzinger, of Reagan's own "indifference." In general, integration and an end to discrimination had no place on the conservative agenda.

The racial dynamics of the 1964 elections, the liberal landslide notwithstanding, offered a portent of how these conservative doctrines could appeal to a broader constituency. In the Democratic primaries, Alabama Governor George Wallace, running against Johnson as a segregationist, had fared surprisingly well among midwestern blue-collar voters. Goldwater himself carried five southern states that had never before gone Republican and had fared ably among usually Democratic Catholics. Indeed, Johnson's victory had relied heavily on his near unanimous support in the African-American community. The most obvious harbinger of discontent among white voters about the progress of civil rights appeared in California. In 1963 Governor Pat Brown had pushed the Rumford Fair Housing Act through the state legislature. In keeping with the growing national commitment to civil rights, the bill banned discrimination in the sale or rental of most private dwellings in the state and posed penalties for real estate brokers found guilty of racial bias. It offered the mildest type of remedy against the pervasive racism in the California housing market. It neither compelled any individual to sell or rent to another, nor did it force a property owner to sacrifice his home at a financial loss. It simply forbade people from refusing to sell or rent to qualified buyers on the basis of race.

The California Real Estate Association nevertheless condemned the Rumford Act as "forced housing." Conservatives denounced the measure as an attack on the rights of property. The California Republican Assembly proclaimed "the right to own and manage property" as a "God-given right not to be retracted by the whim of government." The opponents of the Rumford Act collected signatures, and placed an initiative, Proposition 14, on the 1964 statewide ballot seeking to overturn the civil rights legislation.

In some instances the proponents of Proposition 14 expressed blatantly anti-black sentiments. "Negroes are not accepted because they haven't made themselves acceptable," commented one leader. But for the most part, the advocates steered away from openly racist appeals and instead harped on the issue of property rights. With ample financing and lavish flag-waving campaign materials, they portrayed the Rumford Act as a violation of American principles. They defined a new right, the "right to sell," and played on the fears of white voters that they no longer would control their homes and their communities. They openly defended what one Republican leader called "the right to discriminate" over the ability of minorities to escape bias. Ronald Reagan, an ardent supporter of Proposition 14, later explained, "If an individual wants to discriminate against Negroes or others in selling or renting his home, he has a right to do so."

Governor Brown and Democratic leaders invoked the images of Abraham Lincoln and John F. Kennedy to win support for the principle of fair housing. They warned, correctly, that both state and federal courts would find Proposition 14 unconstitutional. But Californians turned an unsympathetic ear. In the same year that California voters rejected Goldwater by a margin of over a million votes, they approved Proposition 14 and the right to discriminate by almost a two-to-one margin.

Proposition 14 revealed the limits of white California's acceptance of civil rights measures. Other developments on both the national and state scene offered added promise for conservative mobilization. Between 1962 and 1965 the United States Supreme Court, which had provoked states rights' advocates with its declaration in favor of school desegregation, handed down a series of judgments that enraged religious traditionalists. Rulings in 1962 and 1963 banned prayer in the schools and further prohibited school invocations of the Lord's Prayer and compulsory Bible readings. Other decisions narrowed the ability of local governments to outlaw "obscenity," and in 1965 the court approved the sale of contraceptive devices, defining a "right to privacy" on sexual matters. These rapid-fire rulings confirmed for many the dangerous moral drift of modern liberalism.

In California, in the waning weeks of the 1964 campaign, a new force appeared to reshape the state's political landscape. Students at the University of California's flagship campus at Berkeley, many of them veterans of the civil rights crusades of the South, protested vigorously against new campus restrictions on political activism. In October campus officials attempted to arrest a former student for violating the policy. Hundreds of students blocked the police car, giving birth to the Free Speech Movement. In December, students occupied the administration building. Police forcibly removed and arrested more than 700 demonstrators. Regardless of the legitimacy of their concerns, commented conservative Berkeley Professor Henry Stapp, "In expressing these grievances the students used methods not sanctioned by traditional morality." Over the next several years, Berkeley became a tempestuous battleground between rebellious students and state and university officials. Militant students challenged not just restrictions on speech, most of which disappeared quickly, but the very nature of the modern university, and implicitly American culture and values.

Growing opposition to the war in Vietnam further fueled the campus unrest. As Lyndon Johnson escalated America's military involvement in Southeast Asia in 1965, liberal professors and students increasingly questioned not just the war itself, but Cold War assumptions and anti-communist values. The burgeoning anti-war movement merged with student protests to create the image of a seemingly endless chaos on Berkeley and other campuses. Young people, brought up in a largely unquestioning atmosphere of post-World War II comfort and affluence, suddenly found their complacency completely upended by revelations of American racism at home and military aggression abroad. By the mid-sixties members of the vast Baby Boom generation had begun to experiment with drugs, adopt outlandish hairstyles and modes of dress, and openly flaunt and challenge prevailing sexual mores and religious conventions. The potent combination of an audacious countercultural lifestyle and often unruly political rebellion appeared alien and immoral to many Americans, leaving those with traditional values bewildered, confounded, and angry.

The drama of race relations also shifted in 1965 and 1966. In previous years, the Civil Rights Movement had focused primarily on ending legal segregation in the South. The Civil Rights Act of 1964 and the Voting Rights Act of 1965 marked the triumph of this campaign. On August 11, 1965, however, less than a week after Lyndon Johnson had signed the Voting Rights Act into law, the African-American community in the Watts section of Los Angeles exploded in a paroxysm of violence following the arrest of a drunk driver. By the time the National Guard could quell the disturbance nearly three dozen people lay dead, 4,000 had been arrested, and $40 million worth of property, mostly white-owned businesses, had been destroyed. Many liberals viewed the outburst as the result of the oppressive conditions in Watts and other black neighborhoods. Conservatives, like Los Angeles Police Chief William Parker, who described the rioters as acting "like monkeys in a zoo," saw the uprising as further evidence of the breakdown of the civil order and rampant permissiveness.

The events in Watts, the first of many urban riots that would plague the nation in the mid-1960s, signaled a transformation of the nation's racial focus from the South to the North and West, and from issues of integration to those of discrimination and economic opportunity that brought African-American demands into more direct conflict with middle- and working-class whites across the nation. In the summer of 1966, black militants raised the banner of "Black Power," a nebulous concept the rhetoric of which often implied a new racial separatism, visions of violence, and a rejection of American capitalism. In addition, other minority groups began to question the status quo and protest their own conditions. In the fields of California's San Joaquin Valley, Mexican and Filipino farm workers walked off their jobs in September 1965. After a nine-month struggle under the able and inspirational nonviolent leadership of Cesar Chavez, the farm workers won major victories, upsetting the traditional social and economic relationships in California farmlands.

In each of these areas—student militancy, Black Power, minority rights, and the counterculture—California appeared in the forefront of the maelstrom. Television coverage, with its predilection for extreme images, offered a chronicle of social and political unraveling. Thus the political environment in 1966, when the state would choose a new governor, differed greatly from that of 1964, when it had rejected Barry Goldwater. Republican leaders desperately needed a candidate who could unify the factions within the party and reach out more effectively than Goldwater had to moderate voters who were now increasingly sympathetic to a conservative message. A group of businessmen and Republican campaign contributors believed that Ronald Reagan could be that man.

In 1965, more than forty wealthy Republicans, led by auto dealer Holmes Tuttle, oilmen A.Y. Rubel and Henry Salvatori, and chain-druggist Justin Dart, formed "The Friends of Ronald Reagan," to explore a Reagan candidacy. They sent a letter to other Republican donors calling for them to demonstrate their support for the actor in order to encourage him to run. The appeal raised $135,000 to underwrite the prospective campaign. Convincing Reagan posed another problem. Reagan had no qualms about entering the political arena, but both he and Nancy feared the impact of the move on their personal finances. Taft Schrieber and Jules Stein of MCA, Reagan's old talent agency, solved this dilemma. They arranged for Twentieth Century Fox, the film studio headed by Richard Zanuck, a member of the "Friends," to purchase Reagan's ranch in the Santa Monica Mountains. The studio paid Reagan, who rarely seemed to recognize a conflict of interest, $8000 an acre, giving him a $2 million windfall to cushion his plunge into politics. Twentieth Century Fox later resold the property for $1800 an acre, taking a substantial loss on the transaction.

Converting Reagan into a viable candidate still seemed a daunting task. Registered Democrats outnumbered Republicans in the state by a 3–2 margin. Two-term incumbent Pat Brown had already defeated Republican stalwarts William Knowland and Richard Nixon, and had compiled a legislative record unrivaled in the state's history, revamping California's systems of social services, water, and higher education while presiding over dramatic population and economic growth. Polls revealed that while most Californians were familiar with Reagan, a substantial proportion thought that he would be a poor choice for governor. Having focused most of his energies on national and international issues, Reagan possessed, in the description of one of his advisers, "zero" knowledge about California.

The Friends of Ronald Reagan recruited the political consulting firm of Stu Spencer and Bill Roberts, usually identified with the moderate wing of the Republican Party, to run Reagan's campaign. Spencer and Roberts feared that voters might find Reagan's right-wing loyalties unacceptable. But they discovered in the candidate "an open and candid person, easy to talk to, and a good listener." They also learned that after years of accepting instructions from film and television directors, Reagan could readily adapt to the orchestration of a campaign. The campaign also employed the services of the Behavior Sciences Corporation (BASICO), the brainchild of psychologists Kenneth Holden and Stanley Plog. BASICO normally counseled businesses on employee relations. In 1966 it organized the candidate's informational needs, summing up the fundamental issues on five-by-eight-inch index cards that Reagan could study and refer to during his appearances. Throughout the campaign, Holden and Plog coached Reagan, revising the cards to keep him up to date.

Together, Spencer and Roberts, BASICO, and Reagan constructed the themes that would guide his candidacy. Reagan would not try to deny his political inexperience; instead he would convert it into an asset. Like the founding fathers, who had not been professional politicians, Reagan would become a "citizen politician," an outsider uncorrupted by exposure to government. "I am not a politician," proclaimed Reagan. "I am an ordinary citizen with a deep-seated belief that much of what troubles us has been brought on by politicians; and it's high time that more ordinary citizens brought the fresh air of common-sense thinking to bear on these problems."

Reagan also had to overcome the general perception of conservatives as negative people who rejected the modern world. As Holden explained, "You had to be for things, and everything we developed for him was focused on developing a positive program, with conservative underpinnings."

The campaign developed the theme of "The Creative Society." "There is already or potentially present with the incredibly rich human resources of our state the full solution to every problem we face," explained a campaign memo. Big government, however, through high taxes and wasteful welfare spending, had blunted this creativity. Unchained from these restrictions, a glorious future would unfold for California. This uplifting message proved a perfect match for the preternaturally upbeat and optimistic Reagan, redefining conservatism in the process.

As a candidate, Reagan needed to dispel his own image as a right-wing zealot and appeal to moderates without alienating the extremists in the Republican coalition. Employing the relatively liberal Spencer and Roberts helped to allay the fears of many centrists. Reagan further understood that in order to keep the party "glued together," he also had to "keep some of the kooks quiet." Goldwater's failure to condemn the conspiracy-obsessed John Birch Society had haunted his campaign. Early on, Reagan found the right note to neutralize this issue. He would not, he said, reject the Society's support, but "Any members of the Society who support me will be buying my philosophy. I won't be buying theirs." Reagan readily adopted the "eleventh commandment" handed down by Californian Republican party chairman Gaylord Parkinson: "Thou shalt speak no ill of any other Republican." This credo, of course, also discouraged his opponents from openly attacking him.

Campaign leaders further attempted to isolate Reagan from potential embarrassments. Reagan distanced himself from Goldwater and other controversial conservatives. Daughter Maureen, eager to work in her father's campaign, was ordered not to participate, so as not to offend traditional conservatives with reminders of her father's divorce.

Reagan breezed through the primary elections, easily defeating liberal San Francisco Mayor George Christopher.

The relatively effortless victory revealed Reagan's strengths and limitations as a candidate. Reporters found him, in the words of Lou Cannon, "monumentally ignorant of state issues," but because of their minimal expectations they created a low threshold for the substance of his performance, giving him "high grades for average answers," and ignoring his frequent errors and misstatements. Reagan himself suggested that he might dispel doubts about his capabilities by minimizing his scripted speeches and regularly accepting questions from his audience. Equipped with BASICO's five-by-eight cards and always a master of self-deprecating humor, Reagan flourished in these question-and-answer sessions. After years on the stump, he had the remarkable ability to appear spontaneous even when repeating the same stock remarks.

In an era in which television had come to play an increasingly significant role in the political process and the line between news and entertainment gradually had begun to disappear, Reagan's experience as a performer stood him in good stead. His campaign made extensive use of highly effective commercials in which Reagan simply spoke directly into the camera, personally addressing the viewers at home. He effectively and instinctively turned news coverage into engaging video opportunities to advance his candidacy. In each of the venues that he had previously mastered—personal appearances, radio, and television—Reagan, as one Democratic analyst commented, appeared in the role he had mastered in his Hollywood years, that of a "plausible, persuasive 'good guy.'"

His handlers also learned of the need to keep Reagan well rested, lest he lapse into careless mistakes. On one occasion, an exhausted Reagan countered environmental concerns with the quip that "A tree is a tree, how many more do you need to look at?" Reagan stormed out of a meeting of the Negro National Assembly after mistakenly assuming that his rival Christopher had called him a racist.

To overcome his "battle" fatigue, exacerbated by a linger-ing viral infection, Reagan took a nap each afternoon. Some saw this as a sign of laziness, but it really reflected a necessary and wise husbanding of resources.

While Reagan coasted through the Republican primary, Pat Brown faced a surprisingly stiff challenge from Los Angeles Mayor Sam Yorty for the Democratic nomination. Yorty scored Brown for his handling of the Watts riots, attacking the governor and other "irresponsible" liberals for being soft on crime, soft on communists, and soft on anti-war protestors. Yorty's message appealed to many Democratic voters. He polled nearly one million votes in a losing cause.

After surviving this scare from Yorty, Brown welcomed the chance to face Reagan. "We . . . rubbed our hands in gleeful anticipation of beating this politically inexperi-enced, right-wing extremist and aging actor in 1966," he later wrote. But divisions in his own party hampered Brown. His support for the Vietnam War and his seeming lack of leadership during the Watts riots and Berkeley dis-turbances made him vulnerable. Reagan, like Yorty, had discovered that these issues resonated powerfully among the middle-of-the-road voters whom he had to woo away from the Democratic fold.

Even before he had announced his candidacy and be-fore professional pollsters had detected it, Reagan had discovered that wherever he spoke "this university thing comes up." People repeatedly asked him about "the mess at Berkeley." In his announcement speech in January 1966, Reagan had raised this issue with rhetorical vehemence. "Will we meet [the students'] neurotic vulgarities with vacil-lation and weakness," he asked, "or will we tell those en-trusted with administering the university we expect them to enforce a code based on decency, common sense, and dedi-cation to the high and noble purpose of the university?" Throughout the campaign, Reagan returned to this issue. In

May, after a state senate committee issued a report calling the Berkeley campus a "haven for Communist influence and sexual misconduct . . . teeming with Communists, homosexuals and other unsavory types," Reagan pounded away at the issue in a major speech. "There is a leadership gap, and a morality and decency gap in Sacramento," he exclaimed, which had made it possible for "a small minority of beatniks, radicals and filthy speech advocates" to bring "shame to . . . a great university." Reagan also blamed liberal professors, members of a self-important intelligentsia, divorced from reality, for fomenting disorder. He promised, if elected, to create a commission to investigate communism and "blatant sexual misbehavior" on the Berkeley campus.

As historian Matthew Dallek has written, the issue of morality, as exemplified by Berkeley radicals, became "a convenient catchall, an umbrella that allowed [Reagan] to weave together an effective and articulate assault on everything that happened in the state during Brown's tenure." Reagan decried hippies as people who "act like Tarzan, look like Jane, and smell like Cheetah." He charged antiwar protestors "who send blood and money to the enemy" with treason masquerading as "freedom of expression." People, Reagan argued, were "urging change for change's sake. . . .Who among us doesn't feel concern for the deterioration of old standards, the abandonment of principles time-tested and proven in our climb from the swamp to the stars?" He linked this theme to the rise of welfare costs, asserting that working people had been "asked to carry the additional burden of a segment of society capable of caring for itself," but preferring to make welfare "a way of life freeloading at the expense of more conscientious citizens." He falsely claimed that people flocked to California knowing that "in 24 hours they could be taken care of by the rest of us."

Similarly he blamed the state's racial problems on liberals who had lured African-Americans from the South with promises of "streets paved with gold," leading to the lawlessness of the Watts riots. The growing volume of Black Power voices gave Reagan additional ammunition. An inflammatory appearance by militant firebrand Stokely Carmichael at Berkeley gave Reagan the opportunity to connect Black Power and campus activism. "We cannot have the university . . . used as a base to foment riots from," retorted Reagan. The candidate pitched his appeal almost exclusively to white voters (with an occasional nod to the Hispanic electorate), rarely stopping in African-American communities or addressing black audiences.

Pat Brown, the incumbent governor, had little success in responding to these issues. Although he supported the war in Vietnam, moved aggressively against protestors at Berkeley, and had worked hard to address concerns raised by the Watts riots, he nonetheless had come to embody the failure of liberalism to maintain the moral and social order. Brown's efforts to tar Reagan with the stain of extremism, the burden of inexperience, and the sin of demagoguery all fell flat. On election day, voters overwhelmingly chose the actor over the veteran politician, giving Reagan a margin of almost a million votes. He outpolled Brown in all but three of California's 58 counties.

Reagan's victory was in part a triumph of personality, of his ability to convey a sense of likable, unflappable affability and optimism. It also reflected a national trend; Republicans in nine other previously Democratic states won governorships. But, more importantly, Reagan had won because he sensed the growing disillusionment among many white Americans with racial integration and the excesses of the cultural and political protests of the 1960s.

The success of Reagan's campaign signaled a transformation of the American political landscape. He had managed to create a fusion between economic and traditional conservatives and to reach out to moderates, unifying the

Republican Party. Campaigning as an outsider and a representative of hard-pressed, white middle- and working-class Americans, he had helped to transform the message of conservatism from an ideology of the privileged elites to one with a populist base. Reagan's rhetoric encouraged a culture of victimhood among the affluent white majority wherein unsung working people paid "exorbitant taxes to make possible compassion for the less fortunate," having "to sacrifice many of their own desires and dreams and hopes" in the process. These appeals enabled him to siphon off 40 percent of the traditionally Democratic labor vote and run extraordinarily well in the middle-class suburbs of southern California. Over the next few decades, this coalition would shift politics rightward and, ultimately, vanquish the liberal alliance that had dominated America since the days of Franklin Roosevelt.

7

From Governor to President

Ronald Reagan took the oath of office to become governor of California at 12:10 A.M. on January 3, 1967. The unusual time was chosen, some have suggested, because Nancy Reagan's astrological advisers deemed the stars favorable to her husband at that moment. Later that day, the "Friends of Ronald Reagan" staged a lavish inaugural celebration, the most expensive in California history, orchestrated by Walt Disney studios.

Reagan assumed the governorship of the nation's most populous state one month shy of his fifty-sixth birthday. Handsome, trim, and vigorous, he conveyed an image of outgoing vitality. Both his personality and ideology had become fixed and hardened into the patterns that would characterize his new career. He appeared in public charming and affable, yet he was in all personal relations distant and private. Biographer Edmund Morris described him as a man of "benign remoteness . . . possessed of no inner warmth." His closest friends, advisers, and family members all complained of their inability to pierce what even Nancy Reagan called "a wall around him." Reagan embodied an essential simplicity that extended into his life and worldview. "There are no easy answers," he liked to say, "but there are simple ones." He possessed and purveyed a buoyant optimism that another journalist, George Will, would label a "talent for happiness." His favorite story depicted an optimistic boy, digging through a room full of manure, confident that "There must be a pony in here someplace."

Reagan seemed totally at peace with himself, relaxed and composed in all settings, to the point of a seeming passivity and disinterest. At policy briefings he rarely responded or asked questions about the subjects before him. On issues that mattered to him, he acquired a great deal of knowledge, but on most matters he lacked curiosity or analytical interest. Critics and supporters alike commented on the extent of his ignorance. Reagan remained an avid reader and continued to take delight in writing most of his own speeches, allowing him to advance his ideals and beliefs. But his reading seemed designed not to accumulate information or stimulate his intellect, but rather to identify quotations and examples that he might use to support his existing viewpoints. These beliefs had grown ossified, virtually impermeable to change. Longtime aide Lyn Nofziger observed that Reagan excelled at convincing "himself that the truth is what he wants it to be."

This intractability became one of Reagan's great political strengths. He saw his primary role as one of a spokesperson for his ideals. He cared less about facts and details and more about the broader truths that he represented. Reagan reigned as one of the nation's most gifted storytellers, but the tales he conveyed were often riddled with factual errors or flatly untrue. He lived, wrote Morris, "in his own imagination," believing whatever fit into his moral worldview. Reagan saw himself as a man of deep religious convictions, with a strong personal relationship to God, even though he rarely attended church. He could extol the virtues of "family values," although he generally ignored his own children and grandchildren. Reporter Lou Cannon, a usually sympathetic commentator, noted that Reagan tended to memorize "dangerous scraps of information," which, when combined with his "off-the-cuff style of saying whatever came into this head," led to numerous episodes of embarrassing gaffes. But to Reagan and his supporters, the truth, as in a Biblical allegory, lay in the moral message, not in the details. His unyielding certainty in his core beliefs allowed him to remain impervious to ridicule and confident in the ultimate triumph of his convictions.

In the most memorable line from his inaugural speech, the new governor promised, "We are going to squeeze and cut and trim until we reduce the cost of government. It won't be easy and it won't be pleasant." Reagan would quickly learn, however, that imposing his will on the government of California would be far more difficult than he, in his inexperience and naiveté, had envisioned. Indeed, Reagan's first year in office seemed to demonstrate the pitfalls, rather than the benefits, of a "citizen politician." Cannon, a veteran Sacramento newsman, wrote, "He was ignorant of state government, and most of those he brought to Sacramento knew little more than he did. Reagan had goals, but no programs . . . He did not know how government functioned or the processes by which it reached its objectives." In March, when asked to outline his legislative program, Reagan could not respond. At press conferences, he startled reporters by the frequency with which he honestly answered questions, "I don't know."

The new governor's most immediate challenge emerged from the state budget. Pat Brown, unwilling to raise taxes in an election year, had left the state with a massive budget deficit. Reagan had campaigned on the assumption that California government was bloated with waste that could easily be pared. He promised to analyze all departments as a businessman might and eliminate inefficiency. Once in office, however, he proposed a simplistic ten percent across-the-board cut in spending that penalized all divisions equally, regardless of how well they were run. Based on these assumed cuts, Reagan proposed a relatively economical $4.6 billion budget. Within four months, however, spending projections shot upward, and Reagan found himself calling for the state's first $5 billion budget.

The new administration also discovered that many of California's largest expenditures defied reduction. Education constituted the biggest single financial commitment, but state law limited cuts in this area. Although Reagan had railed against welfare cheats, he found that most recipients included elderly people ineligible for Social Security and the clearly needy and disabled. Federal law mandated the maintenance of basic payments to these and other groups. A public outcry emerged when Reagan announced the elimination of nearly 4000 jobs in the Department of Mental Hygiene, which ran the state's mental hospitals. Although Reagan ultimately rescinded a quarter of the layoffs, he callously refused to visit the hospitals to see what the effects of the cutbacks might be.

Ultimately, it became obvious to Reagan and his administration that, his campaign rhetoric notwithstanding, a massive tax increase offered the only solution to the budget shortfall. Since Reagan's advisers had minimal understanding about the tax system, he had to rely heavily on Democratic assembly leader Jesse Unruh in formulating the schedule of increases. The new levies reduced property taxes but raised income, corporate, and sales taxes. Reagan, who believed that "taxes should hurt," successfully resisted the introduction of income tax withholding. The results of these maneuverings undermined many of Reagan's longstanding principles. Reagan now signed into law a billion-dollar tax boost, the largest in California or any state history, the revenues of which far exceeded the state's needs. Furthermore, the tax structure became more progressive, hitting businesses and middle- and upper-income people harder than those at the bottom.

Reagan also ran into difficulties on the issue of abortion. The legislature passed a bill allowing abortion in the event of rape or incest or if a physician specified that the pregnancy endangered the mother's health. It was sent forward for Reagan's signature. Abortion in 1967 was not yet the highly charged issue it would become in the 1970s and 1980s. Nor was it a politically partisan controversy. Supporters and opponents of abortion reform sat on both sides of the legislative aisle. Even the Reagan family split on the matter. Reagan himself had strong religious doubts about the morality of abortions, while his father-in-law, Dr. Loyal Davis, ardently supported reform. Reagan promised Republican lawmakers who had supported the bill that he would sign it if they removed a section that allowed the termination of a pregnancy that might yield a disabled child. "I cannot justify morally . . . taking of an unborn life simply on the supposition that it is going to be less than a perfect human being," asserted Reagan. When legislators removed the offending clause, Reagan still wavered. Francis Cardinal McIntyre of the Roman Catholic Church urged him to veto the bill, arguing that the mother's health provision would lead to an avalanche of abortions. A veto, however, would have violated his promises to Republican legislators. Reagan signed the bill with great misgivings, his equivocation offending partisans on both sides of the issue. As Father McIntyre's forecast came to pass and abortions in California soared in to the tens of thousands annually, Reagan came to greatly regret this decision.

But even as Reagan stumbled through his first year in office, he managed to present a positive public impression. Although he did not "cut and trim," government, he projected the image of a budget cutter. Californians tended, with considerable justification, to blame Pat Brown and not Reagan for the tax increases. Most significantly, Reagan could always rely on "the mess at Berkeley" and the excesses of the burgeoning New Left, Black Power advocates, and counterculture to bolster his support among the electorate.

Reagan had made clear, even before taking office, that the situation at Berkeley would be among his first priorities. "No one is compelled to attend the university," he announced one month after the election. "Those who do attend should accept and obey the prescribed rules or pack up and get out." On inauguration day, Reagan's finance director prematurely announced plans to not only cut the higher education budget by ten percent, but to institute tuition in the University of California (UC) and California State University systems. Higher education leaders, with UC Chancellor Clark Kerr in the lead, reacted with dismay. Reagan had determined to remove Kerr, whose permissiveness he blamed for much of the chaos on the Berkeley campus, even requesting damaging information on the chancellor from the FBI. At the first Regents meeting on January 27, Kerr played into the governor's hands, demanding a vote of confidence from the new administration. The Regents voted 14-8 to dismiss him, Reagan voting with the majority.

Reagan also continued to joust with political militants of various kinds. In February a group of demonstrators, many of them longhaired and bearded, picketed the capital, protesting Reagan's policies. Reagan, knowing that the television news cameras were running, unexpectedly confronted his antagonists, amidst jeers and boos. "If they represent the majority of the student body of California, then God help the university and the college system," he told reporters in a sound bite that played exceedingly well on the evening news. He repeatedly ridiculed the unkempt protestors. "Their signs say make love, not war. But they don't look like they could do much of either," he quipped. When students hoisted signs outside his limousine proclaiming, "We are the future," Reagan held up a piece of paper to the window on which he had written, "I'll sell my bonds."

Reagan also received repeated boosts from African-American militants. On May 2, 1967, nineteen Black

Panthers, a self-proclaimed revolutionary group, descended on Sacramento provocatively displaying guns and rifles. State police hustled Reagan, who was giving a speech on the capitol lawn, inside for protection. The Panthers marched to the capitol building, made their way inside, and after an apparent wrong turn, found themselves fully armed on the floor of the assembly. The resulting photographs evoked horror throughout the nation. Reagan unhesitatingly attacked all such manifestations of radicalism and violence. African-Americans, he proclaimed, "have to make a choice and quit listening to false prophets. You settle one thing with [black radicals] and they will be back with another point. Some of them think they have found a pretty good thing." When in 1968 the Regents refused to allow Black Panther leader Eldridge Cleaver to teach a course at Berkeley, Cleaver led a crowd of 5000 people in Sproul Plaza in a "Fuck Ronald Reagan" jeer, challenging the governor to a duel. Reagan accepted if he could choose the weapons—words composed of more than four letters.

Reagan's defiance of the political left allowed him to sustain his popularity even as he learned how to govern. As his first year in office came to an end, a new efficiency and competence had replaced much of the ineptitude that had characterized the early months of the administration. Although several of Reagan's earliest appointments had proven disastrous, he had now begun to assemble an able team that would serve him throughout the remainder of his public life. William Clark, and later Ed Meese, served as chief of staff. The doggedly loyal Lyn Nofziger became his popular press secretary. Caspar Weinberger, initially blackballed as budget director by conservatives for being too liberal, assumed that position and brought cohesion to Reagan's economic policies. Clark made the cabinet meeting the pivot for all policy making. Each department head would present a four-paragraph "mini-memo" to the governor for discussion, outlining the basics of the issue and proposed action. Since Reagan did not like discord and had little interest in the details of policies, most differences were resolved before they reached his attention, and simply received his affirmation.

Reagan freely delegated authority to his subordinates, viewing his own role as both a ceremonial one, in which he enacted the important public aspects of the office, and that of spokesperson and salesman for the policies agreed upon. Reagan, himself, worked a nine-to-five day, usually retreating to his home to watch television in the evenings and each weekend to his new ranch in southern California.

As indicated by the tax increase, Reagan proved more flexible than his critics expected or his rhetoric indicated. He learned to work with the legislature, which for all but two years of his tenure, was controlled by the Democrats, using his charm to cajole concessions on key votes. When the issue of repeal of the Rumford Act came before the legislature Reagan withheld his support, citing how much the issue "meant morale-wise" to African-Americans and even conceding that "in some cases . . . the problem is solved at the expense of taking away the constitutional rights of others." Even as he railed against the problems on the state's college campuses, he consistently accepted increased spending for higher education.

In 1968 Reagan made a brief, half-hearted attempt to attain the Republican presidential nomination, projecting himself onto the national political scene, but withdrew in the face of the inevitability of Richard Nixon's nomination. The governorship of California would, for the time being, remain his forum for advancing the conservative cause.

Despite Reagan's harsh condemnations and tough talk, California campuses continued to spin out of control. Much of the left, oblivious to political reality and their increasing isolation from mainstream Americans, triggered confrontations that they imagined would radicalize students and lead to revolution. At San Francisco State College, efforts to create a black studies program evolved into mass protests, violent intimidation, and a student strike in late 1968. When President Robert Smith closed down the college, Reagan called it "an unprecedented act of irresponsibility," vowing "Those who want an education, those who want to teach, should be protected at the point of a bayonet, if necessary." The California State College Trustees, with Reagan's support, ultimately replaced Smith with S.I. Hayakawa, who captured the imagination of the nation, if not the campus, with his colorful defiance of militant students and faculties. Their actions often worsened rather than pacified conditions on campus, but in the popular mind, Reagan and Hayakawa earned respect for standing up to the protestors.

Reagan took a similarly hard line in February 1969, when the Third World Liberation Front blocked Sather Gate and threatened to close down the Berkeley campus. "I have just one message for the dissidents outside the gate," announced a dismissive Reagan. "Grow up." Reagan proclaimed a state of emergency and assigned the California Highway Patrol to quell the disturbance. In May radicals seized on an unpopular plan to convert an empty lot into a parking area in order to, in the words of one leader, Stew Albert, "suck Reagan into a fight." Proclaiming the area a "People's Park," demonstrators blocked university construction efforts. The protests degenerated into riots with militants hurling firebombs at assorted targets. Reagan concluded, not inaccurately, that "a revolutionary organization of professionals," determined "to [destroy] the nation's education system," now ran rampant in Berkeley. In a show of force, Reagan called out the National Guard, an action that did little to resolve the overall chaos in Berkeley, but played well in the public arena.

Reagan ran for re-election in 1970. His first term had yielded little in the way of legislative achievements, nor had it produced any noticeable conservative revolution in government. On the other hand, it had not been the disaster that liberals had predicted. Reagan had done a competent if unspectacular job. He campaigned, once again, on a platform of reducing government. As his aide Michael Deaver later wrote, "I saw Reagan run for reelection as governor by running against the government. He campaigned as if he had not been part of it for four years." He won 53 percent of the vote, a smaller margin of victory than he had scored in 1966. But in a year that saw the Republicans lose eleven governorships and incumbent California U.S. Senator George Murphy go down to defeat, Reagan had staged an impressive triumph.

During the campaign, Reagan had resurrected his attacks on the welfare system. "Public assistance," he intoned, "should go to the needy and not the greedy." Welfare, claimed Reagan, had become "the greatest domestic problem facing the nation today," the primary cause of the rising cost of government. Statistics, particularly those related to the federal Aid to Families with Dependent Children Program (AFDC), seemed to bear out these assertions. The AFDC caseload in California had doubled during Reagan's first term and was increasing at a rate of 40,000 a month. In large part the escalation had resulted from a new awareness of the existence of poverty and its consequences. In an attempt to stem the rising tide of lawlessness and disorder in the cities, federal officials had moved to better identify and cover those needing assistance. Welfare rights organizers had also extended their efforts to make sure that people received the benefits the law entitled them to. "They go out and actually recruit people to get on welfare," observed Reagan incredulously. Welfare, he charged, exposed almost a million children in the state to "the stultifying atmosphere of programs that reward people for not working," dooming them "to repeat the cycle in their own adulthood." Nor did the system adequately care for those deserving of assistance. Support levels had remained constant even under the liberal Pat Brown. More than a dozen years had passed since the last increase. "The system does not adequately provide for the truly needy," explained Reagan. "Virtually everywhere in California the truly needy are barely subsisting."

Reagan assembled a task force to explore the welfare issue, instructing it to "place heavy emphasis on the taxpayer as opposed to the tax taker; on the truly needy as opposed to the lazy unemployable." The committee's report called for tighter eligibility requirements, greater efforts to force absent fathers to support their children, and higher benefit levels. To achieve these changes, Reagan would have to negotiate with the Democratic-controlled legislature. When new assembly speaker Bob Moretti proposed that he and Reagan "set aside our personal and philosophical disagreements and work to assure the people that our state will prosper," the governor accepted the challenge. The two men spent more than two weeks hammering out an agreement. Reagan battled Moretti, according to the speaker, "line by line, statistic by statistic." Moretti found that Reagan believed his own rhetoric and was "convinced that a handful of cheats represented all the people on welfare." Moretti discovered that Reagan lacked compassion for welfare recipients "or anyone else." But Moretti also learned that Reagan could be flexible and realistic.

Reagan and Moretti's efforts resulted in the California Welfare Reform Act of 1971, a landmark bill that became a model for similar measures across the nation. The act simultaneously tightened eligibility requirements while simplifying the needs standards employed to determine inclusion. It elevated benefits for those remaining on the rolls by 43 percent and streamlined bureaucratic costs. Although a one-year residency requirement demanded by Reagan would later be declared unconstitutional, the remainder of the law proved sound. The welfare caseload immediately began to plummet. More than 300,000 people were eliminated from the rolls during Reagan's second term. Much of this decline came from economic changes and a nationwide end to the "welfare explosion" of the 1960s. The growing number of abortions in the state resulting from the liberalization of abortion laws also probably contributed to the reductions in the welfare rolls.

In addition, Reagan began to preach the virtues of what he called "workfare," the idea that welfare recipients, including mothers with dependent children, should be required to find work to supplement or replace their benefits. He successfully lobbied the Nixon administration for waivers from federal rules that would allow state experiments in this area. California launched a small pilot workfare program and the concept entered the national debate over welfare reform.

Reagan received justifiable credit for his leadership in the field of welfare reform, and the Welfare Reform Act proved the high point of his governorship. Other achievements proved modest at best. At his urging, the legislature passed more than 40 "law and order" bills, imposing harsher sentences for malefactors and strengthening the state's criminal justice system. The state's crime rate nonetheless continued to soar during his two terms as governor. Reagan's final major initiative came in the area of taxes. In 1973 he sent an initiative to the ballot that he dubbed "the taxpayers' bill of rights." Proposition One proposed limiting state expenditures based on the level of personal income. It also called for a two-thirds vote of the legislature to initiate a new tax. The proposition met widespread opposition and was doomed when Reagan joked that even he did not understand its complexities. But if the measure failed, the issue of tax reform that Reagan had raised would blossom forth in ever more potent forms in the following years.

Reagan left office in January 1975, succeeded by Democrat Jerry Brown, and Reagan had proved to be an able and popular governor. His record could pass as easily as that of a liberal rather than that of a conservative. Under his governance, California had raised taxes and made its revenue system less regressive. The state budget had grown dramatically, though at a slower rate than in earlier years or in other states. He had increased welfare benefits, even while trimming the caseload. Through it all, he had continued to speak as a conservative; in later years he would describe his tenure as a triumph of conservative principles. To a degree it had been. Reagan had waged war against the forces of the New Left, black militants, and the counterculture and had won acclaim for his steadfast defense of anti-communism and traditional values. He had advanced the causes of welfare and tax reform. These issues would become the bedrock of the conservative resurgence of the 1970s and 1980s.

Even before Reagan stepped down as governor, he had set his sites on a run for the presidency in 1976. Reagan had long assumed that when Richard Nixon completed his two terms, the path to the Republican nomination would be wide open. In 1973 he began speaking throughout the nation and appearing on network television to enhance his visibility. The Watergate scandal that drove Nixon from office, however, changed the perspective of the race. Gerald Ford, who had replaced Nixon, would now run as an incumbent. A Reagan entry might split the Republican Party, leaving it vulnerable in the general election. Nonetheless, Reagan became determined to seek the presidency. At age 65, many feared that waiting another four years might leave Reagan too old to run in 1980. Furthermore, Ford, who had achieved the office only when scandals had forced both Nixon and his elected vice-president, Spiro Agnew, to resign, had angered conservatives by proposing an amnesty for those who had evaded the draft or deserted during the Vietnam War and by appointing their longtime nemesis, Nelson Rockefeller, as his vice-president.

In 1975, free of the responsibilities of the governorship, Reagan began to position himself to run. He made as many as ten speeches a month throughout the nation and began writing an opinion column that appeared in 174 newspapers. Hundreds of radio stations carried a daily commentary from Reagan that reached from 10 to 15 million people. These activities proved financially lucrative and, more importantly, gave Reagan a broad exposure. On November 20, 1975, he formally announced his candidacy.

Reagan's 1976 presidential campaign began amid a flurry of mismanagement, missteps, and miscalculations. He lost early primaries in New Hampshire, Florida, and Illinois that he had been expected to win. By the end of March his campaign had run out of money, and his advisers seemed ready to concede defeat. Reagan steadfastly decided to continue. He shifted the focus of his campaign from issues of taxes, social security, and welfare to those of foreign policy and suddenly found new life. Reagan attacked Ford and his secretary of state, Henry Kissinger, for pursuing détente and arms control talks with the Soviet Union. He charged that Russians now had military superiority over the United States. Reagan condemned Ford's plan to turn the Panama Canal over to Panamanian control and invoked the dismay of many Americans over the defeat in Vietnam, vowing, "Let us tell those who fought in that war that we will never again ask young men to fight and possibly die in a war our government is afraid to win."

Reagan suddenly began winning primary after primary. By the time of the convention in July, neither he nor Ford had the requisite votes to secure the nomination. The president, however, controlled the party apparatus and managed to squeeze past his challenger on the first ballot. Reagan, magnanimous in defeat, made a stirring address to the convention. At age 65, he might have announced his withdrawal from public life. Instead, he promised, quoting an old English ballad, "Though I am wounded, I am not slain. I shall rise and fight again."

Reagan campaigned ardently for Ford in the general election, but the burdens of Watergate and a faltering economy proved too much for the incumbent. Democrat Jimmy Carter, campaigning as a fresh face and political outsider, won a narrow victory to become the thirty-ninth President of the United States.

Jimmy Carter had the great misfortune to assume the nation's helm at one of the more inauspicious times in modern history. The American defeat in Vietnam and the Watergate revelations that drove Richard Nixon from office had diminished people's faith in government. More significantly, the American economy, an engine of growth and prosperity throughout most of the post–World War II era, had entered its deepest recession since the 1930s. The Arab-Israeli War in 1973 had sent oil prices soaring and produced fuel shortages, leading to long queues at gas pumps and reduced highway speed limits to save gasoline. The rising costs of energy flowed over into the economy as a whole, generating a pervasive inflation. According to traditional liberal economics, inflation could be tamed by an increase in unemployment. But as unemployment rates approached double digits, inflation continued to rise. Economists described the dilemma as "stagflation," and offered few remedies. As prices rose, people's real incomes dropped, causing widespread alarm and discontent.

Carter fared no better in the realm of foreign policy. American power in the post-Vietnam era seemed to be on the wane. Most people, encouraged by Reagan and other conservatives, falsely believed that the Soviet Union had now surpassed the United States in nuclear armaments. The United States seemed powerless to influence events in the Middle East. Many Americans, their anxieties fanned by Reagan's continued misrepresentations about the centrality of the Panama Canal to American security and the details of the treaty that would hand control of the Panama Canal over to Panama, opposed the giveaway as a further sign of weakness.

Political leaders and intellectuals began to talk about an "age of limits," in which the growth and rising standards of living of the past could no longer be taken for granted. A 1980 poll would reveal that 72 percent of the people believed "We are fast coming to a turning point in our history. The land of plenty is becoming a land of want." Carter appeared to accept these pessimistic projections. In July 1979 he spoke of a "crisis of confidence," abroad in the nation. The address, which came to be known as the "malaise speech," reinforced his image as a weak leader.

The nation's declining fortunes gave great impetus to an already burgeoning conservative movement in America. The political right had scored a substantial victory when Richard Nixon had won the presidency. Nixon had governed in many respects as a liberal—expanding the federal bureaucracy, seeking détente rather than confrontation with the Soviet Union, and opening relations in China. But following the blueprint outlined by Reagan in 1966 in California, Nixon calculatingly used race and cultural issues to break up the venerable New Deal Democratic coalition, wooing white southerners and northern blue-collar workers into the Republican fold. Although he publicly embraced integration and the 1964 Civil Rights Act, Nixon lashed out at policies like busing and affirmative action that pitted African-Americans more directly against white working-class voters. Nixon appealed to an implicitly white "silent majority" of "Middle America," "the forgotten Americans, the non-shouters, the non-demonstrators." Like Reagan, Nixon criticized intellectual and media elites who allegedly deflected the will of this majority.

Americans also increasingly questioned the very wisdom of government itself. Belief in an enlightened, activist government had always been at the center of liberal ideology, but by 1980 almost half of the population believed that government had grown too powerful. Polls showed that a substantial majority felt that public bureaucrats did not "really care what happens" to people, and less than a third felt that officials "knew what they were doing." The conservative argument that government programs had "unintended consequences," which often made conditions worse rather than better, attracted a growing number of adherents. A call for fewer government regulations arose from Democrats and Republicans alike, leading to the deregulation of brokerage commissions, air travel, and trucking during the Ford and Carter administrations.

The rise of a highly politicized religious right accelerated the nation's drift from liberalism. The Christian movement, strengthened by the popularity of flamboyant televangelists, focused on lifestyle issues, many of them stemming from the rise of women's rights and feminism and the sexual revolution encouraged by the countercultural proclivities of the 1960s. Evangelicals criticized rising divorce and out-of-wedlock birth rates, the growing acceptance of homosexuality, and the easing of anti-pornography laws. They opposed the Equal Rights Amendment and equated feminism with a decline of "family values."

The elimination of restrictions on abortions and the continuing separation of church and state in education particularly energized Protestant activists. Women's groups had long called for the right to abortion on demand. The 1972 Roe v. Wade United States Supreme Court decision made this a reality, infuriating both evangelical Christians and the Catholic hierarchy alike. These groups had long bristled at Court limits on prayer in the schools. A Carter Administration plan to withdraw tax exemptions from church schools that refused admission to African-Americans further mobilized Christian political activism. In 1979, televangelist Jerry Falwell created the Moral Majority, a political action group that pledged to get Americans "saved, baptized and registered," vowing "to mobilize at least two million Americans to work for pro-God, pro-family policies in government."

Reagan and other conservatives quickly recognized the potential of an alliance with the new religious right. Both religious and non-religious conservatives believed that the nation had suffered a profound decline that they attributed to the liberal doctrines of secular humanism and moral relativism. "The time has come," stated Reagan in 1977, "to see if it is possible to present a program of social action based on political principle that can attract those interested in the so-called 'social issues' and those interested in economic issues." Donations from wealthy conservatives poured into new think tanks, non-profit foundations, and political action committees designed to advance the conservative agenda. Conservative political consultants pioneered in the use of computerized fundraising to underwrite these activities and political campaigns.

The "tax revolt" launched in California in 1978 laid another foundation stone for the conservative resurgence. Americans remained among the most lightly taxed people in the industrial world, but the burgeoning inflation rates of the late 1970s skewed American taxes. Rising incomes drove people into higher tax brackets, increasing their tax burden. Furthermore, skyrocketing real estate values led to upward reassessments of tax rates. In California taxes on residential properties quadrupled in some areas. Many elderly Californians living on fixed incomes feared they might lose their homes. Moreover, as California political writer Peter Schrag argues, tax revenues generally flowed from "white elderly taxpayers who vote, as against the younger preponderantly black and Latino people who use [government] services, but vote in much lower numbers." The Democratic-controlled California legislature failed to pass tax relief, even as budget surpluses grew. This provided a tantalizing opening for conservative tax reformers, many of whom, like California's Howard Jarvis, called taxes "felony grand theft" and believed that the way to limit the size of government was "not to give [it] money in the first place."

Jarvis and his ally, Paul Gann, placed an initiative on the June 1978 ballot far more radical than Reagan's ill-fated Proposition One in 1975. The measure, listed as Proposition 13, not only rolled back property tax rates to pre-inflation levels and limited future increases, it necessitated a two-thirds vote in each house of the legislature to impose higher taxes. Proposition 13 commanded that a majority of voters had to approve all general tax hikes, like increases in the sales tax, and required a two-thirds vote to approve local "special taxes." In June 1978 California voters overwhelmingly passed the measure. Reagan likened the result to the "dumping of those cases off the boat into Boston Harbor," as the tax revolt spread across the country. Congressional candidates in November called for similar reductions at the federal level. Throughout the nation voters and legislatures would pass tax relief packages.

The tax revolt reinforced the notion that an inefficient government had grown too large and needed to be trimmed. As Schrag argues, it not only limited the ability of lawmakers to raise taxes to pay for essential services, or long-accepted government functions like parks, schools, and libraries, it eroded people's perceptions of social responsibility, replacing a communitarian ethos with a faith in market-driven individualism. Fee-based facilities replaced free common areas, transforming assumptions about public access and well-being.

Reagan, preparing for his presidential run, linked the growing consensus for lower taxes with a new economic philosophy gaining credence among conservatives. Mainstream economics had long been dominated by the Keynesian vision that emphasized stimulating demand or consumer purchasing power as the key to economic growth. "Supply-side" thinkers contended that the economy had stagnated because of excess regulation and taxation that discouraged investment. Cutting tax rates, they believed, particularly for those at the top of the income ladder, would encourage entrepreneurial activity, improve productivity, curtail inflation, and, because of the increased economic activity, actually raise overall tax revenues. Reagan readily seized upon this rosy panacea in his campaign, making supply-side economics the key to his economic platform.

If the tax revolt reinforced Reagan's domestic message, the Iranian hostage crisis supported his warnings that the United States had fallen prey to a "Vietnam syndrome" in foreign policy, afraid to use its military might to impose its will on the world. On November 4, 1979, Iranian students, with the implicit approval of the Iranian government, stormed the American embassy in Tehran and took 53 Americans hostage, demanding that the United States surrender the former Shah of Iran, who had entered the country for medical treatments. The Carter administration had no response to this provocation, which dragged on unresolved throughout the 1980 presidential campaign. The subsequent Soviet invasion of Afghanistan one month later again highlighted the seeming weakness of the United States on the world stage. These shifts in public perception brought the electorate closer to Reagan on tax reform, deregulation, anti-communism, and military preparedness, issues that he had long advocated.

Throughout the 1970s, when not officially running for the presidency, Reagan presented a daily radio address heard by millions of Americans. In a sense, this return to radio marked the completion of a cycle. As Garry Wills has noted, in a career that spanned the evolution of mass media from radio to film to television, and on into an increasingly media-dominated political realm, Reagan's voice had always been "his most valuable professional skill." In the 1970s, long before the advent of "talk radio," Reagan's broadcasts helped conservatives to rediscover the power of the airwaves for dispensing and advancing ideas.

The radio speeches of the late 1970s, which Reagan wrote and edited himself in longhand on yellow pads, indicate his personal formulation of the key issues facing the nation and foreshadow many of the policies he would introduce as president. The broadcasts rarely mentioned social topics like race or immigration, and despite the growing importance of the religious right, largely ignored issues of religion and morality. They focused rather on international issues like the threat of worldwide communism, the importance of bolstering national defense and intelligence agencies, the failures of arms control, and on the domestic side, on tax reform, reducing the size of government, and the power of a free marketplace, liberated from regulation.

Reagan regularly predicted the downfall of the Soviet Union. Communism, he proclaimed in 1975, "is neither an economic or a political system—it is a form of insanity—a temporary aberration which will one day disappear from the earth because it is contrary to human nature." Reagan believed the Soviet system to be exceedingly fragile and that an American acceleration of the arms race could bankrupt its shaky economy. On national defense, he expressed concerns about the wisdom of the U.S.-Soviet reliance on the doctrine of Mutually Assured Destruction, the notion that the vast stockpiles of nuclear weapons held by the two superpowers acted as a deterrent to nuclear war. This, he said, was like "two men pointing cocked and loaded pistols at each other's heads." He worried that "If the Soviets push the button, there is no defense against them, no way to prevent the nuclear destruction of their targets in the United States." The Soviets, on the other hand, charged Reagan in 1977, "have a laser beam capable of blasting our missiles from the sky if we should ever use them, and apparently we have no inkling such a weapon was being added to their arsenal."

Reagan's speeches extolled the virtues of the free market economy. "My belief has been strengthened," he commented in 1976, "that if government would someday quietly close its doors; if all the bureaucrats would tiptoe out of the marble halls; it would take the people of this country quite a while to miss them or even know they were gone." In 1979, at the start of his presidential campaign, he introduced the notion of a "North American Accord," a massive free-trade zone that would include Canada, the United States, and Mexico.

Throughout the 1970s Reagan returned to an idea that he had first addressed as early as 1952, what political scientist Hugh Heclo has called his "sacramental vision" of America. Reagan deeply believed in the providential nature of the American experience, that God had chosen the United States as a beacon of freedom, a special place with a spiritual mission for the betterment of the world. Surrounded by evil, the United States embodied goodness. Both by action and example, it addressed God's will. Thus, though it might err at times, its motives remained pure. "I always felt that from our deeds it must be clear to anyone that Americans were a moral people who starting at the birth of our nation had only used our power as a force of good in the world," he would write in his memoirs. These ideas, as Heclo notes, derived from the country's colonial era, but in the aftermath of the 1960s, in a world characterized by modernism, skepticism, and secularism, they seemed fresh in Reagan's optimistic rendering.

To this Reagan added a rejection of the notion that the United States had entered into a cycle of irreversible decline.

"I don't believe that. And I don't believe that you do either," he proclaimed in his December 13, 1979, speech announcing his candidacy for president. He experienced little difficulty in securing the Republican nomination. His major competition came from George Bush, who memorably dismissed supply-side theory as "voodoo economics." But Reagan triumphed in 29 out of the 33 primaries that he contested, ultimately selecting Bush as his vice-presidential nominee.

Throughout the late summer and fall of 1980, Reagan attacked Carter on his handling of the economy and foreign policy. Four years earlier, Carter had computed a "misery index" that totaled the inflation and unemployment rates to defeat Gerald Ford. In 1976, the index had stood at 15.3; by election day in 1980 it had reached 20.1. Reagan employed the misery index to skewer Carter. "Are you better off now than you were four years ago?" Reagan repeatedly asked. He charged that Carter's foreign policy represented a "sorry chapter" in American history, as Carter had "skimped" on defense spending and been "totally oblivious" to the growing strength of the Soviet Union. He scored Carter's pessimistic demeanor. "Does history still have a place for America, for her people, for her great ideals?" he asked in his final campaign speech. "There are some who answer 'no,' that our energy is spent, our days of greatness at an end . . . I find no national malaise. I find nothing wrong with the American people."

Reagan committed his usual number of gaffes and missteps, blurting out positions and opinions that often undermined his campaign. He called for the teaching of evolution in the schools, failed to identify the president of France, and displayed a distressing ignorance of environmental issues. In an October 7 speech in Steubenville, Ohio, he incredulously proposed that the volcanic eruption at Mount St. Helens "has probably released more sulfur dioxide in the world than has been released in the last ten years of automobile driving . . ." and that trees and decaying vegetation caused most pollution. For several weeks of the campaign, his handlers isolated him from the press to minimize his misstatements.

Yet at the most critical moment of the campaign, in a debate just one week before the election, Reagan clearly outclassed the incumbent president. Carter, armed with facts and information, appeared tense and besieged. Reagan, though under constant attack throughout the confrontation, appeared calm and in control, skillfully deflecting Carter's jabs. After Carter accurately portrayed Reagan's longstanding opposition to Medicare and national health insurance, Reagan sadly shook his head, and commented, injecting a line that he had rehearsed beforehand, "There you go again." As Lou Cannon has noted, "It seemed such a wonderful, natural summation of an opponent's excess that overnight it became part of the political language." Reagan concluded the debate with a masterful recapitulation of his campaign themes. "Are you happier today than when Mr. Carter became president of the United States?" he asked. "Is it easier for you to buy things in the stores than it was four years ago? Is there more or less unemployment in the country than there was four years ago? Is America as respected in the world as it was?"

Seven days later Reagan easily unseated Carter, winning 51 percent of the vote to Carter's 41 percent (with third-party candidate John Anderson polling seven percent). Reagan ran surprisingly well among Democrats and union members. He attracted a majority of independents. Riding his coattails, Republicans seized control of the Senate and cut deeply into the Democratic majority in the House of Representatives.

Exit polls revealed that the triumph had resulted more from a rejection of the failed Carter Administration than an affirmation of Reagan's policies. Two-thirds of the voters cited economic concerns as their prime motivation.

Only 11 percent reported supporting Reagan because of his conservative views. Reagan and his entourage, however, interpreted the election as a mandate for change, a call for a revolution that would roll back the liberal tide that had long engulfed the nation. Ronald Reagan, approaching his seventieth birthday, had completed his lengthy, unlikely political and personal odyssey. On January 20, 1981, the former actor became the fortieth president of the United States.

8

"Stay the Course"
The Reagan Presidency: 1981-1982

The Ronald Reagan White House offered an unusual paradox. To those working within, it often seemed like a chaotic, rudderless enterprise, lacking in coherence or direction from the president. Reagan, according to economic adviser Martin Anderson, one of his most ardent supporters, "made no demands, and gave almost no instructions." At meetings, Reagan often seemed bored, distracted, and uninterested. When faced by conflicting opinions or courses of action, he frequently left his cabinet and staff members baffled as to what, if anything, he had recommended. The battle for Reagan's mind seemed to speechwriter Peggy Noonan, "like the trench warfare of World War I—never had so many fought so hard for such barren terrain." Yet, from the outside, to the American people, Reagan projected an aura of strength and decisiveness. More significantly, the Reagan Administration proved remarkably successful in defining its goals and achieving them, and, as Reagan liked to emphasize, "staying the course," maintaining faith that its policies, even those that seemed misguided in the short run, would ultimately prove correct.

Among the unique features of the Reagan regime was, not surprisingly, the extent to which it resembled a Hollywood production. His "troika" of top advisers, Edwin Meese, counselor to the president; James A. Baker, chief of staff; and Michael Deaver, the deputy chief of staff, orchestrated Reagan's public appearances and carefully controlled access to the president, limiting his contact with even top cabinet officials. They meticulously organized his daily activities. As Donald Regan, who served Reagan as treasury secretary and later chief of staff, wrote, "Every moment of every public appearance was scheduled, every word was scripted, every place where Reagan was expected to stand was chalked with toe marks." Reagan rarely held press conferences, which might require spontaneous answers, but embraced the well-coordinated ceremonial role of the presidency. He enjoyed hosting visiting dignitaries, overseeing military extravaganzas, and presenting speeches to a variety of audiences. Not only his public appearances, but his less visible activities, received the same degree of planning and attention. The president, in effect, received a daily "shooting script," like an actor preparing for a movie, that he scrupulously followed. He often addressed visitors from cue cards created by his staff, rarely deviating from the text to respond to their questions or concerns.

Reagan's departures from routine often came in the form of anecdotes. The president usually began meetings with a joke or humorous tale, told stories to entertain staff members and guests, or used these digressions to deflect his own boredom or disinterest. Reagan's reliance on anecdotes reflected his entrée into the world. He used anecdotes, as economic adviser Alan Greenspan observed, "to express his fundamental ideas and attitudes toward life." His advisers knew that Reagan responded most favorably to ideas presented in narrative or vivid visual form. Journalist Leslie Gelb found "It is not the logic of an argument that he remembers . . . but a circumstance or story that connects the issue at hand to his basic principles." To Reagan, anecdotes were parables that expressed broader truths. Once a tale entered his repertoire, it stayed, regardless of its accuracy. Longtime staffers heard the same jokes and stories over and over again. At times Reagan offered anecdotes at inappropriate times or inappropriate to the occasion, embarrassing aides and visitors alike.

Reagan's outwardly passive and seemingly distracted nature often confounded and frustrated his subordinates. He rarely dealt with the details of policy, issuing broad, general directives and expecting his cabinet and other staffers to fill in the contours. He disliked conflict and infrequently interceded to resolve differences among his cabinet members and other advisers. A growing hearing loss complicated matters, as staffers never could be sure of what Reagan heard or understood. Beneath his generally calm, laid-back, and dispassionate demeanor, however, lay a fiery temper and fierce stubbornness. Once convinced of the wisdom of a given course, Reagan could not be deflected by reason, argument, or the persuasive talents of his closest aides or even his wife.

The presence of Nancy Reagan added another element of ambiguity into this already uncertain mix. Mrs. Reagan, by most accounts, had a limited influence on policy decisions in the White House, but she was fiercely protective of her husband, his health, his reputation, and his perceived legacy. A firm believer in astrology, the first lady dictated the president's travel schedule based on daily consultation with her personal astrologer. Mrs. Reagan also made sure that aides understood her husband's need for regular rest. Since Reagan himself abhorred making even obvious personnel decisions, his wife often became the administration's hatchet person. If she believed that a staffer did not adequately serve the best interests of the president, that person would invariably be removed. On these matters, her instincts were strong and generally correct, but people in the White House feared her wrath.

Yet, amid this sea of apparent dysfunction, the Reagan Administration forged a considerable trail of accomplishment. Most of this resulted from the president's innate strengths as a leader. Reagan possessed and projected a substantial reserve of self-confidence, which allowed him to make decisions without second guessing himself. He governed, to an unusual extent for a modern politician, based on ideas and values. His policies came primarily from his core beliefs, rather than the dictates of public opinion. Richard Wirthlin, Reagan's longtime pollster, explained, "He consulted the polls to identify areas where a majority of his fellow citizens disagreed with him so that he could use the power of persuasion to change their minds." Reagan was impervious to most criticism and skeptical of experts. "One thing you learn in show business," he told a beleaguered cabinet secretary, "there's a difference between the critics and the box office. Don't worry about the critics, just keep doing your job." To most Americans Reagan appeared forceful, decisive, and always in control.

Reagan earned a reputation as "The Great Communicator." Part of this came from his background as an actor. He was aware of the importance of creating a rapport with the viewers. "An actor knows two important things," he explained, "to be honest in what he's doing and to be in touch with the audience. That's not bad advice for a politician either. My actor's instinct told me to speak the truth as I saw and felt it." Although Reagan uttered more untruths and misstatements than most presidents, he always believed what he said, conveying an aura of sincerity.

Reagan was confident that he instinctively expressed the will of the American people. Unlike earlier presidents, he asked people not to sacrifice, not to ask what they could do for America, but rather to simply believe in the power of the American ideal. "Reagan asked Americans to dream great dreams," writes journalist Bill Keller, "but he rarely asked them to give up anything." His vision of the United States as a "City On a Hill," his buoyant optimism, and robust patriotism struck a chord in the post-Vietnam, post-Watergate, post-Jimmy Carter decade.

The Reagan Administration also understood another key to effective governance: that a limited program with a focus on a handful of key issues could yield substantial results. The Reagan agenda consisted primarily of the issues that Reagan had long since defined as his own. It embraced a staunch anti-communism, the importance of building the nation's defenses, the necessity of cutting taxes and reducing the size of government, and the need to redirect the nation's judiciary on a more conservative path.

On foreign policy, Reagan brought to office a team of hard-line anti-communists, as many as 50 drawn from the ranks of the neo-conservative group, the Committee on the Present Danger (CPD). The CPD had grown in power and influence during the 1970s. Reagan had joined its executive board in 1979. The CPD believed that Cold War policies of peaceful coexistence and détente, Richard Nixon's strategy of negotiations with the Soviet Union, were fatally flawed and one-sided in favor of the Soviets. CIA analysts, they argued in the mid-1970s, had greatly underestimated the Soviet threat. The Soviets not only had achieved military and nuclear superiority over the United States, but had begun to develop strategies to allow them to survive and win a nuclear war. Under pressure from CPD members, the CIA, under the leadership of George Bush, had reevaluated its assessments of Soviet strength to reflect CPD beliefs. The CPD also rejected arms control treaties like the Anti-Ballistic Missile (ABM) pact negotiated by Nixon and the Strategic Arms Limitation Treaties (SALT I and II). It disdained American cooperation with international organizations like the United Nations and World Court. It favored a unilateralist foreign policy based on a reliance on unbridled American military strength.

Reagan, and most of his foreign policy team, including Secretary of State Alexander Haig, Defense Secretary

Caspar Weinberger, and CIA Director William Casey, embraced this view. On January 29, 1981, just nine days after assuming office, Reagan told a national television audience that "détente's been a one-way street the Soviet Union has used to pursue its own aims." Arms control negotiations would prove fruitless because "The only morality they recognize is what will further their cause, meaning they reserve unto themselves the right to commit any crime, to lie, to cheat, in order to attain that." Reagan and other administration officials labeled the 1970s a "decade of neglect" during which the Soviets, who in Weinberger's words had "outinvested us by 80 or 90 percent," had a decided military advantage. "Up until now, we have been making unilateral concessions allowing [our arms] to deteriorate, and they've been building the greatest military machine the world has ever seen," asserted Reagan. "The truth of the matter is that on balance the Soviet Union does have a definite margin of superiority." He believed that a "window of vulnerability" existed in United States defenses. Faced by a confrontation, Reagan feared we would be left with a choice of "surrender or die."

During the 1970s, according to this conservative worldview, the United States suffered from a "Vietnam syndrome," a fear of using American strength in the aftermath of our defeat in Southeast Asia. The Soviet Union had thus achieved an uncontested ascendancy. South Vietnam, Laos, and Cambodia had fallen to communism. Angola, Mozambique, and Ethiopia in Africa, and more ominously, Nicaragua and Grenada in the Americas, had accepted a pro-Soviet ideology. The Soviet invasion of Afghanistan in 1979 offered further proof of communist aggression, as did the decision of the Soviet Union and Cuba to arm a proclaimed "final offensive" by Salvadoran guerrillas during Carter's final days in office. "All over the world we can see the face of declining American power, the Soviets and their friends are advancing," warned Reagan.

Administration officials blamed the Soviet Union and its "proxies" or "surrogates" like Cuba and Nicaragua for most of the world's problems. "Let's not delude ourselves," asserted Reagan in his campaign. "The Soviet Union underlies all the unrest that is going on. If they weren't engaged in this game of dominoes, there wouldn't be any hotspots in the world." On January 21, 1981, Haig's first day in office, the secretary of state blamed the Soviet Union for "training, funding, finding, and equipping international terrorism."

Much of the conservative perspective came from selective reading of intelligence reports and willful distortions of reality. The 1970s, rather than a "decade of neglect," had witnessed dramatic increases in United States defense spending. Military outlays grew each year under Carter, with massive expenditures on Trident submarines, Intercontinental Ballistic Missile (ICBM) warheads, cruise missiles, and the B-2 Stealth bomber. Americans not only possessed superiority in the numbers and quality of nuclear warheads, but in their versatility. While the Soviets relied heavily on land-based missiles, the American nuclear triad of land-based, airborne, and submarine attack forces offered greater diversity and flexibility. Each Polaris submarine had the capability of destroying every significant city in the Soviet Union. The revamped CIA estimates of the 1970s proved to have wildly overstated Soviet defense spending, which had plateaued rather than increased since the mid-1970s. But the Reagan Administration refused to acknowledge the more accurate assessments that conflicted with their perspective. Similarly, when the State Department Bureau of Intelligence and Research questioned Soviet involvement in world terrorism, Haig and CIA director Casey criticized the reports.

The major escalation in defense spending also served a more ambitious purpose. The Soviet Union, Reagan had long maintained, could not match the United States in an arms race. "They cannot vastly increase their military productivity because they've already got their people on a starvation diet," stated Reagan in October 1981. "But now they're going to be faced with [the fact] that we could go forward with an arms race and they can't keep up." The United States, hoped Reagan, would then be able to negotiate arms reductions from a position of strength rather than weakness. Indeed, increased military spending might exert so much pressure on the precarious Soviet economy that it could bring the whole edifice toppling down.

Reagan and other hardliners like Casey firmly believed that the United States should not settle for peaceful coexistence with the Soviets, but rather strive for victory in the Cold War. Casey regularly offered Reagan CIA analyses that would support this view, omitting those that would not. Casey advocated a variety of economic stratagems and a sharp augmentation of covert activities in Afghanistan, Nicaragua, and Eastern Europe that would challenge the Soviets throughout the globe and bring their communist system closer to collapse. Reagan wholly supported these schemes. Casey became, according to journalist Bob Woodward, a "shadow secretary of state," advancing a secret undeclared war against the Soviets and their real and imagined proxies.

Although foreign policy matters would dominate much of the Reagan era, domestic concerns took priority during his early months in office. In his inaugural address, he promised to "curb the size and influence of the federal establishment," restoring the distinction between the powers exercised by the federal government and those granted to the states and the American people. Reagan moved quickly to attack what he saw as an excess of regulation. In his first official act, immediately after his January 20 inaugural address, he imposed a hiring freeze on all federal agencies. On January 29 he barred these bodies from issuing new rules. The president also created a Task Force on Regulatory Relief, chaired by Vice-President Bush. In mid-February he issued an executive order requiring a cost and benefit analysis by the Office of Management and Budget before any new regulation could be propagated.

At many agencies Reagan named administrators who advocated and implemented a reduced role for their departments. At the Securities and Exchange Commission the president appointed Wall Street executive John Shad as chair. Shad immediately began cutting staff and reducing enforcement activities. Mark S. Fowler, a leading advocate of deregulation, took command of the Federal Communication Commission. Fowler revised the rules for licensing stations that had prevailed since 1934. He ended the requirement that radio and television outlets offer public service programs, eliminated the "fairness" doctrine that called for equal time for advocates of controversial issues, and more than doubled the number of television stations a single company could own. Reagan's Commerce Department identified the "terrible twenty" federal regulations deemed most onerous by American businesses and targeted many health and safety protections for elimination.

To head the Department of the Interior Reagan selected James Watt. The administration's leading representative from the religious right, Watt had founded the Mountain States Legal Foundation, an anti-environmental advocacy group. He vowed to remove obstacles to economic growth, under the guidance of the "scriptures which call on us to occupy the land until Jesus returns." "We will mine more, drill more, cut more timber," he promised. To head up the Environmental Protection Agency (EPA), Reagan appointed Watt's equally zealous protégé, Anne Gorsuch Burford.

The Reagan team also moved aggressively to reshape the nation's judiciary by appointing conservative federal judges. The new administration hoped, in the words of Ed Meese, "to institutionalize the Reagan revolution so it can't be set aside no matter what happens in future presidential elections." Under previous presidents, the selection of judges had rested with the Department of Justice and relied greatly on rewarding party loyalty and observing recommendations from U.S. senators. The Reagan Administration moved the operation to the White House and established a Judicial Selection Committee (JSC), described by one scholar as "the most thorough and comprehensive system for recruiting and screening federal judicial candidates of any administration ever." The JSC relied less on the advice of professional groups like the American Bar Association or the National Bar Association, which represented African-American lawyers, and imposed its own rigid ideological criteria. All candidates underwent day-long screening sessions in which they answered questions about their positions on crime, affirmative action, abortion, and other issues. These interviews determined their suitability for nomination.

Many of these activities took place out of direct public view. The primary open battleground of the early Reagan presidency involved the nation's economy. Reagan assumed office at a moment of dire economic portent. Inflation remained above ten percent; interest rates hovered at more than double that. Eight million Americans were unemployed. To remedy these ills, Reagan favored a massive supply-side tax cut, slashing rates for those in higher income brackets to stimulate investment. Responsibility for formulating the president's plan fell to David Stockman, his energetic director of the Office of Management and Budget. Unlike Reagan and many of his senior advisers, Stockman recognized the fundamental flaw in supply-side thinking. Tax cuts would slash revenues and dramatically increase deficits. Stockman, however, saw this as an opportunity. Faced by mounting deficits, politicians would have little choice but to eliminate costly programs like Social Security, Medicare, and even defense, thereby achieving the conservative dream of reduced government.

In his negotiations with Reagan and his political team, Stockman discovered that while they embraced his proposed tax plan, they resisted all of his major cost-cutting suggestions. The Reaganites did not hesitate to destroy most 1960s-initiated Great Society programs, a relatively small part of federal expenditures. But political realities prevented tampering with Social Security and Medicare, which accounted for 48 percent of the budget. Both Reagan and Defense Secretary Weinberger were determined to greatly enhance defense allocations, which already absorbed a quarter of all spending. "Defense is not a budget item. You spend what you need," contended Reagan. Furthermore, the president proved even more aggressive on tax cuts than Stockman. Reagan opposed removing tax breaks like the oil depletion allowance that favored the wealthy and insisted on across-the-board cuts for the less affluent as well.

As the date approached when Reagan would present his economic proposals, Stockman's computers predicted unprecedented, ever-mounting deficits. Although for decades Reagan and other conservatives had railed against deficit spending, the president did not allow this prospect to deter him from his broader goals. The need for tax cuts and military spending far outweighed the dangers of budget shortfalls. Furthermore, if supply-side theorists were correct, tax revenues would rise, not fall. Reagan's optimistic nature embraced this economic chimera. He believed that the budget could be balanced "by 1984 at the latest."

On February 18, Reagan presented his economic agenda, "America's New Beginning: A Program for Economic Recovery," in a major speech to the nation. He attacked waste and fraud in the government as a "national scandal." He denounced the Democrats for pushing the national debt upwards toward a trillion dollars, predicting that the present course would produce a "day of reckoning." He proposed a 30 percent tax cut for individuals over three years and an acceleration of depreciation on business investments. This, coupled with a scaling back of government and a tight monetary policy would, he predicted, generate 13 million new jobs and curb inflation.

During the next month the battle for the passage of his budget proposal dominated the president's time. White House lobbyists testified in Congress offering extravagant projections of economic growth. Reagan himself met with and telephoned legislators to garner support. On March 30, however, these activities came to an abrupt halt. As Reagan departed from the Washington Hilton after delivering a speech on behalf of his economic plan, John Hinckley, a young man obsessed with the movie *Taxi Driver*, which culminated in an attempted political assassination, fired several shots at the presidential party. A Secret Service agent pushed Reagan into his limousine, which sped off with the president seemingly uninjured. Reagan suddenly began to cough up blood and the agent ordered the driver to detour to George Washington University Hospital. Though Reagan felt increasingly constricted in his breathing, he insisted on walking into the hospital. Once inside he collapsed. Doctors discovered that a bullet had bounced off the limousine and struck Reagan, hitting his lung and lodging an inch away from his heart. He had lost more than half his blood supply to internal bleeding and his blood pressure had plummeted. When he entered the hospital he was moments from death.

The seriously injured president endured his ordeal with remarkable wit, courage, and grace. When he first saw Nancy Reagan, he borrowed a line from boxer Jack Dempsey, quipping "Honey, I forgot to duck." He joked with surgeons that he hoped they were all Republicans. Although 70 years old, Reagan had a strong physical constitution honed by years of regular exercise that allowed for a relatively rapid recovery. He left the hospital on April 11. On April 28, he made a nationally televised address before Congress calling for the passage of his economic program. Popular admiration of Reagan soared to new heights, rendering him, at least for the time being, immune to personal criticism. Reagan himself believed that God had spared his life to enable him to fulfill whatever plans Providence had in store for him.

Reagan's post-assassination popularity facilitated the passage of his budget and tax plans. Although Democrats held a majority in the House of Representatives, Reagan ardently wooed a group of more conservative Democratic Southern congressmen, known as the "boll weevils," to support his proposals. On July 29, 48 boll weevils joined the Republican minority to pass Reagan's Economic Recovery Tax Act. Reagan demonstrated, as he had as governor of California, that he could be what historian Gareth B. Davies calls a "pragmatic ideologue, willing to compromise and accept partial victories." The legislation had slightly reduced the president's original 30 percent proposal, but it had cut the top individual tax rates from 70 percent to 50 percent, reduced the capital gains tax, indexed tax brackets to shield taxpayers from increases due to inflation, and accelerated depreciation allowances for businesses. Two days later Congress approved the entire Reagan budget complete with its extraordinary increases in defense spending.

These triumphs demonstrated the ability of the Reagan Administration to enact its policies. The victory, however, had not been unalloyed. Early in the budget debate, Stockman had proposed closing the deficit by making adjustments in the Social Security system. He suggested severely penalizing workers who opted for early retirement at age 62 rather than 65. Stockman presented his idea to Reagan in a document deliberately written, in Stockman's own words, "in perfectly incomprehensible . . . format and jargon which obscured almost everything." Uncharacteristically, Reagan instantly approved the plan without consulting his political advisers. Democrats and Republicans alike reacted with dismay. House Speaker Tip O'Neill attacked the scheme as "despicable." The Senate voted 96-0 to bury the proposal. Controversial new regulations on child nutrition issued by the Department of Agriculture (USDA) in September reinforced the image of Republican insensitivity. The USDA attempted to cut spending in federal school nutrition programs by reducing meal sizes and counting ketchup as a vegetable. The resulting uproar forced the USDA to retreat.

The totality and embarrassment of these defeats allowed Democrats to remind voters of Republican hostility to Social Security and other social programs for years to come. This effectively curtailed conservative hopes of limiting the entitlement and welfare systems during the Reagan years. Meanwhile deficits continued to mount unchecked. On August 3, less than a week after the passage of the administration's budget package, Stockman warned the president of the "budget hemorrhage" transpiring under his watch.

On that date, however, Reagan was preoccupied with the first major crisis of his tenure. At 7:00 that morning, the Professional Air Traffic Controllers Organization (PATCO), the union for the federal employees responsible for directing all commercial air traffic at the nation's airports, declared a strike, threatening to bring airplane travel to a halt. PATCO had supported Reagan in the 1980 election, one of the few unions to do so, and everyone agreed that the controllers had legitimate grievances. However, the strike violated a ban on strikes by federal employees in critical industries. Reagan announced that the workers had 48 hours to return to work before they would lose their jobs. He refused to negotiate with union leaders. "Dammit, the law is the law," he exclaimed. Two days later, when only 38 percent of the air traffic controllers reported to work, Reagan fired the strikers and replaced them temporarily with military personnel. Air travel quickly returned to normal without any accidents. The strikers lost their jobs. The crushing of the PATCO strike highlighted the arrival of an anti-union regime in Washington, but more importantly it burnished Reagan's image as a forceful leader, willing to take risks and act decisively on matters of principle. More than two-thirds of Americans supported his stand.

Two weeks later Reagan asserted his leadership in matters of foreign affairs. Libyan leader Muammar al-Qaddafi had confronted the United States by underwriting a series of terrorist attacks in the Middle East and Europe. He now claimed the Gulf of Sidra as Libyan territory and threatened to attack American naval forces if they resumed maneuvers there. Reagan ordered the Sixth Fleet into the gulf. When asked at a cabinet meeting whether American jets could chase Libyan planes that might challenge the fleet, Reagan responded vehemently, "All the way into the hangar." On August 19, two Libyan planes fired on American jets. The U.S. airmen quickly destroyed the attackers. "Let friend and foe alike know that America has the muscle to back up its words," warned Reagan.

The combination of Reagan's budget triumph, his intransigence in the PATCO strike, and his defiant response to Qaddafi's provocations cemented American perceptions of a president firmly in command of his office. The incipient defense build-up reinforced this image. The Reagan commitment to defense spending far exceeded anything that the Pentagon and Joint Chiefs of Staff had requested or expected. The military services, according to one official, were stunned by the administration's largesse: "They simply went to the shelf and took off everything that had been on their wish lists, even low-priority items." Secretary of Defense Weinberger refused to countenance even the slightest decrease in military spending, declining to yield even billions of dollars mistakenly allocated to him by a

David Stockman miscalculation. On October 2, Reagan announced plans to upgrade B-1 bombers and Trident submarines, construct 100 MX multiple warhead missiles, and build a new Stealth aircraft that would be invisible to radar.

The Reagan Administration also launched a departure in the realm of arms control negotiations with the Soviets. In a speech before the National Press Club on November 18, Reagan reaffirmed his displeasure with the SALT II pact engineered by Jimmy Carter that aimed at limiting the growth of nuclear arsenals. He declared that the United States would continue to honor this agreement, but called for new talks seeking actual reductions in the numbers of current nuclear weapons. He dubbed this new round of negotiations Strategic Arms Reduction Talks (START). Reagan offered as his opening proposal a "zero-zero option" developed by adviser Richard Perle, one of the hardliners recruited from the CPD. The United States, pledged Reagan, would withhold its scheduled deployment of land-based missiles in Europe if the Soviet Union would remove its own intermediate-range nuclear force (INF) armaments targeting Western Europe.

Although on the surface, this seemed a major breakthrough, a proposal to actually eliminate a level of nuclear weaponry, the "zero-zero option" was remarkably one-sided. The Soviets would eliminate weapons already in place; the United States would simply not make future deployments. The Soviets would give up five weapons systems, the United States none. The reductions would affect only land-based missiles, the heart of the Soviet armaments, but exclude sea- and air-based strike capability. No mention was made of British and French nuclear forces. Most observers considered "zero-zero" a non-negotiable proposal deliberately designed to undermine serious arms control discussions.

Behind the scenes, the Reagan Administration sought to step up its pressure on what it saw as Soviet "surrogate" states operating to spread communism in Central America. Although Secretary of State Haig advocated committing U.S. military forces to stop the insurgency in El Salvador, neither Reagan nor his political advisers favored entering into what they feared might become another Vietnam. The president turned instead to covert action. Within weeks of taking office, Reagan had approved a clandestine plan to staunch the flow of arms from Nicaragua to guerrillas in El Salvador. On November 16, Reagan agreed to secretly allocate $20 million in funds to arm and train the contras, a group seeking to overthrow the communist Sandinista government in Nicaragua. The Sandinistas were a major supplier of arms to the Salvadorean rebels. White House officials told Congress they simply sought to stop weapons from reaching El Salvador, making no mention of plans to overthrow the Sandinistas.

Even as Reagan moved aggressively in foreign affairs, considerable doubts were forming regarding his economic policies. In the immediate aftermath of the acceptance of Reagan's budget and tax programs, the economy entered an even sharper recession than had existed in the Carter years. The unemployment rate jumped to almost nine percent. The recession resulted in large part from the efforts of Federal Reserve Board Chair Paul Volcker to control inflation. Volcker, a Carter appointee, ratcheted up interest rates in an attempt to curtail the money supply. This drove down inflation, but made it harder for businessmen to borrow money. Many in the Reagan Administration protested this harsh regimen, but the president himself fully supported Volcker, believing that short-term suffering would produce long-term benefits. Reagan was not fazed by the growing deficit numbers. "I did not come here to balance the budget—not at the expense of my tax cutting program and my defense program," he proclaimed in November 1981.

Reagan's economic acumen came even further into question when advance copies of journalist William Greider's article, "The Education of David Stockman," appeared on November 10. Stockman admitted that he had tampered with OMB computers to produce more optimistic economic projections and that he had presented Congress with misleading figures. "None of us really understands what's going on with all these numbers," he confessed. He described the tax cuts as a "Trojan Horse," in which the middle class had received small reductions in order to pass on a windfall for the rich. Supply-side economics, conceded Stockman, was really a reversion to "trickle-down economics," wherein tax cuts for the wealthy stimulated investment and produced jobs for the middle and working classes. This theory had been largely discredited since the Great Depression.

In December, as the economy continued to unravel, the focus again shifted to the foreign arena. On December 13, military leaders in Poland moved to suppress the anticommunist Solidarity movement by declaring martial law. It was widely believed that Moscow had ordered the Polish crackdown. Reagan responded angrily. He lashed out at Soviet support for the "forces of tyranny" and asked Americans to light "candles of freedom" on behalf of the beleaguered Poles. For months the Reagan Administration had threatened sanctions should the Soviet Union send troops into Poland. Although the Soviets had not invaded, on December 29 Reagan imposed sanctions anyway. The United States barred Soviet airline service and moved to block the transfer of high-technology research and products from the West.

The declaration of martial law in Poland also strengthened the determination of hardliners within the Reagan Administration to move more aggressively against communism throughout the world. In February 1982 Reagan approved CIA Director Casey's covert plan to assist Solidarity. The CIA began to supply the Polish insurgents with funds, communications equipment, and intelligence information and to support Polish émigré groups. Casey recruited the AFL-CIO's Free Trade Urban Institute to further help the Polish workers to organize. The CIA also continued to increase its aid to the rebels fighting Soviet troops in Afghanistan.

In March, the administration approved a secret "defense guidance" plan that redefined its policies toward the Soviet Union. The document called for preparations to wage a prolonged conventional war with the Soviet Union and to "prevail" in a nuclear exchange. Furthermore, it urged the United States to take advantage of its technological superiority to build new weapons, including space-based weapons, that would be "difficult for the Soviets to counter, impose disproportionate costs . . . and obsolesce previous Soviet investment." The United States would also attempt to apply pressures to further weaken the Soviet economy. In addition, the new blueprint urged the United States to "develop more effective linkages with the people of Eastern Europe so as to deny Soviet confidence in the reliability of its allies," and to "exploit political, economic, and military weaknesses within the Warsaw Pact." In short, the "defense guidance," formalized in May as the National Security Defense Directive (NSDD-32), proclaimed a broad, far-reaching strategy to not only resist Soviet expansion, but to destabilize communist control of Eastern Europe and the Soviet Union itself.

These documents remained secret, but within weeks of the approval of NSDD-32, President Reagan moved forward with bold new assertiveness. In June he traveled to Europe to meet with Polish-born Pope John Paul II. The two leaders cemented a covert U.S.-Vatican collaboration to channel aid to Solidarity. On June 8, speaking before the British Parliament, Reagan delivered one of the most important and prophetic addresses of his career. The uprising in Poland, he averred, was but the beginning of "a great revolutionary crisis," shaking the Soviet empire.

There would be "repeated explosions against repression" in Eastern Europe. The Soviet Union itself had become mired "in deep economic difficulty," Reagan asserted, and "the dimensions of this failure are astounding." In the end, predicted Reagan, "The march of freedom and democracy will leave Marxism-Leninism on the ash-heap of history as it has left other tyrannies which stifle the freedom and muzzle the self-expression of the people."

In conjunction with his June European tour, the Reagan Administration fired a sharp shot in its economic offensive against the Soviet Union. The Soviets had been building a Siberian gas pipeline that would connect its oil supplies to Western Europe and bring badly needed income into the country. The United States blocked not only the sale of American equipment and technology to the pipeline project, but transfers of technology licensed in the United States by firms in Western Europe. Europeans protested this infringement on their economic activities, but the American boycott remained in place. At the same time the START nuclear weapons talks began with an American proposal that each side limit its land-based missile force to 2500 warheads. Since the Soviets had 5500 such weapons and the Americans only 2152, this would have been a decidedly one-sided bargain. Not surprisingly, the negotiations quickly bogged down.

Events in the Middle East also attracted increasing attention. A long-festering civil war in Lebanon had violently escalated. Since the mid-1970s, Lebanon had become a base for the Palestine Liberation Organization (PLO). The PLO used its outposts there to wage war not only against Lebanese Christian forces, but to launch attacks on Israel as well. On June 6, Israel dispatched troops into Lebanon, ostensibly to clear out PLO border camps and then leave. The Israeli troops, however, continued their onslaught, attacking both PLO and Syrian troops and marching toward the capital city of Beirut. The Reagan

Administration took no action until August 12, when Israeli planes bombed West Beirut for 11 hours. A livid Reagan called Israeli Prime Minister Menachim Begin and demanded that the Israelis stop the bombing. After an agreement had been reached to remove the PLO from Lebanon, the United States dispatched 800 marines as part of a multinational force to oversee the withdrawal.

By September 10, American troops in Lebanon had completed this mission and began their evacuation. Four days later, however, Muslim militants assassinated Lebanese president-elect and Christian leader Bashir Gemayel. In response, Gemayel supporters, with the tacit cooperation of the Israelis, massacred more than 700 people in Palestinian refugee camps. Reagan reacted by committing U.S. marines to a new multinational peacekeeping force, in what Lou Cannon describes as an "ill-defined mission," seeking to maintain order in a lawless Lebanon.

At home, what his supporters called the "Reagan Revolution" had crawled to a halt. The economy had dropped to one of its lowest levels since the Great Depression. Seventeen thousand businesses failed in 1981 alone, the second highest total registered since 1933. The housing industry experienced its worst performance since 1946 and automobile sales declined to a 20-year nadir. Unemployment reached its highest point since 1940, peaking with more than 11 million people out of work and millions more forced into lower-paying jobs. Economists estimated that the average American family lost $3000 during the downturn, with the losses disproportionately affecting those in the lower half of the income pyramid. At the same time, the Reagan Administration had sharply cut welfare benefits, food stamps, and school lunch programs. In July 1982, the economic system received another shock when the Penn Square Bank in Oklahoma City shut down, raising the specter of a wave of bank failures. Meanwhile, deficits continued to climb at an unprecedented rate. The Congressional Budget Office projected $200 billion annual shortfalls for years to come.

Many now blamed "Reaganomics," as the president's policies had come to be known, for the slide. In reality, however, Reagan's tax cuts and budget priorities had little to do with the downturn. The economy was completing the unsettling restructuring begun during the 1970s and feeling the effects of the tight fiscal policy imposed by Volcker at the Federal Reserve to combat inflation. On the one hand, Volcker's strategy had succeeded. High interest rates combined with declining energy prices due to an increased flow of oil from the Middle East had more than halved inflation to only five percent. But the extreme cost of borrowing had muted any potential impact of the supply-side tax cuts; with interest rates so high, few dared to borrow money. The dangers posed by the Penn Square collapse forced Volcker to relent. In October, the Federal Reserve began to lower interest rates.

The careening economy severely dented the president's popularity, making it more difficult for him to control Congress. The rising deficits forced Reagan to retreat from his tax policy. In June 1982, he signed into law the Tax Equity and Fiscal Responsibility Act, which, while not interfering with the overall structure of his 1981 tax bill, effectively negated about one-third of the earlier cuts by closing off numerous business loopholes. Reagan denied that this represented a tax increase, preferring instead to label it a "tax reform" that restored "simple fairness" to the codes. In September, the Senate killed a constitutional amendment seeking to outlaw abortion despite Reagan's active intercession on its behalf.

The Reagan Administration did register one major legislative success in the realm of banking deregulation. The economic crisis of the 1970s and early 1980s had greatly destabilized the savings and loan segment of the banking industry. Savings and loan banks specialized in historically safe mortgage loans for home buyers, paying out small but steady interest rates to depositors. The federal government guaranteed these deposits from loss. During the inflationary 1970s customers had shifted their funds into investments that paid higher rates, triggering staggering losses for the banks. In 1980, during the Carter Administration, Congress, hoping to strengthen the industry, lifted restrictions on interest paid to depositors and more than doubled the amount of money covered by federal deposit insurance from $40,000 to $100,000. This helped but failed to stem the tide of losses. The Reagan Administration saw the solution in deregulating the savings and loan industry, allowing the banks to make not just housing loans, but more speculative investments as well. On October 15, Reagan signed the Garn-St. Germain Act into law, unshackling the savings and loan banks from federal regulation. The president called the legislation "the most important . . . for financial institutions in fifty years," boasting, "All in all, I think we've hit the jackpot."

The savings and loan victory, however, proved a rare bright light in a dismal autumn. By election day in November, Reagan's popularity had slipped to 41 percent, and Democrats gained 26 seats in the House of Representatives during the midterm elections. Emboldened by their gains, and with the support of many Republicans, they handed Reagan a series of defeats even before the new Congress was seated in January.

Democrats had grown increasingly restive with the president's environmental program. Since coming into office, Interior Secretary James Watt had dramatically reversed earlier priorities. He had opened more federal land to mining and logging and allowed more offshore and Alaskan oil and gas drilling. He had frozen new acquisitions for the national parks and additions to lists of endangered species, and proposed selling off millions of wilderness acres. His appointees within the agency had adopted more lenient regulations and reduced enforcement of federal laws. When environmental groups charged that EPA head Ann Burford had mismanaged funds for the Superfund program dedicated to toxic cleanups, a House subcommittee subpoenaed Burford to produce documents related to the Superfund. The White House invoked executive privilege and advised Burford not to cooperate. The House, in an unprecedented action, cited her for contempt by an overwhelming 259-105 vote.

Congress also turned back the Reagan Administration's plans to develop the land-based nuclear multi-warhead MX missiles. The MX, originally conceived under the Carter Administration, became a centerpiece of Defense Secretary Weinberger's military build-up, designed to close an alleged "window of vulnerability" in America's nuclear defenses. From the start, however, opposition had arisen because of both the proposed location of the MX weapons and the task of protecting them from incoming missiles. Congress had earlier defeated plans for mobile launchers running along hundreds of miles of track in western states and a more static basing in super-hardened silos. On December 7, 1982, it rejected as impractical a "Dense Pack" solution that would have placed a hundred missiles tightly bunched together, in hopes that some might escape a Soviet nuclear first strike. Meanwhile, a grass roots Nuclear Freeze Movement, calling for an end to the testing, production, and deployment of nuclear weapons, had taken shape in Europe and the United States. Despite Reagan's warnings that a freeze posed a threat to national security, 70 percent of Americans supported the concept.

As 1982 drew to a close, Congress dealt Reagan one final setback. Throughout the year covert assistance to the contras in Nicaragua had grown. Ostensibly designed to halt the flow of arms to rebels in El Salvador, it had become increasingly obvious that, despite repeated government denials, the real purpose of CIA efforts in Central America was to overthrow the Sandinista government. This policy was of questionable legality. Congress responded by passing the Boland Amendment capping assistance to the contras and barring both the CIA and Department of Defense from using federal funds in any effort to supplant the Sandinistas. The House of Representatives voted 411–0 in favor of the measure. Nor did Reagan's efforts in Poland seem to be bearing fruit. Widespread protests from European nations forced the president to withdraw the technology sanctions affecting the Soviet-Western Europe pipelines. In Poland itself the military government had declared Solidarity illegal.

In January 1983, polls showed that Reagan's popularity rating had plummeted to 35 percent, the lowest midterm assessment of a president in 40 years. Less than one in five Americans expressed confidence that the economy was improving. Yet Reagan, ever the optimist, seemed unfazed. He retained faith in what, to many people, increasingly seemed yet another failed presidency. All will turn out well, he urged Americans, if we simply "stay the course."

9

The Road to Reelection
The Reagan Presidency: 1983-1984

At the start of 1983, Ronald Reagan looked like yet another one-term leader, soon to be denied re-election by an intractable economy. In March, however, a remarkable resurgence began with two controversial speeches that displayed the president in his most audacious and peculiarly visionary form. In the first, he condemned the Soviet Union as an "evil empire"; in the second, he advanced the idea of a space-based Strategic Defense Initiative (SDI) that would protect Americans from nuclear attack. These orations launched the start of one of the most confrontational periods of the Cold War. They also, along with a sudden reversal in the economy, triggered a rise in Reagan's political fortunes. By fall 1984, he symbolized a newly emboldened America and his re-election had become a foregone conclusion.

In late 1982 and early 1983, the Reagan foreign policy team laid out the parameters of its aggressive hard-line Soviet policy in a pair of top secret National Security Defense Directives. NSDD-66, issued in November 1982, called for a series of strategies designed to undermine the Soviet economy. Two months later, NSDD-75 implemented a policy of modernization for United States nuclear and conventional military forces to show Soviet leaders that this nation would never accept a second-class status. Furthermore, the United States would block any economic trade or technology transfers that might strengthen the Soviet military and would launch "an ideological thrust which clearly affirms the superiority of U.S. and Western values . . . over the repressive features of Soviet Communism." At the same time the United States would press for liberalization within the Soviet system, exploit "vulnerabilities and weaknesses within the Soviet empire," and press for negotiations over international differences predicated on American strength and Soviet concessions on human rights issues at home and abroad. As Reagan would state later in the year, "The goal of the free world must no longer be stated in the negative, that is, resistance to Soviet expansionism. The goal of the free world must be stated in the affirmative. We must go on the offensive with a forward strategy for freedom."

Reflecting this approach, on March 8, 1983, President Reagan issued his most strident attack on the Soviet Union since taking office. Speaking before the National Association of Evangelicals, Reagan assailed communism as "another sad, bizarre chapter in human history whose last pages even now are being written." Reagan urged his religious audience to "pray for the salvation of all those who live in totalitarian darkness," so that "they will discover the joy of knowing God." The struggle we face, he asserted, was one "between right and wrong, good and evil." The Soviet Union was "the focus of evil in the modern world," an "evil empire."

The shock over Reagan's sharp, provocative rhetoric had barely subsided when two weeks later, on March 23, he gave a televised speech on national defense. He began with his standard assault on Soviet militarism. The "enemies of freedom grow stronger every day," he warned. Reagan criticized the Soviet arms buildup and assailed them for their deployment of SS-20 intermediate-range (INF) missiles in Europe. This justified his administration's defense buildup. Suddenly, however, Reagan changed his tone and direction. He decried the doctrine of Mutually Assured Destruction (MAD) that governed defense thinking as "a sad commentary on the human condition." In the place of MAD he offered a "vision of the future which offers hope." Reagan proposed a program to "save lives rather than avenge them . . . to counter the awesome Soviet missile threat with measures that are defensive." Instead of American security resting on the threat of retaliation as a deterrent to a Soviet attack, he foresaw a system that would allow the nation to "intercept and destroy strategic ballistic missiles before they reached our own soil or that of our allies," a space shield that would act as an umbrella to protect Americans from a rain of nuclear bombs. Current technology allowed us to begin such an effort, affirmed Reagan, adding, in an elegant sentence he had written himself, "I call upon the scientific community in this country, who gave us nuclear weapons, to turn their talents to the cause of mankind and world peace; to give us the means of rendering these weapons impotent and obsolete."

Reagan's Strategic Defense Initiative, as he entitled his innovative prescription, caught virtually everyone by surprise. Secretary of Defense Weinberger and Secretary of State George Schultz, who had recently replaced Alexander Haig, did not learn of Reagan's intentions until two days before the speech. The Joint Chiefs of Staff (JCS), whom Reagan indicated had given support for SDI, also seemed startled. They had recently discussed the possibility of a space-defense project as one of several options for development, but according to JCS Chairman General John W. Vessey, "There was no program definition. It was [simply] the idea that defenses might enter into the equation more than in the past." Media commentators labeled the initiative "Star Wars" after the popular series of movies, and the phrase, originally meant to be derogative, attached itself to the plan, enhancing its popular appeal.

SDI, as much as any other policy adopted during Reagan's administration, was his personal inspiration. SDI emerged from a blend of optimism, science fiction, politics, spiritualism, ignorance, and long-term conservative ideology. Early accounts attributed the plan to Reagan's epiphany while touring a national defense facility in 1979. He had suddenly realized that the nation, which spent millions on offensive weaponry, had no way to defend itself against a nuclear attack. But the idea of a space umbrella had long percolated among many conservatives, who bristled at the restrictions placed on defense technology imposed by the 1972 Anti-Ballistic Missile (ABM) Treaty.

The ABM pact resulted from the general consensus in both the United States and the Soviet Union that costly systems designed to block incoming missiles could always be offset by counter technologies. Barring development, though not research, on these systems offered a cost-saving predictability to the arms race. The ABM Treaty specified that "Each party undertakes not to develop, test or deploy ABM systems or components . . . that are space-based." Many conservatives, including Reagan, believed that the Soviets had nonetheless developed a missile-defense system. Indeed, the 1980 Republican platform rejected Mutually Assured Destruction and proposed "vigorous research and development of an effective anti-ballistic missile system, such as is already at hand in the Soviet Union."

In reality both the Americans and the Soviets had spent billions of dollars in research into ABM systems in the 1970s, but neither had unearthed any realistic prospects. Most American research focused not on protecting populations, but rather on defending U.S. land-based missiles from a first-strike nuclear attack. Several parties, most notably retired Air Force Lt. General Daniel Graham and famed nuclear physicist Edward Teller, advocated versions of space-based defense. Teller met with Reagan in September 1982. Reagan reported in his diary, "He's pushing an exciting idea that nuclear weapons can be used in connection with Lasers to be non-destructive except as used to intercept and destroy any missiles far above earth." The Teller concept included x-ray lasers mounted on platforms orbiting in space and powered by nuclear bombs.

The idea of creating a "Star Wars" system played well into many recesses of Reagan's soul. Leaders of the religious right had introduced him to the biblical prediction of Armageddon, a final battle for the soul of the world. The prophecy held that in the end-times an evil empire led by an anti-Christ would emerge. After a period of plague and widespread destruction, Christ and his saints would rout their enemies on the field of Armageddon, bringing about a 1000-year period in which Christ would rule on earth. The Bible listed many portents of these events: a return of the Jews to the Holy Land, freak weather phenomena, plague, and natural disasters. Reagan, like many fundamentalist Christians, believed "that we may be the generation that sees Armageddon." The predicted plague, he feared, might be nuclear war. As president, he might be able to stave off this devastating holocaust and the suffering that it entailed by creating his space shield and using it to ultimately eliminate the threat of nuclear weapons. Logically this might delay the arrival of Christ's reign on earth; Reagan's own messianic longings to save the world blinded him to this contradiction. But this did not seem to enter into his thinking.

SDI also appealed to Reagan's love of science fiction and fascination with movies. The idea of a beam that could immobilize enemy aircraft had appeared in both *Murder In the Air*, one of Reagan's Brass Bancroft films, and Alfred Hitchcock's 1966 film, *Torn Curtain*, starring Paul Newman. Indeed, the sentence that Reagan inserted into his March 23 speech faithfully echoed a line spoken by Newman, who stated, "We will produce a defensive weapon that will make all nuclear weapons obsolete, and thereby abolish the terror of nuclear warfare." The idea that the United States might ultimately share the SDI system with its enemies, which would become an important part of Reagan's plan, also appeared in both *Torn Curtain* and one of Reagan's favorite science fiction movies, *The Day the Earth Stood Still*.

The fact that none of the technologies needed to develop SDI were even remotely possible or that even a shield of 99 percent effectiveness would still allow a hundred devastating missiles to annihilate American cities did not bother Reagan. Nor did he ever acknowledge that a space-based defense system might be used for offensive purposes. His personal knowledge of nuclear weaponry was minimal. On several occasions he shocked members of Congress, telling them that our submarines and bombers did not carry nuclear armaments, that missiles fired from a submarine could be recalled, and that he had not realized that the Soviet Union relied on land-based projectiles. His optimistic nature and broad faith in American science and technology convinced him that any obstacles could ultimately be overcome. And, as journalist Frances Fitzgerald has observed in her major study of SDI, perhaps only Reagan could have credulously transformed a program designed primarily to protect missiles into one that offered "a shield that could protect [all Americans] from nuclear missiles just as a roof protects a family from rain," making it not only more palatable, but more desirable to anxious Americans.

Reagan's aides did not take his SDI proposal seriously. National Security Adviser Robert MacFarlane viewed it as at best a bargaining chip in upcoming arms control negotiations. The Soviets, MacFarlane believed, faced by a new technological battleground they could not afford to compete in, would make concessions at the bargaining table. MacFarlane also recognized the political benefits of a defense designed to neuter or eliminate nuclear weapons as a counterpoint to Reagan's arms buildup and a response to the Nuclear Freeze Movement. "You have thrown the left into a tizzy," he told Reagan. "They are left with the most bloodthirsty strategy—Mutual Assured Destruction—as a means to keep the peace." In addition, as Secretary of State Schultz, who initially opposed SDI came to realize, Reagan "spoke to national pride in American technological prowess." Reagan, on the other hand, while recognizing the geopolitical and political dimensions of "Star Wars," was a true believer. SDI, he felt, was the path to nuclear disarmament and world peace.

While the world attempted to absorb Reagan's astonishing new proposal, the president kept up the pressure on the Soviet Union. On April 27, he defended United States policies in Central America as a bulwark against Soviet expansionism. One week later he praised the Nicaraguan contras as "freedom fighters," a term that Reagan would increasingly use to evoke sympathy for peoples fighting communism throughout the world. The Reagan Administration, however, invoked a rather narrow definition of freedom. It included not the Four Freedoms defined by Franklin Roosevelt in World War II—which included not only freedom of speech and religion, but also freedom from want and fear—nor an overall rejection of dictatorship and tyranny. Freedom, in the Reagan sense, meant only a release from communism.

The Reagan Administration embraced a philosophy, advanced by United Nations Ambassador Jeane Kirkpatrick, which distinguished between authoritarian and totalitarian governments. "Right-wing autocracies," though brutal and corrupt, argued Kirkpatrick, were less onerous and rigid than communist dictatorships. Authoritarian regimes "do sometimes evolve into democracies," but totalitarian nations, built on ideology and controlling all aspects of their citizens' lives, could never change. The United States therefore should not hesitate to ally with those brutal dictatorships resisting communism to advance this nation's larger objectives. Events would ultimately expose Kirkpatrick's rationalizations as sheer sophistry, but in the 1980s "this doctrine of the lesser evil" justified the Reagan Administration's broader policy of supporting the enemies of our enemy.

Throughout the world the United States offered aid and assistance to a variety of despots. In El Salvador and Guatemala, American officials turned a blind eye to right-wing death squads that murdered tens of thousands of civilians. The United States underwrote the Nicaraguan contras, led by officers of the brutal pre-Sandinista National Guard, who used terrorist tactics to undermine the Nicaraguan government. The CIA engaged President Manuel Noriega of Panama to supply arms to the contras, despite Noriega's repressive regime and close ties to Colombian cartels exporting drugs to the United States. As Bill Casey liked to remark, "He's a bastard, but he's our bastard." In Liberia the United States backed the murderous anti-communist Sidney K. Doe, whose reign destabilized Liberia and neighboring countries for decades. The Reagan Administration also demonstrated scant inclination to assist those seeking to unseat dictatorships and oppression in Haiti and the Philippines. Regarding South Africa's treatment of its black population, Reagan incorrectly maintained that that nation had "eliminated the segregation that we had in our country," and later praised South Africa's government in the face of the international campaign to end apartheid.

In Afghanistan Reagan continued and expanded the Carter Administration's support of fundamentalist Muslim mujahedin forces resisting the 1979 Soviet invasion. According to Zbigniew Brzezinski, Carter's national security adviser, the United States had deliberately lured the Soviets into a "trap" in Afghanistan. In July 1979 Carter signed a secret finding giving aid to opponents of the communist regime in Afghanistan. Brzezinski predicted to Carter that this would "induce a Soviet intervention" and give them their own debilitating Vietnam-type war. The United States expanded its assistance in December and the Soviet Union, citing covert American involvement, invaded Afghanistan on December 25, 1979.

Like the Carter Administration, the Reagan team saw Afghanistan as an ideal place to bleed the Soviet Union and began channeling hundreds of millions of dollars of supplies through Pakistan into Afghanistan. The Afghani resistance became a cause for Muslim fundamentalists throughout the Middle East, who flocked to join the mujahedin. While Kirkpatrick, Reagan, and other American officials would call them "freedom fighters," the mujahedin had few democratic attributes. The effort in Afghanistan also increased collaboration with the Saudi Arabian monarchy, which sought, among other goals, to spread its militant brand of Wahhabi fundamentalism into Central Asia. In May 1984, the Reagan Administration, evading congressional opposition, secretly sold Stinger anti-aircraft missiles to the Saudis.

Although unrelated to its anti-communist doctrine, the Reagan Administration also implemented a similar policy in the Iran-Iraq war. Iran had released the hostages taken during the Carter era on the first day of the Reagan regime. Nonetheless, the United States sought to contain the Islamic revolution underway in Iran. In late 1980, Iraq, led by the brutal Saddam Hussein, had attacked neighboring Iran. In the early months the Iraqi offensive had made inroads into Iran, but the tide had quickly turned and the fundamentalist Shiite state now threatened to overrun Iraq. Fearing Iranian dominance in the oil-rich Persian Gulf, the United States began to shore up Hussein's regime. As one official later explained, "Our long-term hope was that Hussein's government would become less repressive and more responsible." In February 1982, the

State Department removed Iraq, which gave safe haven to some of the world's most notorious terrorists, from its list of terrorist nations, enabling it to trade with American companies. In November 1983, despite growing evidence that Iraq was violating international law with its use of chemical weapons, Reagan signed NSDD-114, pledging the United States to do "whatever is necessary and legal" to block an Iranian victory. The next month, Reagan dispatched Donald Rumsfeld as a special presidential envoy to meet with Hussein and discuss opening normal diplomatic relations with the dictator. The United States offered vital military intelligence assistance and billions of dollars in credits to Iraq.

At home the conservative domestic agenda continued to stall. In the spring, the President's Committee on Social Security headed by economist Alan Greenspan deeply disappointed many conservatives who favored ending Social Security. The Greenspan committee recommended that Congress "should not alter the fundamental structure of the Social Security program or undermine its fundamental principles." Based on the prescriptions in the Greenspan report, Congress instituted several key reforms designed to stabilize the Social Security system into the twenty-first century. The changes included a hike in payroll taxes. Reagan rationalized these increases as adjustments to an earlier timetable rather than a deviation from his tax cut priorities. Neither Democrats nor Republicans were prepared to seriously address the longer-term problems posed by Social Security.

The Reagan Administration also touted its success in the realm of deregulation. In August 1983 Vice-President George Bush's Task Force on Regulatory Relief projected savings of $150 billion over the next ten years by eliminating unnecessary governmental proscriptions. But the problems of a deregulated system had also begun to surface. Staffed increasingly by conservatives who did not believe in the oversight responsibilities of government, federal agencies deliberately evaded enforcing laws or viewed programs as ways of personal aggrandizement or rewarding political cronies. At the Department of Housing and Urban Development (HUD), Assistant Secretary Emanuel S. Savas, a key figure in the campaign to cut federal aid to the cities, resigned before he could be fired for "abuse of office." Savas had worked as a consultant to a firm which received a half-million-dollar HUD contract after he took office. He ran up $14,000 in travel expenses for trips to Europe and weekends in New York and used workers to prepare a book manuscript on *Privatizing the Public Sector: How to Shrink Government*. He became the first of many HUD employees who would be tainted by scandal.

Scandals also emerged at the EPA. As a congressional investigation would reveal, EPA officials regularly ignored public health and environmental legislation and turned much of the toxic clean-up Superfund into a political slush fund. In February 1983 EPA head Burford fired Superfund manager Rita Lavelle. Lavelle was later convicted of lying to Congress to cover up abuses of the Superfund. Several weeks later, Burford herself resigned under a cloud of corruption.

Secretary of the Interior Watt, perhaps the most controversial of all Reagan appointees, survived a firestorm of criticism over his stewardship of the environment, only to fall to a callous display of insensitivity. On September 21 he described a commission he created as having "every kind of mix you can have. I have three Democrats, two Republicans. I have a black. I have a woman, two Jews and a cripple." The resulting uproar over these comments forced Watt to resign. His tenure, however, had given voice to and greatly empowered a conservative counterforce to the environmental movement that had blossomed in the 1960s and 1970s.

These instances of outright corruption or willful negligence on the part of government officials would characterize much of the Reagan years. More dramatic events in fall 1983, however, overshadowed news of the scandals. On September 1 Soviet military personnel in Asia mistook a Korean Air Line (KAL) flight that had drifted off course for an American reconnaissance plane. When the passenger jet failed to respond to warnings, the Soviets shot it down, killing all 269 people on board, including 61 Americans. U.S. intelligence reports quickly established that Soviet incompetence, not malevolence, had caused the tragedy. Nonetheless, Reagan took the opportunity to excoriate the Soviets in an address to the nation on September 5. He described the downing of the KAL flight as a "massacre," and "an act of barbarism born of a society which wantonly disregards individual rights, the value of human life, and seeks to expand and dominate other nations." Nor should Americans be surprised at "such inhuman brutality," in light of Soviet suppression of Eastern Europe and Afghanistan. Five days later Reagan again invoked the incident to "dispel any lingering doubt about what kind of regime we are dealing with." As journalist Seymour Hersh later wrote, "The President of the United States, relying on information that was wholly inaccurate and misleading, was accusing the other side of telling lies." The Soviets responded with their own charges. Yuri Andropov, Leonid Brezhnev's successor as the Soviet general secretary, protested Reagan's "military psychosis" and "extreme adventurism."

While Cold War tensions flamed anew in the wake of the KAL incident, the situation in Lebanon continued to bedevil the United States. On April 18, 1983, suicide bombers had driven a van full of explosives into the American Embassy in Beirut, killing 63 people. The Reagan Administration responded by shelling Muslim militia positions in Lebanon. This action further reinforced the notion in the Middle East that the American and other peace-keeping forces were pro-Christian and pro-Israel, rather than neutral peacekeepers in the conflict. Most American military advisers saw no vital interests at stake and favored removing the highly vulnerable U.S. troops from the volatile battleground. Reagan, however, defended the deployment on the grounds that the free world could not "stand by and see the Middle East incorporated into the Soviet bloc." On October 23, suicide bombers attacked both French and American positions in Beirut. Fifty-eight French paratroopers perished in one attack. At the U.S. marine barracks, an explosion with the force of 12,000 pounds of dynamite ravaged the compound, killing 241 Americans.

The catastrophe in Lebanon might have had devastating political consequences for the Reagan Administration if not for events thousands of miles away in the Caribbean. Communist leaders had seized control of the island of Grenada in 1979. Cuban leader Fidel Castro had dispatched hundreds of Cubans to Grenada to build an airstrip for the new communist regime. On October 12, 1983, a rival communist group had overthrown the existing Grenadan government, executing its former leaders. Most members of the United Nations, Organization of American States, and even Reagan ally Prime Minister Margaret Thatcher of Great Britain opposed an intervention. Several neighboring Caribbean states, however, asked the United States to restore order. Fears also arose over the safety of several hundred American medical students attending school in Grenada. On October 22, one day before the Lebanon bombing, President Reagan authorized an "outright invasion" of Grenada.

Three days later American forces easily overran minimal resistance from the Grenadan army. It took two more days to root out the armed Cubans at the airfield. United States forces removed the medical students from the island.

Nineteen Americans died in the fighting, most in accidents or from friendly fire. Reagan reported the discovery of secret documents that justified the incursion. The Cubans, he claimed, were building not an improved airport to welcome tourists, but something "which looked suspiciously suitable for military aircraft, including Soviet-built long-range bombers." U.S. forces had found enough weapons to supply thousands of terrorists. These charges later proved to be unfounded, but approval for the Grenada invasion was secured when a rescued American medical student knelt down and kissed the ground as he deplaned in the United States.

President Reagan addressed the nation on October 27 about the week's momentous occurrences. Grenada, he argued, "was a Soviet-Cuban colony being readied as a major military bastion to export terror and undermine democracy. We got there just in time." Moreover, "The events in Lebanon and Grenada, though oceans apart are clearly related," he informed Americans, since the Soviet Union had supported "the violence in both countries . . . through a network of surrogates and terrorists." Reagan's charges had no foundation. As former CIA analyst Raymond L. Garthoff writes, "The heart of Reagan's case was not even circumstantial; it was mythical and ideological." Yet Americans largely ignored the debacle in Beirut and celebrated the foregone victory over tiny Grenada as if a massive weight had been lifted off the nation's shoulders. "The Grenada rescue helped to exorcise the ghost of Vietnam from the American psyche," argues Dinesh D'Souza. "For the first time since the Vietnam War, the United States had committed ground troops abroad, sustained casualties, emerged victorious and won the support of the American people." Conservatives vested an even greater significance in Grenada. According to the Brezhnev Doctrine, promulgated by the late Soviet leader, no country which became communist would ever be allowed to retreat from that sphere. Grenada, however, had now fallen. The Brezhnev Doctrine, writes D'Souza, "was dead."

The American response to the KAL shootdown, the Lebanon bombings, and the invasion of Grenada caused grave concern in the Soviet Union. Soviet leaders increasingly saw Reagan as an irresponsible "cowboy" intent on dangerous confrontation. These fears almost exploded into reality in November 1983 during "Able Archer 83," a large-scale military exercise undertaken by the United States and NATO. These war simulations were commonplace on both sides of the Cold War, but Able Archer exceeded previous exercises in its scope and realism. The Soviet Union watched Able Archer unfold with growing alarm. The Soviets included within their own war scenarios the possibility of attacking under the cover of a planned rehearsal. When Soviet intelligence agents mistakenly advised that the United States had upgraded the alert status of its forces, panic set in. "The international situation at present is white hot, thoroughly white hot," a Politburo member informed the Soviet Congress. Moscow placed some of its nuclear fighter fleet on alert. The Americans watched this response with incredulity. The Soviets seemed to honestly believe that the United States might launch a first-strike nuclear assault.

Ronald Reagan was shaken by these events. In early October he had watched an advance screening of *The Day After*, a soon-to-be televised movie that graphically depicted the aftermath of a nuclear attack on Lawrence, Kansas. Confronted by scenes of death, radiation burns and sickness, and general suffering, Reagan wrote in his diary, "It is very effective and left me greatly depressed. My own reaction: we have to do all we can . . . to see that there is never a nuclear war." Shortly thereafter Reagan received a military briefing in which he discovered, "There are still some people at the Pentagon who claim a nuclear war is winnable. I thought they were crazy." Exercise

Able Archer reinforced Reagan's fears. On November 11, the day the simulation ended without further incident, Reagan stepped back from the steady stream of militant rhetoric that had dominated his administration. "A nuclear war can never be won and must never be fought," he announced. "I know I speak for people everywhere when I say our dream is to see the day when nuclear weapons will be banished from the face of the earth."

Nothing in American policy seemed to back up Reagan's words. At the START talks, the Soviet Union offered to reduce the number of INF nuclear missiles aimed at Western Europe if the United States would cancel its plans to place nuclear weapons on the continent. The United States responded with renewed insistence on the imbalanced "zero-zero option" as the basis for negotiation. When America began to deploy its missiles on November 23, 1983, the Soviets walked out of the talks. For the first time in 14 years the two sides had ceased negotiating on arms control.

But Ronald Reagan had crossed a personal divide. Ever since George Schultz had become secretary of state, the Reagan Administration had been divided between hard-line anticommunists like Caspar Weinberger and Bill Casey and moderates like Schultz, who favored opening negotiations with the Soviets. Nancy Reagan also urged the president to tone down his rhetoric and stake his historical legacy on disarmament talks. On January 16, 1984, in a nationally televised speech, Reagan adopted a markedly more conciliatory tone toward the Soviet Union. Reagan reiterated his plea for banishing nuclear weapons, stressing the common interests rather than the differences between the two countries. "Living in a nuclear age makes it imperative that we . . . talk," stated Reagan. He urged "a better working relationship, one marked by greater cooperation and understanding," calling for "a dialogue as constructive as possible," and "high-level consultations as a regular and normal component of U.S.-Soviet relations." Reagan did not place his usual emphasis on the Soviet threat or expansionism, but acknowledged that most of the world's conflicts "have their origins in local problems." In a veiled reference to Abel Archer, he made reference to "dangerous misunderstandings and miscalculations" and reassured the Soviet Union that the United States "poses no threat to the security of the Soviet Union." He concluded with an anecdotal fantasy of a Russian family and an American family meeting and discussing their common dreams of a peaceful future.

Reagan clearly meant this to be a major address, but most observers dismissed it as election-year rhetoric designed to ameliorate the president's belligerent image. The Soviets seemed skeptical that any change had occurred. Nonetheless, although it would take a long time to manifest in concrete actions, the January 16 address marked the beginning of a profound shift in Reagan's policy toward the Soviet Union.

On other foreign fronts the administration faced a series of setbacks. Although Reagan proclaimed in his January State of the Union Address that the marine presence in Lebanon was "central to our credibility on a global scale," two weeks later, he requested "a plan for redeployment of the marines from Beirut Airport to their ships offshore." Although Reagan pointedly declined to call this a withdrawal, the American military mission in Lebanon had drawn to an ignominious end.

In March a Soviet tanker struck mines laid off the coast of Nicaragua. Congress had banned the use of U.S. funds to dislodge the Sandinista government in Nicaragua. CIA Director Casey had offered repeated reassurances of his agency's noninvolvement. But the *Wall Street Journal* now reported that the CIA, with presidential approval, had mined Nicaragua's harbors. The subterfuge angered even conservative Senator Barry Goldwater. "I am pissed off," he wrote to Casey. "This is an act violating international law. It is an act of war." The Senate voted to demand a halt to the mining, and both Reagan and Casey vowed to keep the Senate Intelligence Committee informed of all future covert actions. In June, Congress rejected Reagan's request for additional funds to support the contras.

These stumbles, however, could not offset the groundswell of pro-Reagan sentiment that had been building since the Grenada invasion. A resurgent nationalism gripped the United States. In June Reagan traveled to France to attend the fortieth anniversary of the World War II D-Day landings. He embraced the reassembled survivors who had stormed the beach, bringing tears to their eyes in a moving speech at Omaha Beach in which he promised, "We will always remember. We will always be proud. We will always be prepared, so we may always be free." At the Summer Olympics in 1984 in Los Angeles, the Soviet Union and most of its eastern European allies boycotted the games in retaliation for the American embargo on the Moscow games in 1980. As a result, American athletes won an unusually large number of medals. Unabashed fans waved large American flags and chanted "U.S.A.! U.S.A.!"

A suddenly resilient economy also worked in Reagan's favor. Since Paul Volcker had begun to lower interest rates in 1983, business activity had picked up. The inflation rate dropped below two percent; interest rates, once as high as 21 percent now hovered near 11 percent. The recovery was in part a normal bounce back from the bottom of a recession, and, ironically, a classically liberal Keynesian economic response in which increased government spending and massive deficits generated jobs and business growth. Nonetheless, the improved conditions seemed to validate "Reaganomics."

By the time the 1984 presidential campaign got underway, there seemed little doubt that Reagan would win in a landslide over his Democratic opponent, former Vice-President Walter Mondale. A Republican staff memo instructed, "Paint Reagan as the personification of all that is right with, or heroized by America. Leave Mondale in a position where an attack on Reagan is tantamount to an attack on America's idealized image of itself—where a vote against Reagan is, in some subliminal sense, a vote against a mythic AMERICA." The campaign embraced this blueprint. Advertisements depicting Reagan at Normandy, Reagan greeting Olympic champions, and the post-Grenada medical student kissing United States soil proclaimed "America Is Back" and the dawning of "Morning in America." "Under the leadership of President Reagan, our country is stronger, prouder, and better," extolled one ad.

Reagan's aides carefully husbanded his impromptu appearances to guard against embarrassments. In one instance, however, the president slipped. During a warm-up for a radio address, not realizing that the microphone was live, he joked, "My fellow Americans, I am pleased to tell you I just signed legislation outlawing Russia forever. The bombing begins in five minutes." Many Americans loved it; the Soviets were appalled.

During the campaign Reagan sent mixed messages to the Soviets. In August he spoke of Eastern European countries as "captive nations" and vowed that the United States could not accept "the permanent subjugation of the people of Eastern Europe." In a speech to the United Nations, on the other hand, he made no criticisms of the Soviet Union, and called for "constructive negotiations" characterized by "ten-fold trust and thousand-fold affection."

Reagan's re-election never seemed in doubt until October 7, when Reagan and Mondale met in the first of two televised debates. As Mondale attacked Reagan's record, the president seemed unprepared and unable to respond. Reagan's poor performance raised questions about his age and whether, at age 73, he could still meet the demands of leadership. A psychologist expressed concern about Reagan's "ability to think on his feet, disjointedness of his sentences, and his use of the security blanket of redundancy." A *Wall Street Journal* headline wondered, "Is Oldest U.S. President Showing His Age?" Polls showed Reagan's lead, although still healthy, shrinking.

Two weeks later Reagan and Mondale faced off again. Nancy Reagan and campaign aides had worked to rebuild the president's confidence and be sure he was well rested. Early on in the debate Reagan addressed the age controversy with a characteristic quip. "I will not make age an issue in this campaign," he joked. "I am not going to exploit for political purposes my opponent's youth and inexperience." As the audience roared with applause and laughter, the campaign effectively ended. Lou Cannon later explained, "For Reagan the burden of proof was exceptionally light and he more than met it with his inspired one liner."

On Election Day Reagan received 59 percent of the vote. He registered a plurality in every state but Mondale's home of Minnesota. Reagan won a majority of the vote in almost every demographic group, although tellingly he received a minority of support from those earning under $10,000 a year and African-Americans. Reagan polled only 9 percent of the African-American vote, the lowest percentage of any candidate in history. These exceptions notwithstanding, the American people had planted a decisive stamp of approval on Reagan's first term and a strong mandate for the continuation of his policies.

10

The Reagan Doctrine
The Reagan Presidency: 1985-1986

During the 1984 campaign year Ronald Reagan had adopted a markedly more temperate stance in his comments on the Soviet Union. With the start of his second term, the earlier hard-line emphasis of his administration reasserted itself. In his inaugural address on January 21, 1985, Reagan again chastened the Soviets for amassing offensive weapons in "the greatest military buildup in the history of man." He demanded a concerted American military response, including a renewed pursuit of the SDI. In his State of the Union message, Reagan issued a clarion call to Americans to assist anti-communist insurgents throughout the world as an act of self-defense. "We must stand by all our democratic allies," he exhorted. "And we must not break faith with those who are risking their lives—on every continent, from Afghanistan to Nicaragua—to defy Soviet-supported aggression and secure rights which have been ours from birth." On March 1, Reagan called the Nicaraguan contras "the moral equivalent of our Founding Fathers." Two weeks later he sent a message to Congress requesting funds to combat "Soviet adventurism in the developing world."

Viewing these developments, *Time* magazine columnist Charles Krauthammer observed that a "Reagan Doctrine" had now taken shape. The Reagan Administration, which for years had covertly supported anti-communist movements across the globe, had now openly proclaimed these activities as essential to our national security. Although neither Reagan nor his associates ever explicitly embraced a formal Reagan Doctrine, the concept clearly reflected their outlook and determination to aggressively invalidate the Soviet Brezhnev Doctrine and overturn existing communist governments.

Afghanistan and Nicaragua continued to be the most important applications of the Reagan Doctrine. In Afghanistan the mujahedin, with American and other international assistance, had fought the Soviets to a standstill. The CIA channeled assistance to the mujahedin through Pakistan's Inter-Services Intelligence Agency (ISI), which distributed arms and funds primarily to Islamic radicals. Many Afghani rebels also raised funds through the drug trade. A February 1985 report revealed that Afghanistan had become "the world's leading source of illicit heroin exports to the United States and Europe." The Reagan Administration chose to overlook these developments in pursuit of its broader objectives. In March, Reagan signed NSDD-166 which established American determination to break the stalemate and force the Soviets out of Afghanistan "by all means available." In the next few months the United States increased the flow of arms and information into Afghanistan. Reagan approved an additional $300 million in covert assistance. The mujahedin received advanced satellite photos of Soviet positions and the United States established schools that would train tens of thousands of insurgents in the use of modern weapons. CIA Director Casey, in collaboration with the Saudis, also encouraged the "freedom fighters" to actually make raids into the Soviet Union.

Administration policies in Nicaragua had run into more severe obstacles. Following the mining of Nicaragua's harbor in March 1984, both Reagan and Casey had promised to keep Congress informed of U.S. covert activities in Central America. In the fall, however, Congress learned that the CIA had distributed a manual instructing the contras on terror tactics and assassination. Congress passed a Second Boland Amendment in October 1984, designed to end all assistance to the contras. The act specifically barred the CIA, Department of Defense, or "any other agency or entity" from "supporting, directly or indirectly, military and paramilitary operations in Nicaragua by any nation, group, organization or individual." Despite the seemingly pre-emptive blanket language, and warnings from Secretary of State Schultz that further assistance to the contras could constitute "an impeachable offense," Reagan convinced himself that the law did not cover members of his immediate staff. He instructed National Security Adviser MacFarlane, "I want you to do whatever you have to do to help [the contras] keep body and soul together."

MacFarlane turned this task over to Oliver North, an energetic Marine officer on the National Security Council staff. Barred from using government monies in the operation (although on the federal payroll himself), North began raising funds from private American citizens, some of whom were rewarded with audiences with the president. He and MacFarlane also turned to several foreign countries for assistance, securing money or arms from Israel, Saudi Arabia, South Africa, Brunei, and other nations. To coordinate the flow of materiel to the contras, North recruited arms dealers Richard Secord, a former Air Force major general, and Albert Hakim, an Iranian businessman. North, Secord, and Hakim organized The Establishment, a business operation complete with ships, planes, airfields, advanced communications capabilities, and Swiss bank accounts, camouflaged through a web of dummy corporations. The Establishment employed pilots normally engaged in the drug trade to make their shipments to the contras. The pilots often mingled their arms and drug shipments together or used Establishment-supported contra airstrips for refueling on their drug runs. When initial reports of these activities surfaced in summer 1985, Reagan categorically denied violating any laws and vowed to continue cooperating with Congress. MacFarlane responded to the House Select Committee on Intelligence, "I can state with deep personal conviction that at no time did I or any member of the National Security Council staff violate the letter or spirit" of the Boland Amendments.

The efforts to support the contras in the face of a clear congressional ban reflected a recurrent pattern within the Reagan Administration of ignoring or conveniently misinterpreting laws that did not adhere to the Administration's desires and agenda. Reagan's wholehearted participation in the Nicaraguan subterfuge may also have been made possible by changes that had taken place within the executive office. The troika of James Baker, Ed Meese, and Michael Deaver that had so effectively controlled the president's life during his first term had departed. Baker and Meese had moved into the cabinet as secretary of the interior and attorney general, respectively. Deaver had switched to the private sector to work as a lobbyist. Donald Regan, who replaced Baker as chief of staff, lacked their appreciation of the need to divert Reagan from his most impetuous impulses. This gave Reagan more leeway to initiate his pet policies. The contra and Establishment operations fell into this category.

A greater engagement with the Soviet Union itself emerged concurrent with the Reagan Doctrine. During the early years of his presidency, Reagan had demonstrated little interest in meeting with his Soviet counterparts. When he began calling for a more direct dialogue in 1984, the Soviet Union had fallen into a leadership crisis. Leonid Brezhnev died in November 1982. His heir, Yuri Andropov, in ill health throughout his brief tenure, passed on in February 1984. Konstantin Chernenko repeated

Andropov's performance, lasting only a year before dying in March 1985. "How can I make peace if they keep dying on me?" wondered Reagan.

The elderly Brezhnev, Andropov, and Chernenko had represented the Soviet old guard, shaped by their World War II and Cold War experiences. Their younger successor, Mikhail Gorbachev, brought a fresh perspective to the Soviet scene. Even before Gorbachev's ascent, Soviet leaders had concluded that Ronald Reagan's assessment of their system was correct. "By the end of the 1970s . . . the Soviet economic system was no longer functioning," reports one former official. "About 80 percent of industry, directly or indirectly, was tied into or working for the military-industrial complex . . . truly depressing the economy." In an age of computers and high technology, Soviet expertise had fallen far behind the West. Gorbachev and others had come to realize that an end to the arms race offered the only possible salvation for the socialist system. But the combination of the Carter-Reagan arms buildups and the leadership vacuum of the early 1980s had made it impossible to implement serious reforms.

Once in power, Gorbachev moved quickly to shift Soviet priorities. In spring 1985, even as the Reagan Administration ramped up its efforts to support anti-communist insurgents, Gorbachev addressed the party congress in Moscow on the need to re-evaluate its international commitments. On April 8, he announced a unilateral six-month moratorium on the placement of INF missiles in Europe, offering to make it permanent if the United States halted its deployment. This proposal clearly favored the Soviets, who had already positioned their missiles. But on April 18 Gorbachev called for an end to all nuclear testing, and on April 26 he indicated that the Soviet Union would make extensive reductions in its nuclear armaments in exchange for a United States retreat on SDI. The Reagan Administration doubted the sincerity of these overtures and quickly turned them down. But Gorbachev did have a hidden agenda. On April 23, he informed the Soviet Central Committee that he had decided to move forward on arms control talks, adopt a more defensive rather than offensive stance in international affairs, reduce the size of the military, and seek a way to withdraw Soviet armed forces from Afghanistan.

While Americans pondered the meaning of the changes taking place in the Soviet Union, terrorism in the Middle East again seized the nation's attention. On June 14, 1985, two Lebanese Shiites hijacked a TWA plane in Athens and routed it to Beirut. They beat and murdered a United States Navy diver and threw his body onto the runway. The hijackers threatened to kill the remaining 39 Americans on board if Israel did not release more than 700 Shiites held prisoner. Reagan announced that "Americans will never make concessions with terrorists," but pressured the Israelis to accede to the demands. In a stunning victory for the terrorists, Israel released its prisoners, after which the hijackers freed the American hostages. Americans welcomed the denouement, which had spared their countrymen and women. Reagan triumphantly, if somewhat incongruously, proclaimed, "The United States gives terrorists no rewards and no guarantees. We make no concessions. We make no deals."

The president had also grown increasingly concerned about another group of hostages held in the Middle East. During the previous year, seven Americans had been kidnapped and held in Lebanon. Their families pleaded with Reagan to effect their release, but the president possessed no leverage to achieve that goal. On July 3, however, just three days after Reagan vowed never to deal with terrorists, an Israeli official approached National Security Adviser MacFarlane with a proposition. The Israelis had long supported Iran in its war with Iraq. Operation Staunch, a program launched by the Reagan Administration to prevent the flow of arms into Iran, had left the Iranians desperate for weapons. The Israelis reported that a group of Iranian moderates opposed to the Khomeini regime had offered to arrange the release of the hostages in Lebanon in exchange for American weapons. The Israelis would supply the weapons, if the Americans would then replenish their stocks.

Despite Iran's clear links to terrorism, the initiative won favor with several Reagan officials. Eternal cold warriors MacFarlane and Casey viewed it as a way to position the United States more favorably in a post-Khomeini Iran and to blunt any Soviet designs on the oil-rich nation. Reagan, himself, seemed obsessed with the need to free the hostages. MacFarlane brought the scheme to Reagan in mid-July while the president recovered in the hospital from surgery to remove a pre-cancerous growth. Reagan responded favorably, noting in his diary, "It seems two members of the Iranian government want to establish talks with us. I'm sending [MacFarlane] to meet them in a neutral country." Reagan hoped that this might get "our seven kidnap victims back." When MacFarlane laid out the plan to the national security team on July 22, Secretaries Schultz and Weinberger and Chief of Staff Regan questioned it. But Casey enthusiastically supported it.

As CIA director, Casey should have known better. The key middle man supposedly in contact with the Iranian moderates was Manucher Ghorbanifer, a shady Iranian arms dealer, viewed with contempt by CIA operatives. Ghorbanifer had failed two CIA lie-detector tests. One year earlier the CIA had named him in a special notice as someone who "should be regarded as an intelligence fabricator and a nuisance." Nonetheless, MacFarlane entered into negotiations with Ghorbanifer and on August 2, Reagan approved the transfer of 100 American TOW missiles to Israel to replace weapons to be sent to Iran. Federal law required the president to inform Congress of this transaction, but Reagan declined to do so. On August 20 Iran received 96 missiles from Israel, the first of a series of covert shipments in violation of both United States law and Operation Staunch, designed to liberate the hostages in Lebanon. Ominously, the Iranians reacted not by arranging for a hostage release, but with a demand for more weapons.

The arms control front with the Soviet Union occupied far more of Reagan's time. In March, when Gorbachev had succeeded Chernenko, President Reagan had extended an invitation to hold a summit meeting with the new general secretary. Gorbachev readily accepted and in July plans were announced for the two leaders to meet in Geneva in November.

During the following months the two sides positioned themselves for the meeting. Gorbachev offered significant concessions; the hardliners in the Reagan Administration rejected any prospects of change. On August 19 MacFarlane offered a pessimistic assessment, calling Soviet arms control proposals "unrealistic." Secretary of Defense Weinberger suggested that the United States should jettison the ABM Treaty and, in his annual report to Congress, dismissed as "inherently incredible" any notion that the Soviets had changed course. The United States accelerated its deployments of Pershing Missiles in Europe, staged a test of SDI technology, and dispatched the U.S.S. Iowa to the Baltic Sea. The presence of an American battleship in Russian waters was a provocation without Cold War precedent. On September 17 Reagan told a press conference that he would not sacrifice SDI to win cuts in nuclear armaments. Gorbachev, on the other hand, proposed a 50 percent decrease in offensive strategic weapons in exchange for an agreement on SDI and announced a unilateral reduction of INF missiles the Soviets had already deployed.

The efforts of the United States to develop a space-based "Star Wars" defense system loomed as an ever-broadening obstacle to serious arms control talks. Since the beginning of the year, the Reagan Administration had launched a campaign to build popular support for SDI to force Congress to increase funding for the program. The Pentagon claimed substantial progress on the new defense system, presenting a videotape showing a successful test wherein a ground-based laser had struck an incoming missile. By April 1985 a majority of Americans favored development of SDI. Congress allotted $3 billion for further research. European nations, initially skeptical about the efficacy of SDI, also climbed on board when the Reagan Administration began offering their scientists lucrative SDI research contracts.

In reality, there was little to justify this sudden leap of faith in a space-based technology. Administration officials had admitted to Congress in 1984 that their proposed plan did not include a truly comprehensive shield. American scientists had yet to conceptualize any coherent vision of how a Star Wars system might work. Edward Teller's original concept of x-ray lasers had been abandoned, as had an alternative of chemical lasers. The Pentagon, it would later be learned, had rigged its vaunted 1984 test to guarantee success.

Ironically, the Soviet emphasis on stopping SDI in arms control talks fueled the American belief in its utility. Some elements in the Soviet hierarchy, much like Reagan, believed that American technological acumen might produce a workable system. Most Soviet scientists, however, shared in the general consensus that not only was a true space shield impossible, but any system attempted could be countered at a fraction of the cost it would require to mount it. Indeed, contrary to the expectations of some members of the Reagan Administration, the Soviets never expended substantial resources to develop their own SDI program. The Soviets did, nonetheless, fear the abandonment of the predictability offered by the ABM Treaty and opposed the militarization of space. They worried that

SDI might be designed for offensive first-strike capabilities rather than just defensive purposes. Secretary of State Schultz, who had initially opposed Reagan's SDI vision, began to take it more seriously when he realized how determined the Soviets seemed to be to block it. Schultz hoped this could be used to win concessions on arms control. Hardliners in the administration, like Richard Perle, who opposed all negotiations with the Soviets, saw Reagan's infatuation with SDI as a means to undermine the impending talks.

On October 6, 1985, six weeks before the scheduled Geneva Summit, the hardliners attempted a pre-emptive strike. MacFarlane announced that the Reagan Administration had re-evaluated the ABM Treaty and adopted a new "broad interpretation" of the 13-year-old pact. The administration had decided that the ABM Treaty, despite specific language barring space-based applications, left open the possibility of developing systems based on new technologies not in existence in 1972. American officials claimed that an examination of the original negotiation transcripts supported this conclusion. As classified documents, however, these records remained unavailable to others. This "broad interpretation" constituted not only a rejection of the ABM accord as it had been generally understood for over a decade, but an unprecedented assertion that the executive branch could unilaterally reinterpret any longstanding international agreement. A roar of protest arose from many parties, including those who had negotiated the original treaty. Within a week, President Reagan announced that although the "broad interpretation" was "fully justified," the United States would abide by the original "restrictive" reading of the accord. Several days later, however, Perle indicated that this compromise might only be a temporary state of affairs.

As preparations for the November summit continued, Reagan faced yet another terrorist challenge. On October 7, members of the Palestine Liberation Organization seized control of the *Achille Lauro*, an Italian ocean liner, and brutally killed a wheelchair-bound Jewish-American passenger. After two days the hijackers released the remaining passengers in exchange for their own safe passage. Reagan responded by dispatching F-14 jets to force down an Egyptian airliner carrying Abul Abbas, who had masterminded the plot, turning Abbas over to Italian authorities. Although Abbas would soon be released, the incident reaffirmed Reagan's image as someone who dealt harshly with terrorists. In addition, Reagan's hostage initiative seemed to be bearing at least some fruit. In September Israel had sold an additional 408 missiles to Iran. One day later the kidnappers released hostage Benjamin Weir. Ghorbanifer informed MacFarlane he could secure the freedom of others, but only if the United States would now provide more sophisticated HAWK anti-aircraft missiles.

On November 14, the eve of the Geneva Summit, Reagan addressed the American people about his upcoming meeting with Mikhail Gorbachev. In his most expansive comments yet on the issue of arms reduction, Reagan stated that nuclear weapons, rather than ideological differences, "pose the greatest threat in human history to the survival of the human race." The United States, he stated, "do not wish the Soviet people any harm." Instead, "We should seek to reduce the suspicions and mistrust that have led us to acquire mountains of strategic weapons." But while Gorbachev saw Geneva as place to pursue the arms control agreements the Soviets so desperately needed, Reagan envisioned a more broad-based dialogue on worldwide conflicts and human rights within the Soviet Union.

Privately, Reagan saw the meeting as an opportunity to implement one of his longstanding fantasies. He truly believed that if given the opportunity to speak to a Soviet leader face-to-face, he could convince his counterpart of mankind's common interest and the need for the Soviets to change their behavior. To implement this scenario, Reagan, unbeknown to even many of his senior aides, set his own agenda. Although the schedule called for Reagan and Gorbachev to meet alone for only 15 minutes on the first day, the President invited Gorbachev to join him for a private meeting at a boathouse on the lake.

In the boathouse, for several hours before a roaring fire, the two men became acquainted. Reagan attempted to convince Gorbachev of the need for the two nations to pursue their common interests. Invoking the science fiction movie, *The Day the Earth Stood Still,* Reagan noted that if earth were invaded from outer space, its people would come together to repel the attackers. At the same time he assured Gorbachev that the United States would never allow the Soviets to prevail in the arms race. Gorbachev impressed the president by several times invoking God in his comments, surprising behavior since most communists professed atheism. As they left the boathouse, the two men agreed to hold two more summits, one in Washington and a second in Moscow.

This image of amiability and a genuine chemistry developing between Reagan and Gorbachev permeated the Geneva Summit. The concrete accomplishments of the meeting were less impressive. The United States and the Soviet Union affirmed Reagan's assertion that a "nuclear war cannot be won and must never be fought." They agreed to a vague 50 percent reduction in nuclear weapons, "appropriately applied," and pledged to move toward "an interim agreement" on missiles in Europe. Significantly, Gorbachev, departing from previous Soviet practice, accepted human rights questions as appropriate to the U.S.-Soviet dialogue. The countries also pledged to pursue cultural and scientific exchanges. On the other hand, Reagan refused to negotiate on the issue of SDI. When the Soviets mentioned their intention to withdraw from Afghanistan, the Americans ignored the statement.

In private, both leaders expressed reservations about the other. Gorbachev described Reagan as not "terribly bright or knowledgeable," an ideological "dinosaur." Reagan wrote to George Murphy that Gorbachev "is a firm believer in their system. . . . At the same time, he is practical and knows his economy is a basket case." But the overall image conveyed by the summit was one of progress. Reagan emerged as a strong leader and tough negotiator, further enhancing his popularity at home.

Far from view, the effort to free more hostages from Lebanon continued to wend its unpredictable course. "We have an undercover thing," Reagan optimistically wrote in his diary in late October, "which could get them sprung momentarily." To date the United States and Israel had illegally sold several hundred missiles to Iran and received one hostage in exchange. The Americans had no idea who in Iran had received the weapons. In November the Israelis withdrew their cooperation from the conspiracy. Oliver North and The Establishment stepped into the breach. On November 25 they arranged for the shipment of 18 HAWK missiles to the Iranians. Federal law required the president to sign an "intelligence finding" on all covert actions and report these measures to Congress in a "timely fashion." To date, Reagan had not met these obligations in his Iranian operation. Finally, on December 5 he issued a finding that retroactively authorized the completed transfers. The document specifically instructed CIA Director Casey "not to brief the Congress of the United States . . . until such time as I may direct otherwise."

Two days later MacFarlane, who had recently stepped down as national security adviser, reported on the hostage initiative to Reagan's national security team. Again Schultz and Weinberger raised strong objections. A CIA representative warned, "Whatever arms we give these so-called moderates . . . will end up supporting the present Khomeini regime." Reagan, however, remained adamant on the need to free the hostages. He dispatched MacFarlane to London to meet with North, Secord, and Ghorbanifer to discuss the situation. When MacFarlane suggested that the United States open talks with Iranian moderates without trading arms, Ghorbanifer grew irate. His colleagues, he said, would respond by letting the kidnappers kill the hostages. North also disliked this approach. In the sale of U.S. HAWK missiles, the Establishment had overcharged the Iranians, netting a hefty profit. This had given North what he later described as a "neat idea." He could channel money earned in the sale of weapons to the Iranians to support the effort to bolster the contras in Nicaragua. This brainstorm, though probably begun without the president's knowledge, would link Reagan's two unrelated illegal covert initiatives.

In January 1986, Reagan signed two more findings approving the continuation of the arms trade. By this time the arrangement had degenerated into not merely "arms for hostage" trades as they would later be described, but straight-out arms sales to the Iranians. In February, The Establishment delivered 1000 more TOW missiles to the Iranians. The deal garnered a $6 million to $10 million profit, but again no hostages were liberated. The profits were diverted in part to the contras and in part to pay North's allies, Secord and Hakim. Both parties to the transactions now saw them as part of an elaborate confidence game. North felt that he was getting the better of the Iranians by overcharging them. "I lied every time I met the Iranians," he later testified. The Iranians, on the other hand, had received badly needed weapons for their war with Iraq, while securing the freedom of only one hostage. No openings to the illusive moderates in Iran materialized for the American conspirators.

At home, Reagan took advantage of his immense popularity to try to regenerate support for the contras. In a pair of speeches in March 1986 the president warned of the danger posed by the communists in Nicaragua. In the first he noted that Nicaragua was only a short distance from the Texas border town of Harlingen, implying the danger of a possible invasion from an impoverished nation of only four million people. On March 16, he charged, "Using Nicaragua as a base, the Soviets and Cubans can become the dominant power in the crucial corridor between North and South America. Established there they will be in a position to threaten the Panama Canal, interdict our sea lanes and ultimately move against Mexico." By June Reagan had convinced the House of Representatives to approve $100 million in aid for the previously repudiated rebels.

Reagan also bolstered his image as tough on terrorism. On April 5 terrorists bombed a Berlin night club packed with American soldiers. Two United States citizens died and 50 were wounded. When evidence pointed to Libyan complicity, Reagan dispatched 30 bombers to hit Libyan targets including the headquarters of Muammar Qaddafi. The supposedly "surgical strikes," aimed at military assets, killed mostly civilians, including Qaddafi's two-year-old daughter. Americans welcomed the raid as another sign that under Reagan's leadership, the United States would not appear helpless or intimidated, despite the dubious and dangerous precedent of directly targeting a foreign leader.

The administration seemed less certain about how to deal with the Soviet Union. In the months after Geneva, Gorbachev continued to make major concessions, each one bolder than the last. In December 1985 he withdrew longstanding opposition to on-site inspections of nuclear test sites needed to verify a moratorium on testing. On January 15, 1986, he introduced a plan to remove all intermediate range (INF) weapons from Europe and banish all nuclear weapons by 2000. The proposal, in effect, accepted the "zero-zero" option introduced in 1981 and promised to destroy far more Soviet than American missiles.

In speeches to the Soviet Union's Party Congress in February, the Soviet leader called for a halt to the "confrontation between capitalism and socialism." Gorbachev invoked Reagan's vision of an alien invasion that would bring the two nations together in a common defense. "But isn't a nuclear disaster a more tangible danger than a landing by extraterrestrials?" asked Gorbachev. Security could only be obtained, he argued, by maintaining a minimum defense force and eliminating all nuclear arms.

Two months later Gorbachev offered "a substantial reduction" of Soviet forces in Europe. This minimized the need of the United States to protect Europe from the Soviet Union's conventional military superiority and removed one of the justifications for an American nuclear strike force. In June Gorbachev froze the number of Soviet INF missiles in Asia. He also decoupled British and French compliance with the proposed European ban, allowing them to keep their existing missiles after the United States and Soviet Union dismantled theirs.

The Reagan Administration viewed Gorbachev's overtures as designed for propaganda purposes. If Gorbachev was sincere, they believed, his concessions had been wrung by the massive American military build-up, the covert operations directed at Soviet satellites, and the encumbrances placed on the Soviet economy. As Gorbachev backpedaled, the United States continued to apply pressure. In March, two United States ships on an apparent intelligence-gathering mission entered Soviet territorial waters and ignored warnings to withdraw. On April 8, the United States fired a new nuclear weapons test.

When the Soviet Union experienced a severe accident at a nuclear power plant in Chernobyl on April 26, exposing the inadequacies of Soviet technology and spreading clouds of radiation over Europe, Reagan denounced the beleaguered and confused Soviet Union for its "stubborn refusal" to give a "full account" of the event. In June Reagan announced that the United States would no longer adhere to the arms limitations outlined in SALT II, blaming Soviet noncompliance for undermining the pact and raising "fundamental concerns about the integrity of the arms control process."

Covertly, the United States dramatically escalated its support for the mujahedin in Afghanistan. Despite Soviet indications at Geneva of their intent to seek a withdrawal, in July the CIA began to arm the mujahedin with Stinger anti-aircraft missiles that could bring down Soviet helicopters and aircraft. Both the State Department and Department of Defense feared that the missiles might be used by terrorists to attack commercial airliners. Reagan nonetheless approved the shipment of 1000 Stingers to the mujahedin.

Reagan's popularity continued to soar. In May and June the Gallup Poll revealed that almost 70 percent of Americans approved his handling of his job. Eighty-two percent of younger voters gave the oldest president in American history a favorable rating. This offered a firm base for conservatism to build on in the future. Americans expressed satisfaction not only with his conduct of foreign affairs but with the performance of the economy. Since the turnaround had begun in 1983, the nation had experienced three years of steady growth. On July 4, Reagan joined in a one-hundredth-birthday celebration for the newly renovated Statue of Liberty. Before a worldwide television audience, Reagan proclaimed, "We are the keepers of the flame of liberty, we hold it high for the world to see."

The Iranian hostage initiative meanwhile continued to spin out of control. In May MacFarlane and North flew to Iran to negotiate directly with the "moderates" for the release of the hostages. To hide their identities MacFarlane and North carried false passports; in case of discovery they concealed suicide pills. They finally realized that Ghorbanifer had been running a sting operation and that his contacts in Iran had minimal influence over the kid-nappers in Lebanon. Remarkably, probably to continue the flow of monies to the contras, the trade with Iran con-tinued. In May North sold Hawk spare parts to the Irani-ans to secure the release of two hostages. In July the Lebanese freed only one. In September, as might be expected given the rewards now established for hostage-taking, two more Americans were kidnapped. Nonetheless, in October North sent 500 more TOW missiles to Iran. He callously confessed to one of his associates that he hoped to get a hostage liberated in time to influence the mid-term Congressional elections in November.

As his subordinates implemented their arms-for-hostage machinations, Reagan continued to rail against terrorism. In August he signed an anti-terrorism law bar-ring arms sales to nations that encouraged terrorism. Iran appeared prominently on the list. "We must remain res-olute in our commitment to confront this behavior in every way," admonished the president.

In the Soviet Union, meanwhile, Mikhail Gorbachev had grown restive. Despite all of his arms-reduction pro-posals, he had achieved little in the way of an actual agreement that would give him the political leverage to move forward on his domestic reform program. In late September 1986, Gorbachev surprised the United States with an invitation to a pre-summit meeting before the scheduled gathering in Washington in 1987. Although the Reagan Administration had made no preparations or planned any agenda for such an encounter, Reagan readily agreed to meet Gorbachev on October 11 in Reykjavik, Iceland. Reagan and his aides assumed that the interim summit would contain little substance, but give both lead-ers an opportunity to enhance their popularity at home.

It quickly became apparent in Reykjavik, however, that Gorbachev had arrived determined to seek real reductions in nuclear arms. According to one Reagan aide, "We came with nothing to offer and had offered nothing; we merely sat there while the Soviets unwrapped their gifts." Gorbachev accepted the American zero-zero option on intermediate INF missiles in Europe and proposed an additional 50 percent reduction in long-range ballistic missiles. He called for a ban on nuclear testing and adherence to the conventional interpretation of the ABM Treaty, blocking SDI development for ten years. The Americans were astounded. Veteran arms control negotiator Paul Nitze told Reagan that this was "the best Soviet proposal we have received in twenty-five years."

When the talks recessed, the unprepared American team grappled to devise a response. Reagan returned with an offer to eliminate all land-based ballistic missiles by 1996, after which the United States could still deploy a Star Wars system to defend itself. Gorbachev quickly agreed to the arms reductions, but then countered with a proposal to eliminate all nuclear weapons, including those launched from bombers and submarines. "It would be fine with me," said Reagan. The consequences of this impromptu agreement, had it been allowed to stand, were enormous. Reagan, without consulting either the Joint Chiefs of Staff or NATO allies, had effectively removed the nuclear deterrent that had protected Europe from Soviet invasion throughout the Cold War.

At this point Gorbachev reintroduced the issue of SDI, which he had addressed in his opening comments. All other considerations, he informed Reagan, depended on keeping space-weapons research in the laboratories as provided in the ABM Treaty. This was the type of tradeoff that Secretary of State Schultz had long hoped for. Reagan reacted as if he were hearing about abandoning SDI for the first time at the summit. "I couldn't believe it and blew my top," he later explained. After a brief exchange in which Gorbachev expressed disbelief at Reagan's offer to share SDI technology, the president turned to Schultz and announced, "The meeting is over. . . . Let's go George. . . . we're leaving." When Gorbachev chided him for missing "the unique chance of going down in history as a great president who paved the way for nuclear disarmament," Reagan responded icily, "That applies to both of us."

As the meeting broke up, observers struggled to understand what had happened. "It's been a failure," announced Gorbachev. "We missed an historic chance. Never have our positions been so close." Reagan told John Poindexter, who had succeeded MacFarlane as national security adviser, that he had agreed to eliminate all *nuclear* weapons. "You couldn't have!" exclaimed Poindexter, to which Reagan replied, "John, I was there and I did!"

The administration quickly launched what presidential press secretary Larry Speakes would call "an unprecedented news blitz . . . the super blitz of all blitzes," to present its interpretation of the Reykjavik summit. United States officials described it as a "momentous," "historic," "breakthrough event." Dramatic progress had been made, and Reagan's bold walkout and resolution not to surrender SDI had protected the nation's security. The United States, Reagan informed the American people, ignoring Gorbachev's original initiative, had offered to eliminate all ballistic missiles. This represented "perhaps the most sweeping and generous arms control proposal in history." But Reagan had told Gorbachev that he had pledged "to the American people that I would not trade away SDI. . . . I went to Reykjavik determined that everything was negotiable, except two things: our freedom and our future." Nonetheless, the president reported with characteristic optimism, "The significance is we got as close as we did." The American public backed the president. Seventy-two percent of those surveyed applauded his dealings with the Soviets. A similar number now said they supported developing SDI.

Reporter Strobe Talbot called Reykjavik "one of the strangest episodes in the annals of nuclear diplomacy."

Perhaps the strangest element was, when the smoke had cleared, how much it justified Reagan's optimism. Although the Reagan Administration quickly "clarified" the impression that Reagan promised to eliminate all nuclear weapons, the Soviets had accepted the zero-zero option. The goal of a fifty percent reduction in all long-range ballistic missiles remained. These agreements, achieved without any major American concessions, writes Raymond Garthoff, "broke the mold and opened up new possibilities in arms control." Within a year even some Russian officials would hail it as "a landmark development of the world."

Upon his return from Reykjavik, Reagan got to celebrate one of the rare domestic policy triumphs of his second term, the passage of the Tax Reform Act of 1986. The intense focus on foreign affairs obscured the almost total absence of a domestic agenda. From 1984 to 1986 Reagan initiated only this one major successful piece of legislation. Despite his reputation as a tax cutter, Reagan had actually signed legislation increasing taxes and fees three times since 1981. None of this legislation had significantly dealt with the nature or fairness of federal taxation. Chief of Staff Regan, while still treasury secretary, had pressed Reagan to revamp the tax system. Knowing Reagan's penchant for dramatic examples, Regan shocked the president by noting that in 1982 Reagan's personal secretary had paid more in taxes than sixty major companies combined. He also reminded Reagan that his own speeches had advocated a fairer and simpler system for everyone.

In May 1985, Reagan introduced a set of reforms prepared by Regan designed to bring "fairness, growth, and simplicity" to tax collections. Reagan sounded a populist note. The only losers, he promised, would be "those individuals and corporations who are not paying their fair share, or for that matter any share. These abuses cannot be tolerated. . . . The free rides are over." After a long legislative struggle, the Regan/Reagan bill won enactment in

October 1986. It constituted a major overhaul of the tax system. The top rates on individuals fell from 50 percent to 28 percent, but the top capital gains rate rose. The number of tax brackets dropped from 14 to three. Six million low-income Americans were dropped from the tax rolls entirely. The legislation lowered the top corporate rate, but closed many loopholes that had allowed businesses to completely evade paying taxes. The changes affected the taxes paid by most Americans only minimally, with the greatest benefits going to upper-income citizens. But the system that emerged did, as Reagan had promised, create a somewhat fairer and simpler federal tax mechanism. Reagan proudly signed the bill on October 22. Although no one realized it at the time, the Tax Reform Act would mark Reagan's last triumph of any kind for many months to come.

11

Scandals and Summits
The Reagan Presidency: 1987-1988

As the November 3, 1986, midterm elections approached, Republicans hoped that Ronald Reagan's immense popularity would enable the party to attain dominance in the House of Representatives, giving Republicans control of both branches of Congress for the first time in more than three decades. National Security Adviser John Poindexter and his assistant Oliver North thought they had furthered that goal when they arranged the release of hostage David Jacobsen on November 2. To their disappointment, Reagan's personal stature did not readily transfer to other Republican candidates. On election day, the Democrats not only added to their House majority, they regained power in the Senate, registering a net gain of eight seats.

As the polls closed, an unexpected bombshell dropped in the Middle East. An article appeared in a Lebanese magazine detailing Robert MacFarlane's misbegotten Iranian negotiations. Iranian officials not only confirmed the story, but divulged that the "moderates" who had engaged Mac-Farlane and North were actually agents of the Khomeini government seeking to fleece the gullible Americans. The Iranian revelations marked the second time in less than a month that the covert operations of the National Security Council had been breached. On October 5 in Nicaragua, the Sandinistas had shot down an Establishment supply plane and captured its pilot, Eugene Hasenfus. The president quickly denied that Hasenfus and his crew had any ties to the United States. "While they're American citizens, there is no government connection with that at all," stated Reagan. North, fearing that his connection to Hasenfus might soon be discovered, began shredding documents about the contra supply operation.

The almost simultaneous exposure of both the Iranian and contra initiatives plunged the Reagan Administration into its worst crisis, one that revealed the least appealing aspects of the president's leadership and conceivably could have resulted in his impeachment. The Iran-contra affair, as the scandal came to be known, was the most spectacular of a series of exposés both in and out of government that characterized the final years of the Reagan regime and tarnished his reputation. But Reagan retained his remarkable resiliency, recovering from these setbacks to leave office in a fashion that could have been crafted in the Hollywood of his past.

As the press began to investigate the allegations of arms-for-hostage trades, the Reagan Administration clumsily sought to cover up the president's complicity. On November 6, Reagan issued a categorical denial stating that the reports had "no foundation." Reagan maintained the delusion that neither he nor his National Security Council staff had done anything illegal or ethically wrong. "We will never pay off terrorists, because that only encourages more of it," he stated, seemingly oblivious to the fact that this was precisely what had happened. Indeed, Lebanese kidnappers now held more American hostages than they had when the trades began. Although Secretary of State Schultz and others advised the president to publicly accept responsibility and move on, others in the administration advocated a defensive strategy. Poindexter, North, and CIA director Casey circulated deliberately falsified information and chronologies.

Reagan addressed the nation on November 13, and while admitting that his administration had sold weapons to Iran, he claimed that this had been done to encourage Iranian moderates and bring an end to the Iran-Iraq war. "We did not—repeat did not," he asserted, "trade weapons or anything else for hostages; nor will we." For once, the American people did not believe Reagan. Polls showed that only 14 percent thought that he had told the truth. Six days later Reagan conducted an even more embarrassing press conference. When asked about Israeli involvement in the arms deals, he replied, "We . . . have had nothing to do with other countries or their shipment of arms or doing what they're doing." He insinuated that the press exposures had prevented the release of more hostages. The total amount of arms shipped, he contended, could have fit on "a single cargo plane." As Lou Cannon observes, "Almost every answer that dealt with a question about the Iran initiative was at variance with the facts." Twenty minutes after the press conference, the White House issued a clarification attempting to correct Reagan's comments.

On November 21, with public dissatisfaction building, the president instructed Attorney General Meese to launch an investigation of the National Security Council staff. North, warned by Poindexter of the looming probe, staged what he called a "shredding party," destroying 5000 pages of material. Even in this pursuit he proved less than competent. Evidence survived on computer back-up tapes, and an April 1986 document revealed the diversion of funds from the Iranian arms trades to the contras.

On November 24, Meese informed Reagan of the link between the Iranian hostage initiative and the effort to support the contras. According to Chief of Staff Regan, Reagan's face turned white when he heard the news. In his diary, Reagan recorded, "North didn't tell me about this. Worst of all, John Poindexter found out about it and didn't tell me." At a press conference on November 25,

Reagan announced Poindexter's resignation, North's removal from the NSC staff, and the creation of a Special Review Board to investigate the entire affair. Attorney General Meese then informed a visibly stunned press corps of the newly discovered connection between the Iranian arms transactions and the Nicaraguan resistance. Both houses of Congress indicated that they would launch probes of these events. On December 19, Meese appointed Lawrence Walsh as a special prosecutor to investigate the entire matter.

Reporters dubbed the scandal the Iran-contra affair, linking the two essentially unrelated, but equally illegal, presidential initiatives. This conceptualization obscured as much as it revealed. In both instances, Reagan had encouraged his subordinates to pursue policies expressly forbidden by law. In each case he had committed potentially impeachable offenses. The crimes committed in support of the contras predated and outlasted the hostage-related transgressions. But the Iranian negotiations aroused a greater sense of outrage among the American people. Reagan had not only violated his repeated pledges never to deal with terrorists, but he had done so with the nation that had so baldly humiliated the United States when it had seized the American embassy less than a decade earlier. On December 2, less than a month after the initial revelations, the president's approval rating in the Gallup Poll dropped from 67 percent to 36 percent. The precipitous fall was the largest that Gallup had ever recorded.

In some respects the Iran-contra affair reflected Reagan's impulsiveness and naiveté. More pointedly, it illustrated a brand of lawlessness that often characterized the Reagan Administration. As journalist Haynes Johnson observes, "In the Reagan White House, laws were something to be evaded rather than executed. Instead of trying to change a law by pointing out its inadequacies, the Reagan people chose either to disregard it or find a way to get around it." This tendency manifested itself not only in the Iran-contra affair, but on a wide range of fronts. Clarence Thomas, first as director of civil rights in the Department of Education and later as chair of the Equal Employment Opportunity Commission, refused to process discrimination complaints. The Justice Department failed to investigate alleged violations of the Voter Rights Act. The Department of Energy and Nuclear Regulatory Commission ignored safety violations at nuclear power plants.

When combined with an almost total neglect of standards on conflict of interest and a commitment to cutting back on the regulatory function of government, this mindset led to neglect and corruption that reached into the highest levels of the administration. Corruption ran rampant in the Department of Defense, where payoffs, kickbacks, insider information, overcharges, false claims, and other offenses accompanied the military buildup. As early as May 1985, 45 of the nation's largest contractors faced 131 separate investigations. Deputy Defense Secretary Pat Thayer spent 19 months in prison for providing friends with inside investment information. Special National Security Assistant Tom Reed faced similar charges. A 1988 Justice Department probe resulted in the conviction of more than 50 Defense Department officials and private contractors charged with rigging bids and faking quality control tests. At the Department of Housing and Urban Development (HUD), funds earmarked for low-income housing found their way into luxury apartment complexes, golf courses, and swimming pools. A House subcommittee uncovered numerous abuses at HUD, including influence peddling, fraud, embezzlement, and outright theft, resulting in convictions of several HUD staffers.

Similar ethical lapses compromised several of Reagan's closest advisers. Lyn Nofziger, the president's longtime press secretary, and Michael Deaver, his special assistant, left office during Reagan's first term to trade on their insider connections as political consultants. Both fell afoul of conflict-of-interest statutes. Nofziger was convicted of three violations of the 1978 Ethics in Government Act, Deaver of lying to Congress and a federal grand jury to cover up his lobbying malfeasance. Nofziger's conviction was overturned, but Deaver received a three-year suspended sentence and was fined $100,000.

Special investigators spent years untangling the activities of Ed Meese. Meese served as White House counsel until 1984, when Reagan nominated him as attorney general. Accounts that Meese had never reported reimbursements that he had received for trips made as White House counsel and that he had received favors from those seeking government positions led to the appointment of an independent counsel to look into these charges. The investigation failed to fully exonerate Meese. The independent counsel pointedly stated not that Meese was innocent, but only that there was insufficient evidence to secure an indictment. The Office of Government Ethics concluded that Meese had indeed ignored basic ethical principles. After a long battle, Congress nonetheless affirmed Meese as attorney general in 1985. A second independent counsel was later appointed to probe Meese's connection to the Wedtech Corporation, which had committed numerous acts of fraud in securing federal defense contracts. In 1987 Meese admitted pressuring the Defense Department on Wedtech's behalf. The special prosecutor concluded that Meese probably had broken at least four laws, including filing a false tax return while attorney general. United States Attorney Rudolph Giuliani called Meese "a sleaze" and several Justice Department officials resigned rather than serve under him. Meese finally stepped down on July 5, 1988. A Justice Department report cited him for "conduct which should not be tolerated of any government employee, especially not the attorney general." By the early 1990s, nearly 200 Reagan-era officials had faced investigation and indictment for illegal practices.

Reagan, who throughout his career had demonstrated scant sensitivity to conflicts of interest, failed to offer any type of moral compass for his administration. As the scandals unfolded, he never spoke out on the issue of honesty in government, opting to blame the press and partisan politics for the revelations of ethical lapses of his subordinates. Reagan's blanket condemnation of all forms of government regulation also encouraged corruption and lawbreaking. As a conservative, Reagan was continually attuned to threats to individual freedom imposed by government. He remained oblivious, however, to the potential of abuses emanating from the private sector and the need of a federal bureaucracy to protect against this. As political scientist Hugh Heclo notes, "The positive, constructive role of constitutional government was profoundly and incurably lost on Reagan."

The Reagan Administration took great pride in its efforts to scale back government. The Federal Register, listing the nation's regulations, shrank by 45 percent by 1986. The Office of Management and Budget estimated in 1987 that Americans now performed more than 600 million hours less each year filing government paperwork. But in most respects the costs of deregulation and the concomitant reductions in federal workers far outweighed its benefits. The Customs Department faced a growing influx of drugs and illegal immigrants with a shrinking labor force. The Justice Department cut back sharply on antitrust enforcement, contributing to a wave of mergers, many funded by investors who raised money with high-interest "junk bonds" that offered lucrative commissions for those brokering the deals. This left a substantial debt load for the newly merged companies. Meanwhile, at the Securities and Exchange Commission the number of employees had remained static even as the number of stockbrokers in the nation doubled. The number of unprocessed company annual reports tripled between 1983 and 1986. Amid the merger mania and in the absence of adequate supervision, fraud at the nation's brokerages skyrocketed.

The extent to which this had unleashed the latent corruption in the nation's financial sector became apparent in late 1986. In May, Ivan Boesky, the foremost arbitrageur on Wall Street, had advised the graduating class at the University of California at Berkeley Business School that "Greed is all right . . . Everybody should be a little greedy. You shouldn't feel guilty." On November 14 Boesky pleaded guilty to using insider information and manipulating stock prices in the merger activities that had earned him his fortune. Boesky promised to cooperate with the authorities to expose other Wall Street financiers who had violated the law.

Americans also began to learn the high price they would pay for the Garn-St. Germain Act that had deregulated the savings and loan industry. For a half-century New Deal reforms had effectively stabilized American banking and warded off bank failures. In the 1980s, deregulation reduced accounting oversight and made it easier for individuals to buy or create savings and loan institutions with a minimal personal investment. Speculators flooded into the industry, attracting deposits by offering high interest rates on federally insured accounts, and investing the money in exceedingly risky propositions. Many made donations to curry favor with politicians of both parties and win additional exemptions from official scrutiny. In the Southwest and Far West the unfettered savings and loans encouraged a construction and real estate boom. Properties were traded over and over again at ever higher prices, thus generating lavish commissions but suspect value. Staff reductions at the Federal Home Loan Bank Board, which supervised the savings and loans, made it impossible for the government to adequately monitor the burgeoning industry.

The problems generated by these practices became evident as early as 1984 when the federal government had to bail out the Continental Illinois Bank to prevent its collapse. As other banks began to fail, Ed Gray, the director of the Federal Home Loan Bank Board, looked on in dismay. A longtime Reagan crony from Sacramento and advocate of deregulation, Gray realized that Garn-St. Germain had created a time bomb. He called for the hiring of more examiners and a tightening of lending rules and federally insured deposit limits. White House officials attacked him as a "re-regulator" and called for his resignation. Overextended savings and loans began to collapse with growing regularity, with the federal government paying off investors who had lost their money. Between 1984 and 1986 the federal fund underwriting deposit insurance for savings and loans dropped from $6 billion to $2.5 billion, threatening to bankrupt the system. Deregulation of the savings and loan industry, wrote the *U.S. News and World Report*, had turned "the thrift industry into a huge casino where only taxpayers could lose."

Banker Charles Keating and his Lincoln Federal Savings and Loan in California came to personify the ongoing debacle. Keating advised his employees to go after "the weak, meek, and ignorant" in attracting investors. He hired family members at lavish salaries and distributed millions of dollars in campaign contributions and low-interest loans to politicians. In 1985, auditors questioned Lincoln Savings practices. Gray ordered that Keating be required to invest more of his personal money in the operations. Keating called upon his allies in the U.S. Senate, the beneficiaries of his political spending spree, to pressure Gray into exempting Lincoln Savings from federal rules. When Gray refused, Reagan replaced him in May 1987 as head of the Federal Home Loan Bank Board. The new director compliantly rejected recommendations from bank examiners to shut down Lincoln Savings. The bank finally collapsed two years later, leaving a $2.5 billion liability for the federal government to cover in its wake.

The price of banking deregulation, which would ultimately cost taxpayers upwards of a trillion dollars over several decades, far outweighed the benefits and savings achieved in deregulating other sectors throughout the economy. Yet Reagan barely acknowledged the crisis or allowed it to challenge his views on the need for government oversight.

In the early months of 1987, the administration remained paralyzed by the ongoing investigations into the Iran-contra matter. The Special Review Board, chaired by former Texas Senator John Tower, confronted numerous impediments. On December 15 CIA Director Casey had suffered a debilitating stroke, preventing the Tower board from questioning him. Robert MacFarlane attempted suicide the night before his scheduled testimony. Reagan himself faced a health scare when he underwent prostate surgery on January 5. The operation revealed no cancer, and Reagan appeared before the inquiry on January 26. He admitted having approved the arms sales to Iran. Two weeks later the president testified again, reading from a prepared written statement that completely contradicted his earlier sworn account. "The President was recanting his testimony," wrote Tower. "Words were being put into his mouth." On February 20 Reagan recanted his recantation, which he admitted had been prepared by others. He now told the board, "The simple truth is, I don't remember—period."

On February 26, the Tower board issued a report that, while sharply critical of Reagan's "management style," exonerated him from any illegal acts. The president's notorious inattention to detail had allowed MacFarlane, North, and later Poindexter to "dupe him" into supporting their questionable activities. Reagan's speech to the nation on March 4 reinforced this conclusion. "As angry as I might be about activities taken without my knowledge, I am still accountable for those activities," he admitted. "A few months ago I told the American people I did not trade arms for hostages. My heart and my best intentions still tell me that's true, but the facts and evidence tell me it is not." As the testimony of others and Reagan's own diaries reveal, this statement was no more accurate than any of the earlier explanations that Reagan had offered. Almost all of the activities in question had been taken not only with Reagan's full knowledge, but at his instigation. He had long ago convinced himself that somehow the arms sent to Iran to secure the release of the hostages did not constitute a trade and did not contradict American policy toward Iran and terrorism. But no one else could seriously accept this distinction.

Nonetheless the American people seemed prepared to accept this image of Reagan as a victim of his own gullible mismanagement rather than probe more deeply into the scandal. Reagan remained personally popular and few desired another impeachment confrontation so late in his presidency and so soon after the Watergate ordeal. Furthermore, the objects of the deception—support for the contras in Nicaragua and release of the hostages in Lebanon—were far removed from issues of national security or true national import. The slapstick activities of MacFarlane and North, especially in Iran, appeared so grandiosely farcical, that the broader implications of the secret operations they had engineered became obscured as the story unfolded. The economy continued to prosper and people approved Reagan's handling of arms control talks and the Soviet Union. The Iran-contra investigations would remain a festering sore, but never inflamed into the crippling disaster that once seemed possible.

Reagan also received help from Mikhail Gorbachev. In the immediate aftermath of Reykjavik, Gorbachev had expressed irritation with his American counterpart. He alleged that United States officials had distorted the events of the arms control talks and charged the Reagan Administration with seeking "to exhaust the Soviet Union economically through a race in . . . expensive space-weapons."

His frustration notwithstanding, Gorbachev pressed forward with his reform agenda. In November, the Politburo approved the withdrawal of Soviet troops from Afghanistan and Gorbachev informed Eastern European communist allies that they could no longer rely on Soviet support to maintain their regimes. At the January 1987 meetings of the Central Council, Gorbachev called for *Perestroika,* a restructuring of the Soviet economy allowing for the replacement of strict planning with greater reliance on a free market. In the wake of Chernobyl, where secrecy about the disaster had bred suspicion at home and abroad, he reaffirmed his commitment to *Glasnost*, a new freedom and openness in Soviet society.

Gorbachev's actions reinforced his rhetoric. In December 1986, he ended the internal exile of scientist Andrei Sakharov, the Soviet Union's most famous dissident, and allowed him to return to Moscow. In the early months of 1987 the government released most other political prisoners, expressed a greater tolerance for religious freedom, allowed banned literature to be published, announced it would allow Jews to emigrate from the country, and stopped jamming Voice of America broadcasts into the Soviet Union.

The Reagan Administration seemed oblivious to these changes. In January 1987, a White House report on the *National Security Strategy of the United States* portrayed the Soviet Union in the dark Cold War imagery of the past. Defense Secretary Weinberger, claiming that "some elements of our research have proved successful beyond the expectations of our most optimistic scientists and engineers," called for an accelerated deployment of "Phase One" of SDI before Reagan left office in 1989. In a rare public airing of disagreements on defense policy, Joint Chiefs of Staff Chairman William J. Crowe publicly dismissed Weinberger's exaggerated assertions of progress on SDI.

In the Soviet Union, the freeing of Sakharov paid unexpected dividends. The outspoken physicist immediately weighed in on the SDI debate. The Soviet Union, he proclaimed, should cease its obsession with SDI. A Stars Wars system, he argued, would be at best a "Maginot Line in space," easily and inexpensively countered. More likely the project would "simply die on its own quietly and peacefully." He suggested decoupling SDI concerns from other arms control efforts, predicting that true disarmament would lessen the popularity of SDI in the United States. Bolstered by Sakharov's support, Gorbachev on February 28 delinked all arms control talks from SDI. He announced that the Soviet Union would unconditionally agree to the removal of all American and Soviet INF missiles from Europe.

For Reagan, still embattled by Iran-contra, Gorbachev's overture came at an opportune time. It drew attention away from the dispiriting portrayal of his leadership in the Tower report and reminded Americans of his perceived successes in dealing with the Soviet Union. On March 3, Reagan accepted Gorbachev's offer. In April, Secretary of State Schultz traveled to Moscow to negotiate an INF treaty. In the past the Soviets had always balked at calls for on-site verification of arms control agreements. Now the Soviets surprised the Americans by removing all objections to what Schultz called "strict and intrusive verification," causing concern among U.S. defense and intelligence officials who feared the consequences of Soviet inspections of American sites.

Congressional Democrats, emboldened by their electoral triumph and Reagan's decline in the polls, had begun to flex their muscles. In January, Congress overrode Reagan's veto of an $80 billion Clean Water Act. In March, Congress suspended all aid to the contras, rejected Weinberger's calls for further increases in defense spending, and blocked the administration's attempts to retreat from the ABM Treaty.

Reagan attempted to restore his image by asserting leadership on a variety of issues. Amid great fanfare Reagan proposed an Economic Bill of Rights for all Americans. He belatedly addressed the AIDS epidemic that had escalated dramatically over the previous five years. The predominance of male homosexuals among AIDS victims had forestalled both government compassion and research funding that might have saved lives and slowed the spread of the deadly disease. On April 1, 1987, Reagan, in a speech carefully vetted to avoid offending his supporters on the religious right, pronounced AIDS as "public health enemy Number 1," opening the path to more federal support in the AIDS fight.

Reagan traveled to Germany in June to deliver one of the most impassioned speeches of his presidency. Standing before the wall that divided East and West Berlin, Reagan challenged Gorbachev, "If you seek peace, if you seek prosperity for the Soviet Union and Eastern Europe, if you seek liberalization: Come here to this gate! Mr. Gorbachev, open this gate! Mr. Gorbachev, tear down this wall." The Berlin speech reflected the ongoing commitment of the Reagan Administration to maintain pressure on the Soviet Union to withdraw its support for communism in other countries. The United States continued to pour arms into Afghanistan and give funding and other assistance to Solidarity in Poland.

Throughout the summer of 1987, the televised Congressional hearings on the Iran-contra affair transfixed the nation. Testimony by MacFarlane, Poindexter, North, Secord, and others revealed the bizarre and often bungling nature of the covert world created by the CIA and NSC. North's bravura performance won surprising sympathy from viewers. The handsome, charismatic North, dressed in his Marine uniform bedecked in military decorations, confessed to myriad crimes, but righteously invoked a broader national interest to justify his actions. His attractive secretary, Fawn Hall, who had assisted him in shredding documents, captured the essence of his defense when she told her congressional inquisitors, "Sometimes you have to go above the written law, I believe." That neither the hostage release nor support of the contras rose anywhere close to this overriding level of national interest failed to faze either North or his growing army of admirers.

Fortunately for Reagan, the complex issues raised by the two NSC scandals were largely scaled back into an investigation of the diversion of funds from the Iranian arms sales to the contras in Nicaragua. While North and others testified that Reagan had approved this "neat idea," the president repeatedly asserted that he had "never heard a whisper about funds being channeled from the Iranian arms shipments to the contras." No evidence ever arose to disprove this assertion. Like the Tower report, the congressional investigation held Reagan responsible for all that had transpired on his watch. "If the president did not know what his national security advisers were doing, he should have," concluded the committee. The investigation by Independent Counsel Walsh would continue for seven more years. By fall 1987, however, public interest in the Iran-contra scandal had waned.

October brought more problems for Reagan, both personal and political. On October 5, the White House announced that Nancy Reagan had breast cancer. Two weeks later she underwent a successful mastectomy. On October 19, the stock market, which had risen steadily for several years, a symbol of the Reagan prosperity, suddenly stumbled. The Dow Jones average dropped 508 points, shaving off 22.6 percent of its value, the largest one-day drop since the Great Depression. Some banking leaders, fearing a complete collapse, advised a total shutdown of the New York Stock Exchange. Instead the Federal Reserve Board demonstrated the beneficial effects of a regulated economy. The Federal Reserve moved instantly to lower interest rates and pour money into the banking system. Within two days the ominous crisis had passed.

The Reagan Administration suffered another severe blow on October 23 when Congress rejected Reagan's nomination of conservative Robert Bork to serve on the Supreme Court. Throughout his career Bork had expressed controversial opinions on issues of civil rights, privacy, free speech, and women's rights. He had downplayed the importance of relying on legal precedent to determine constitutional law. Liberal organizations had launched a determined campaign to block his approval. At televised hearings before the judiciary Bork, seeking to appear more moderate, retreated from earlier positions, undermining his credibility. By the time of the vote a majority of Americans opposed his selection. The Senate rejected him by an unprecedented 58–42 margin. Reagan immediately nominated Douglas Ginsberg to replace Bork, only to hastily withdraw his support when it was discovered that Ginsberg had smoked marijuana while a law professor.

Although 1987 had been marked primarily by its travails, the year ended on a triumphant note for Reagan. On December 8, Reagan and Gorbachev met in Washington, their third summit in two years. Gorbachev charmed the American press and public while Reagan graciously accepted a supporting role. "I don't resent his popularity," joked Reagan. "Good Lord, I co-starred with Errol Flynn once." The two leaders signed the INF Treaty, eliminating all intermediate-range missiles from their arsenals. In relative numbers the pact seemed unimpressive. Ninety-six percent of all nuclear weapons remained untouched. But the INF Treaty had both a practical and symbolic significance. For the first time an entire class of arms, including modern recently installed missiles, had been targeted for destruction. The Soviet Union would jettison almost 1000 more weapons than the United States. Both nations had agreed to on-site verification. Issues involving the ABM

Ronald Reagan and Mikhail Gorbachev signing the INF Treaty in 1987. (Courtesy Ronald Reagan Library)

Treaty and SDI remained unresolved. "Mr. President, you do what you think you have to do," advised Gorbachev. "And if in the end you have a system that you want to deploy, go ahead and deploy it. . . . I think you're wasting your money. I don't think it will work." The Washington summit completed Reagan's rehabilitation from the ignominy of the Iran-contra scandal. At the year's end his job approval rating had soared from its low of 36 percent to a solid 58 percent.

In agreeing to the INF Treaty Reagan defied anti-communist hardliners, who refused to acknowledge that the Soviet Union had actually changed. Some called the treaty a "sellout," and accused Reagan of "appeasement." Even within his administration, the image of an ongoing Soviet threat died hard. In his final report to Congress before stepping down as defense secretary in November 1987, Weinberger clung to his vision of an "all the more ominous" Soviet military buildup. The annual *National Security Strategy* review issued in January 1988 contended, "We have yet to see any slackening of the growth of Soviet military power or abandonment of expansionist aspirations." Deputy CIA Director Robert Gates charged that Gorbachev intended "to make the USSR a more competitive and stronger adversary in the years ahead." By this time, however, moderates had replaced hardliners throughout the Reagan foreign policy team and Reagan, once among the most militant of the cold warriors, had come to recognize the sincerity of Gorbachev's revolutionary efforts.

This faith was borne out on February 8, 1988, when Gorbachev publicly announced that Soviet troops would be withdrawn from Afghanistan by the end of the year. Nevertheless, the Reagan Administration, which had promised to stop supplying the rebels if the Soviets pulled out, reneged on that pledge, continuing to supply the mujahedin as long as the Soviets armed the current government in Kabul. The Soviets also offered to help broker a settlement in Nicaragua, but the United States spurned their cooperation. Although the Sandinistas had begun to comply with a regional peace plan and entered into negotiations with the contras, Reagan requested additional contra funding from Congress to "prevent the consolidation of a Soviet military presence on the American mainland." On February 3, the House of Representatives turned him down.

In March, Reagan became embroiled in a controversy that highlighted his administration's characteristic indifference and, at times, hostility to civil rights issues. The Reagan Administration had no positive civil rights agenda. Reagan had opposed the creation of a national holiday honoring Martin Luther King, Jr., and an extension of the Voting Rights Act. Federal agencies had repeatedly refused to enforce civil rights statutes. In the courts, Justice Department officials had opposed all efforts to advance school desegregation and affirmative action. In 1984, the Supreme Court had ruled that federal programs could not deny funds to colleges and other institutions that practiced discrimination, only to the specific programs within the institution that violated the law. In 1988 Congress passed the Civil Rights Restoration Act, designed to reinstitute the earlier intent of the 1964 Civil Rights Act. Reagan vetoed the bill. Twenty-one Republican senators and 52 Republican congressman joined the Democratic majority to override Reagan's veto.

The great debate in the Congress, however, revolved around the INF Treaty. Despite the opposition of some conservatives, the Senate approved the treaty 93–5 on May 27, just in time for Reagan's fourth summit meeting with Gorbachev. Reagan traveled to Moscow, where he resisted Gorbachev's efforts to secure further arms control agreements, and focused instead on the advancement of human rights in the Soviet Union. The president met with a group of dissidents and with Patriarch Aleksei II, the head of the Russian Orthodox Church. He addressed students at Moscow State University about the virtues of freedom. Reagan fully appreciated the symbolism of his visit. He celebrated his personal friendship with Gorbachev and their acknowledgment of common interests as "a cause for shaking the head in wonder." When asked if the Soviet Union was still an "evil empire," he responded, "No, I was talking about another time, another era."

The Moscow summit marked the final high point of the Reagan presidency. In October he signed into law one final piece of domestic legislation, the Family Support Act of 1988. The bill primarily represented liberal Democratic ideas forced upon him by the Congress. But it also included important steps toward the creation of "workfare," a demand that recipients must also hold jobs to earn their benefits, a longstanding Reagan alternative to the current system.

In November, Reagan's vice-president, George H.W. Bush, easily won election to succeed Reagan as president.

Reagan and his most recent and greatest co-star, Mikhail Gorbachev, staged a final curtain call in view of the Statue of Liberty in New York in December. The next day Gorbachev addressed the U.N., promising to pull out 50,000 soldiers and 5000 tanks from eastern Europe and shrink the Soviet military by 500,000 troops. He emphasized "the obligatory nature of international law for all states" and defined "the principle of freedom of choice" as a "universal principle to which there should be no exceptions." A poll taken in the aftermath of his speech revealed that a majority of Americans now regarded the Soviet Union as no more than "a minor threat" to our security.

On January 11, 1989, Reagan made his final address to the nation as president. His popularity stood high with 70 percent of the nation approving his performance. In the speech, he returned to the themes that had served him so well throughout his political career. "We Americans are the keepers of miracles. We are asked to be guardians of a place to come to, a place to start again, a place to live in the dignity God meant for his children," he asserted. The United States remained "a beacon, still a magnet for all who must have freedom." Of his own contribution, he averred, "I wasn't a Great Communicator, but I communicated great things . . . they came from the heart of a great nation—from our experience, our wisdom, and our belief in the principles that have guided us for two centuries." To those who spoke of a "Reagan Revolution," he responded, "Well, I'll accept that, but for me it always seemed like a great rediscovery, a rediscovery of our values and common sense." Ten days later, following the inauguration of President Bush, the Reagans flew home to California.

Reagan left the White House several weeks shy of his seventy-ninth birthday. As in the days before they had gone to Washington, he and Nancy could still depend on the kindness of their California friends. The Reagans leased a mansion in Beverly Hills bought for $2.5 million by 18 millionaires who had posted $156,000 each toward the purchase. The Reagans kept a generally low profile, though the former president made several speeches around the world, receiving as much as $2 million for a series of talks in Japan. Reagan addressed the Republican convention in summer 1992 and in December he traveled to England where he told an audience at Oxford that even after the fall of communism, a new, less-defined "evil still stalks the planet." He proposed "an army of conscience," led by the same United Nations that he had once excoriated, to combat these threats.

During the final years of his presidency, he had experienced several cancer scares, including surgery to remove a growth from his colon and two episodes of skin cancer. But Reagan appeared healthy and vibrant in retirement. In July 1989 Reagan suffered a massive contusion on the brain in a riding accident in Mexico, requiring surgery at the Mayo Clinic. Over the next few years Nancy and others, and even Reagan himself, became aware of a slackening of cognitive function.

In 1993 Reagan visited the Mayo Clinic, where doctors made a provisional diagnosis that the former president now suffered from degenerative cognitive dementia—Alzheimer's disease. One year later the Mayo specialists confirmed that finding. On November 5, 1994, Reagan sat down and in one quick handwritten draft, pausing only once to cross out a phrase, composed his final formal message to the American people. "I have recently been told that I am one of millions of Americans who will be afflicted with Alzheimer's disease," he gracefully wrote. "We feel that it is important to share it with you. In opening our hearts, we hope this might promote greater awareness of this condition." He offered his thanks to "you the American people for giving me the great honor of allowing me to serve as your President. When the Lord calls me home, whenever that may be, I will leave with the greatest love for this country of ours and eternal optimism for its future." He concluded, naturally, on a positive note: "I now begin the journey that will lead me into the sunset of my life. I know that for America there will always be a bright dawn ahead."

The release of the letter naturally caused many people to wonder if the onset of the disease had begun during Reagan's presidency and how that might have affected his performance. Several gerontologists, concerned with indications that Reagan had experienced a cognitive decline, had debated calling for the president to be evaluated for Alzheimer's disease during his second term. Nonetheless, his closest aides say they saw no evidence of deterioration during these years. Edmund Morris reports several minor episodes of memory lapse in 1986 and 1987 that might be attributed to aging. But Morris, who had access to Reagan's daily diaries, also writes that "The diary—all eight years of it—was uniform in style and cognitive content from beginning to end. There was no hint of mental deterioration." Reagan's diaries and letters, concludes Morris, "testify to the fact that he retained a useful intelligence throughout two terms as President, and for three years thereafter."

After November 1994, Ronald Reagan largely disappeared from public view. The Associated Press described him as a "recluse at his Bel-Air home." He remained physically sound, but his mental powers gradually departed. In 2002, when he turned 91, he became the nation's longest-living former president. He had long since reached the point where he did not recognize visitors, his children, or even his devoted wife. For his final act, the actor/politician who had always engaged the world on his own terms and boldly expressed his views and visions, withdrew into silence.

12

Legacy

Ronald Reagan left office in 1989, an extraordinarily popular figure. He had become the first president to complete two terms since Dwight Eisenhower in the 1950s. Reagan, asserts Lou Cannon, had restored "the respect of Americans for themselves and their own government after the traumas of Vietnam and Watergate, the frustration of the Iran hostage crisis, and a succession of seemingly failed presidencies." He bequeathed to his successor, George H.W. Bush, a prosperous economy and a world closer to peace and disarmament than he had inherited. Within two years of Reagan's departure not only the Soviet empire, but the Soviet Union itself collapsed. This momentous event, more than any other, cemented Reagan's reputation as not only a well-beloved, but highly effective president. A torrent of books written from a conservative perspective, with titles or subtitles proclaiming *Victory*; *How an Ordinary Man Became an Extraordinary Leader*; and *When Character Was King* celebrated the Reagan years as a triumphant era.

Yet Reagan's legacy remains highly disputed. A spate of tell-all books written by former members of the Reagan Administration portrayed his presidency, especially his management style, in less than flattering terms. Biographers and other historians wrestled with the gap between his phlegmatic personality and record of accomplishment.

Liberal critics questioned the success of his economic policies, his role in the end of the Cold War, and the overall moral message of his leadership. Amid these disputes, however, there remained the undeniable extent to which Reagan had transformed America. In terms of prolonged political impact, the ability to define the national course for future generations, only Franklin D. Roosevelt, Reagan's early political hero, can rival the former actor's impact on twentieth-century American life. When Reagan entered formal electoral politics in 1966, conservatism had been a fringe ideology. When he left the presidency in 1989, it had become, although not a dominant viewpoint, the belief system around which American politics defined itself.

Reagan was once described as a "Teflon President." Mistakes and even serious misdeeds never seemed to adhere to him or seriously tarnish his image. He retained a reputation for personal morality and honesty even as the waters of corruption and abuse of power swirled around him. The number of exposés of the scandals that had tainted his administration swelled in the years after he left office. In the early 1990s congressional investigations revealed the depth of wrongdoing in Housing and Urban Development. A Justice Department probe depicted the widespread corruption in the Defense Department. The full extent of the savings and loan debacle, a textbook example of the dangers of the unregulated marketplace, grew undeniably apparent. A 1990 report by Reagan's own economists disparaged his administration's mishandling of the savings and loan industry. The General Accounting Office pegged the cost of the scandal to taxpayers at a minimum of one trillion dollars. The independent counsel investigation of the Iran-contra affair produced 14 indictments and 11 convictions of top Reagan aides, including John Poindexter and Oliver North. Defense Secretary Caspar Weinberger escaped prosecution due to a pre-trial pardon from President Bush. In his final report in 1994

Iran-contra Special Prosecutor Lawrence Walsh concluded that while Reagan's actions "fell well short of criminality which could be successfully prosecuted," he had "created the conditions which made possible the crimes committed by others." A disconnection clearly existed between the high moral principles that Reagan espoused, his law-and-order rhetoric, and an environment in which inconvenient laws were evaded and government officials sought to illegally cash in on the very programs they attacked as wasteful.

Reagan largely avoided blame for this state of affairs, seen by most Americans as separate from his performance as president and peripheral to his broader achievements in the more important arenas of foreign and economic policy. On these critical fronts the strategies of the Reagan Administration appear, at first glance, to have prevailed. In the United States at the start of 1989, the Reagan presidency had overseen the longest period of peacetime economic growth in the nation's history, seemingly validating the precepts of "Reaganomics." Within a year of Reagan's departure from office, the "captive nations" of Eastern Europe had liberated themselves from communism and Soviet domination. By the end of 1991, the Soviet Union itself had imploded, with democracy transcending dictatorship and a rudimentary capitalism replacing a moribund communism. Reagan's secret strategy, argues conservative writer Peter Schweizer, had hastened the collapse of the Soviet Union. But surface impressions rarely satisfy the demands of history, and the judgment on Reagan on these and other matters remains highly contested.

In January 1989, when Reagan returned to California, the final outcomes of his foreign policy remained uncertain. The progress made on arms control and Gorbachev's reforms notwithstanding, the Soviet Union remained a formidable foe, its eastern European empire shaken, but still intact. Within a year, however, the extent to which the longstanding Cold War reality had changed grew apparent.

In March 1989, the Soviet Union held its first free elections. In June, elections in Poland propelled Solidarity to power. Soviet General Secretary Gorbachev made no effort to reverse the Polish results, confirming that, as he had promised, the Soviet Union would no longer use repressive military force to impose its rule on eastern Europe. On October 18, the communist government of East Germany collapsed and on November 9 the new government ordered the opening of the Berlin Wall. At the site of Reagan's challenge to Gorbachev just two years earlier jubilant Germans destroyed the wall that had symbolized the Cold War. Before 1989 had ended, the brutal communist dictatorship of Nicolae Ceausescu fell in Romania, and dissident leader Vaclev Havel assumed the reins of government in Czechoslovakia.

The next two years brought equally dramatic changes. In March 1990 Lithuania voted to declare its independence from the Soviet Union. In October, East and West Germany reunited after 45 years of division. The United States and the Soviet Union signed the START I arms control treaty in July 1991, cutting their nuclear arsenals by an additional 50 percent. Most dramatically, in December 1991, the Soviet Union itself dissolved, with its 11 republics forming independent states, the majority of which now pledged themselves to capitalism and democracy. In addition, the communist regimes in Afghanistan and Nicaragua both fell. As Reagan had prophesized, communism had been discredited and the Soviet Union's "evil empire" had fallen into "the ash heap of history."

The sudden and unexpected end of the Cold War and demise of communism in Europe appeared to bear out Reagan's foreign policy. "What was most brilliant about Reagan's view was that it rejected the assumption of Soviet immutability," writes Dinesh D'Sousa. "Reagan dared to imagine a world in which the communist regime in the Soviet Union did not exist." The logic of this argument

seems unassailable. The Reagan Administration definitively changed the terms of the Cold War. From the start they predicted that the Soviets would be unable to counter an American arms buildup and expended tens of billions of dollars to prove that assumption. Reagan's Strategic Defense Initiative upped the ante even further, provoking considerable concern in the Soviet Union. Reagan had predicted that America's new position of military superiority would force the Soviets to the bargaining table, and at Geneva, Reykjavik, Washington, D.C., and Moscow, Gorbachev had capitulated to Reagan's demands. Furthermore, the Reagan Administration had reversed the defensive and reactive policies of previous Cold War presidencies, rejecting the Brezhnev Doctrine and supporting anti-communist insurgencies in Central America, Europe, and Africa. Reagan and his foreign policy team adopted a more aggressive stance against the Soviet Union itself, waging undeclared economic warfare designed to weaken, and ultimately topple, the Soviet regime. In the end, their wildest hopes and dreams had been fulfilled.

Yet, very often in history a wide gap exists between perception and reality, concurrent events and causation. The Reagan Administration enacted a policy to achieve a Cold War victory and victory was won. Whether or not Reagan's policies determined this outcome, however, remains problematical. Viewed from the Soviet rather than the American perspective, a far different analysis of the end of the Cold War emerges. Many scholars who study the Soviet Union downplay the significance of Reagan's role in the fall of the Soviet empire. The Reagan Administration, they argue, based its policies on misconceptions about Soviet military strength and an exaggeration of the Soviet role in Third World unrest and international terrorism. The Soviets never possessed the overweening military superiority projected by the Committee On the Present Danger, and Soviet leaders began to reduce both defense spending and foreign entanglements in the late 1970s before Reagan came to office.

Although Reagan invoked a new American supremacy in 1984 to justify renewed arms control talks, little changed in the existing balance between the two super-powers during the 1980s. Much of the vaunted United States defense buildup had been consumed by waste and inefficiency. The MX-missile program had expended $15 billion, but still lacked an acceptable plan for deployment. SDI had absorbed $26 billion in research funds, but was no closer to viability than it had been in 1983. The Soviets, moreover, did not respond to the Reagan-era defense buildup or the SDI threat with enhanced military spending that disrupted or bankrupted their economy as antici-pated. The Soviet Union might well have muddled along indefinitely, its nuclear deterrent sufficient to ward off American advances, its conventional forces constraining eastern European dissent, if not for the ascension of Mikhail Gorbachev.

"The single most important factor underlying this im-portant shift [in Soviet policy]," writes former CIA ana-lyst and Soviet specialist Raymond L. Garthoff, "was the determination of Soviet leader Mikhail Gorbachev to overcome the military confrontation between East and West." Gorbachev believed that the Soviet political and economic system required a dramatic overhaul to rescue the nation from its inertial malaise. The key to this trans-formation lay in drastic reductions in defense spending that could only be achieved through arms control agree-ments with the United States and an end to the standoff in Europe. Gorbachev acted, according to Garthoff, "almost always because he saw the need for change and not be-cause of Reagan's pressures."

Indeed, while Reagan had signaled his desire to engage in arms reductions talks as early as January 1984, more than a year before Gorbachev assumed power, the United

States never initiated serious proposals at any of the summit meetings. Gorbachev, desperate for agreements that would advance and justify his domestic program, offered concession after concession. But Reagan refused to yield, especially on SDI, an experimental program with at best a distant chance of success. Garthoff suggests that Reagan's anti-Soviet rhetoric and intransigence strengthened hardline opposition to Gorbachev in Moscow and may have delayed, rather than hastened, Soviet military reductions. "All that the Reagan Administration had ever done," writes Frances Fitzgerald, "was talk to the Soviets, pocket the concessions they made, and take credit for having forced Gorbachev to do what he was doing anyway for his own purposes."

Similarly, Garthoff and others argue that communist regimes in eastern Europe collapsed not as a result of the Reagan Doctrine, but rather from Gorbachev's commitment to *Glasnost* and his decision to withhold Soviet repression in the face of change. "What happened would not have happened without [Gorbachev]," argues Garthoff. "That cannot be said of anyone else." In addition, the Reagan Doctrine had broad moral and security consequences for the United States. Throughout the world, "authoritarian" forces embraced by the United States as anti-communist allies caused embarrassments or severe security threats. In 1989, President Bush sent 22,500 troops to Panama to arrest Dictator Manuel Noriega for his drug-running activities. In 1990 Iraq's Saddam Hussein, following his defeat in the Iran-Iraq war, invaded and occupied Kuwait. The United States responded with "Operation Desert Storm," a major American-led military action in 1991, to drive Iraqi troops out of Kuwait.

In Afghanistan, the withdrawal of Soviet support led to the collapse of the communist government and precipitated a civil war among rival warlords and fundamentalist groups. When the United States requested that former "freedom fighters" return their unused Stinger missiles, they met with resistance. "We will not return the Stingers. . . . We ourselves need them most," responded one mujahedin group. In 1991 the CIA initiated a new covert action in Afghanistan, seeking to buy back the Stingers. The agency expended $65 million to reacquire approximately 200 of the dangerous anti-aircraft missiles, but hundreds more remained either in Afghan hands or unaccounted for, available to shoot down both military and commercial aircraft. The Taliban, an extreme Muslim fundamentalist group, seized power in Afghanistan and welcomed the presence of Al Qaeda, a violent terrorist group. Al Qaeda, led by former mujahedin leader Osama Bin Laden, had its roots in the Soviet-Afghan conflict. Al Qaeda used Afghanistan to stage terrorist attacks on United States installations throughout the world, culminating in the September 11, 2001, assaults on the World Trade Center and the Pentagon. The United States responded by invading Afghanistan to drive out Al Qaeda and the Taliban. After more than two decades of invasions, civil war, and Taliban misrule, Afghanistan lay devastated.

The Soviet archives generally support the liberal revisionist view. Yet Reagan's contribution to the end of the Cold War remains significant. The Soviet empire might have ultimately faltered in the face of a less intransigent American policy. But Reagan's support for insurgent forces in Poland, Afghanistan, and elsewhere weakened the hold of communism on these countries. Although Gorbachev's decision to withdraw Soviet power ultimately created the conditions that allowed a change in regimes, American underwriting of resistance movements hastened the day of reckoning and helped to force the issue. On the nuclear disarmament front, Reagan defied hardliners in his own administration by engaging Gorbachev in the talks that led to the INF Treaty and the START I and START II accords completed by Presidents George H. W. Bush and

Bill Clinton. His commitment to reducing the nuclear threat, sincere though erratically applied, made these gains possible.

The second pillar of Reagan's legacy is the nation's economic performance during his tenure. Basic statistics attest to a substantial record of growth. After the rocky "Reagan recession" of 1981–1982, the overall economy expanded steadily. When Reagan entered office, inflation hovered at 12 percent, interest rates had soared as high as 21 percent, and unemployment exceeded seven percent. The so-called "misery index" combining the unemployment and inflation rates stood at twenty points. In January 1989, inflation had dropped to 4.4 percent, the prime rate to 9.3 percent, and unemployment to 5.4 percent. The "misery index" had been halved. Over the course of the Reagan years the nation's gross national product had doubled and per capita income had jumped from $9722 to $11,326. Nearly 18 million new jobs had been created.

The years from 1983 to 1989 marked the longest stretch of uninterrupted economic growth in United States history. Champions of the Reagan presidency hailed it as a triumph of Reaganomics and a validation of the often-maligned supply-side tax cuts. As with foreign affairs, the reality is far more complex. The primary components of the 1980s expansion were the taming of inflation and the stimulus provided by deficit spending. Cannon calls the victory over inflation "the most notable accomplishment of the Reagan years." Lower interest rates, accompanied by a dramatic drop in oil prices after 1985, freed money for investment and consumption, as did lower tax rates for the rich.

Nonetheless, public spending stimulated the economy far more than private investment. Federal budget deficits ranging from $128 billion to more than $200 billion annually pumped desperately needed capital into the system. These unprecedented shortfalls tripled the national debt.

When added to the deficits accumulated by Reagan's successor, George H.W. Bush, the two Republican administrations created more debt than all of the nation's previous presidents combined. The deficits generated widespread concern at the time, as critics predicted that Reagan and Bush had purchased prosperity by creating an economic burden that would saddle Americans for generations. These jeremiads proved ill founded. The economy, as liberals had argued for decades, could sustain a substantial amount of deficit spending; the larger the gross national product, the greater the allowable deficit. An economic boom in the 1990s allowed the United States to project paying off its debts in less than two decades of Reagan's departure from office.

Reagan's vaunted tax cuts probably played a far lesser role than federal spending in generating economic growth. The Reagan tax reforms made fundamental changes in the nation's revenue system and lowered the highest tax rates, but barely affected the overall taxation of Americans. When Reagan came to office, 19.4 percent of the national income was diverted into federal taxes. Upon his departure this figure stood at 19.3 percent. The Reagan Administration passed far more bills raising taxes and fees than lowering them. Increases in payroll taxes to fund Social Security and Medicare offset other cuts, especially for working-class Americans. In addition, many states raised taxes to offset the decline in assistance flowing from the federal government.

The new tax regime proved far more regressive than the old. While most Americans saw modest tax reductions at best, the greatest benefits went to families earning more than $200,000 per year. According to the tenets of supply-side economics, this windfall for the wealthy should have generated greater savings and investment. Economists, however, have uncovered little evidence of a strong correlation between the lower rates and the economic rise in the 1980s. The economy had grown spectacularly in the post–World War II era despite top rates often exceeding 70 percent. Reagan's tax reforms had dropped the top rate as low as 28 percent. According to economist Charles Kindleberger, much of the savings generated "seems to have been spent on consumption: second and third houses, travel, luxury apparel, cars, jewelry, yachts and the like, rather than being saved or invested." A substantial proportion of the available capital was pumped into the paper economy, speculative investments offered in the savings and loan and merger phenomena, rather than underwriting plants, equipment, or production. When these bubbles burst, the capital misallocated to these ventures evaporated. Shortly after Reagan left office, the economy entered a sharp recession. Recovery and a far more dramatic financial boom occurred in the 1990s after Presidents Bush and Clinton raised taxes.

Viewed in a broader historical perspective, the Reagan prosperity, its length notwithstanding, seems far weaker than indicated by an isolated glance. The economy grew at a slower rate in the 1980s than it had in the 1960s and 1970s and than it would in the 1990s. The real gross national product grew no faster during the Reagan era than it had during the much-maligned Carter years. From 1983 to 1989, at the peak of the Reagan prosperity, private wealth grew by eight percent; from 1975 to 1980, during the Carter downturn, private wealth had increased by 31 percent. While the traditional industrial segment of the economy continued the decline begun in the 1970s, only relatively modest expansion took place in computers and technology. The less financially rewarding service sector generated most of the growth. Economists noted that of the millions of jobs created during the Reagan era, about half were minimum- and low-wage posts. Millions of people who lost jobs because of plant closings during the 1980s found new positions that paid less. The unemployment rate, while lower than at the trough of the recession, remained high by recent historical standards.

The supply-side tax cuts and the expansion of low-wage jobs represented parallel attributes of what political commentator Kevin Phillips has called the "Great Inversion." The nation that emerged from the Reagan-Bush era diverged greatly from the more egalitarian United States of the immediate post-World War II decades. In the 1940s and 1950s, notes Phillips, economic gains accrued largely to the broad middle class. From the 1970s onward, prosperity flowed disproportionately to the wealthiest Americans, as a culture that glorified intemperate accumulation materialized. The Reagan years accelerated this trend at mach speed. In 1979, the top one percent of the population held 22 percent of the nation's wealth; in 1989 that figure had almost doubled to 39 percent. Within the top one percent, the greatest gains went to the richest elite as billionaires increased their net worth from highs of $10 billion in 1982 to peaks of $100 billion and more. Compensation for corporate chief executive officers (CEOs) exemplified this phenomenon. In the 1960s CEOs had earned 25 times the income of hourly production workers. During the eighties, top CEO incomes leaped 500 to 700 percent. CEOs now made 93 times as much as their hourly employees, a figure that would skyrocket to 419 by the end of the 1990s. "The gap between the rich and everyone else was yawning to widths unseen since the 1920s and 1930s," writes Phillips.

Contrary to supply-side predictions, these gains did not trickle down to the average Americans. As historian Michael Schaller comments, "The rich got richer, and everyone else trod water." A wide variety of measures indicated that middle-class income stayed the same or actually declined in the 1980s and 1990s, prompting economist Lawrence Summers to lament a "quiet depression" in living standards. By the 1990s, typical Americans worked longer hours for fewer rewards than they had in the recent past. In the 1990s alone, the average American work year expanded by 184 hours, and the American workload surpassed that of all industrial nations. The percentage of Americans saying they always felt rushed jumped from 28 in 1975 to 38 in 1992. In a decade when labor union membership fell from 23 percent to less than 17 percent, fringe benefits, one of the perquisites of the "affluent society" lifestyle of the 1950s won by unions, also declined. In 1982, 49 percent of all workers in the bottom ten percent of the economy had health benefits provided by their employers. By 1996 this figure had plummeted to 26 percent. Slippage had also occurred for middle-ranked employees. Employers of those who received health coverage were also far less likely to pay the entire costs of the plan.

Individuals at the lower rungs of the economic ladder fared particularly poorly during the Reagan years. The average family income for the bottom fifth of Americans fell by seven percent during the 1980s. One out of five children dwelt below the poverty level. At the same time the proportion of government assistance expenditures, including food stamp and school lunch programs, shrank. The Reagan Administration tightened eligibility requirements for welfare and cut benefits for many of those on the rolls. Other indicators of social conditions also revealed the deterioration of life among the poor. In the nation's cities, homelessness increased, the use of hard drugs climbed, and the numbers of people in prison doubled.

Reagan's true legacy rests, however, neither in foreign policy nor in the economic sphere. Reagan's greatest accomplishments lay in the realm of ideology and politics. American conservatives came to embrace Reagan as a visionary, the triumphant personification of their beliefs and the foundation on which to consolidate their hold on the American electorate. There is some irony in this. Although his boosters had hailed a "Reagan Revolution," many conservatives in 1989 expressed disappointment with the timidity with which he advanced their cause. Some, on the far right, remained distrustful of his liaison with Mikhail Gorbachev and the Soviet Union. Economic conservatives expressed discontent with Reagan's failure to shrink the federal domain. The number of government workers actually expanded more under Reagan than under Jimmy Carter. In part this resulted from the defense buildup, but Social Security and Medicare had not only survived the "revolution," but expanded their expenditures. Total welfare spending in 1989 exceeded 1981 levels. Nor had the Reagan regime significantly enhanced states' rights. As Schaller observes, "In practice, the Reagan Administration shifted costs, not power, to local government. . . . Washington burdened state, county, and city governments with many new, expensive-to-administer regulations . . . but provided less federal money than before." The burgeoning deficits concerned many conservatives who had railed for generations against Democratic profligacy.

The religious right also had cause for complaint. Although Reagan had courted and legitimized political evangelists with appearances before their gatherings and his regular invocations of God and morality, he had done little to advance their social agenda. Reagan was unwilling to invest too much of his political capital in the "culture wars" so dear to the evangelical Christians, but so polarizing in the nation as a whole. During the Reagan years, the religious right made little headway in its calls for banning abortion, protecting school prayer, and warding off the growing acceptance of homosexuality in America.

Nor had Reagan established the type of durable political coalition that Franklin Roosevelt had. His vice-president, George H.W. Bush, won election in 1988, effectively decrying liberalism as the "L-word," but Democrats still controlled Congress, muting further conservative advances.

The Republicans could not even hold the White House. In 1992 maverick billionaire Ross Perot, running as an independent candidate, sheared off the populist element of the Reagan vote, allowing Democrat Bill Clinton to unseat Bush as president.

But Reagan had advanced the conservative agenda in ways beyond the national ballot box. From the 1930s to the early 1980s, a large majority of Americans had identified themselves as Democrats. By the end of the Reagan era, the Republicans had drawn even. The nation's political discourse had shifted dramatically to the right. To win election, Clinton had had to portray himself as a "new Democrat," less wedded to public solutions to social problems, more committed to a rhetoric of individual responsibility and law and order. Despite the often spectacular failures of deregulation, Americans remained suspicious of bureaucratic agencies. They also maintained a heightened hostility to taxation, making it difficult for governments at the federal, state, or local level to generate additional revenues for basic purposes such as education and infrastructure.

Americans had also become determined to clean up the "welfare mess," long a target of Reagan's wrath. In 1987, the White House granted states the right to attain waivers from federal regulations to test experimental "workfare" programs, a goal advocated by Reagan when he was still governor of California. By the mid-1990s half the states had implemented workfare projects. President Clinton in 1996 would lead the fight to end "welfare as we know it," with a program that reflected Reagan's longtime demands, and declare with Reaganesque bluntness that "The age of big government is dead."

Conservatives also had made extraordinary gains in the federal judiciary. Robert Bork's bitter defeat in 1987 obscured the extent to which not only the Supreme Court, but the lower courts as well, had shifted to the right. Reagan

appointed three new justices to the Supreme Court—
Sandra Day O'Connor, Antonin Scalia, and Anthony M.
Kennedy—and elevated Nixon appointee William
Rehnquist to chief justice. The High Court thus moved
closer to a conservative majority. Of greater long-term import, by the time he left office Reagan had appointed almost half of all federal judges. Carefully selected by the
Judicial Selection Committee centered in the White House,
the judges tended to be, according to legal historian David
M. O'Brien, "predominantly young, upper middle-class
white males, with . . . reputations for legal conservatism."
Their relative youth would guarantee a longstanding
rightward swing in the federal courts. The heated Bork
dispute notwithstanding, Senate Democrats acknowledged
the presidential prerogative in judicial selection, rejecting
only three out of almost 400 Reagan appointments. Although for years conservatives had decried "judicial activism" on behalf of liberal causes, the new judges would
often move aggressively to implement their own political,
cultural, and social agendas.

The generation that came of age during the Reagan
presidency also proved more conservative than its predecessors. Much as the New Deal had cemented their grand-
parents' allegiances to the Democratic Party, the "Reagan
Revolution" led many young Americans, particularly
white Americans, to identify as Republicans and conservatives. They viewed Reagan as a symbol of a renewed
American spirit and shared his distrust of government.
The rise of the religious right that began in the 1970s and
lasted beyond the Reagan years brought many evangelical
Christians not just to the ballot box, but into political office as well. In the 1994 midterm elections, the Republican leadership delineated a "Contract with America,"
which espoused a decidedly conservative agenda for the
nation. Under its banner the Republicans gained control
of both houses of Congress for the first time in 40 years.

The conservative coalition that emerged in the 1990s illustrated how the fusion between traditional social conservatives and economic and libertarian conservatives engineered by Reagan and others in the 1960s had evolved. Those who supported the "Contract with America" embraced proposals for deregulation, lower taxes, loosened environmental controls, and a dismantling of the welfare state. But the dominance of the religious right in the alliance largely overwhelmed the libertarian influences of earlier conservatism, calling for a greater role of government in imposing a more authoritarian social order on issues like abortion, gay rights, the right to privacy, and the tolerance of dissent. Federalism also became a more inconsistently held value, with conservatives advocating a reversion of powers to the states in areas of social welfare and regulation, but an enhanced national role on issues that concerned their moral and political agenda.

The results of the 1994 election seemed to complete the "Reagan Revolution." But the presence of Democrat Bill Clinton in the White House and his 1996 re-election over a Republican Party still hampered by the Perot schism muted the impact of conservative control of Congress. The 2000 elections highlighted how much the national debate revolved around conservative ideals and how narrowly divided the American electorate had become. George W. Bush, the Republican candidate and son of the former president, secure in his support from the religious and far right, portrayed himself as a more moderate, "compassionate conservative." Clinton's vice-president, Al Gore, another exemplar of the centrist "new Democrats," ran more of a populist campaign, but still extolled his support for welfare reform and shrinking the federal bureaucracy. At both the congressional and presidential levels the election demonstrated the failure of Reagan's heirs to mobilize a majority-governing coalition. Republicans retained a narrow majority in the House of Representatives, but Democratic victories in a majority of the Senate races, many of them tightly contested, left the upper house divided in a 50–50 split.

The presidential race proved the most dramatic of all. Both Gore and Bush polled 48 percent of the vote, with Gore receiving a half-million more votes than his opponent. A leftist Green Party insurgency led by consumer advocate Ralph Nader garnered most of the remaining votes, preventing a Gore victory. Neither Bush nor Gore, however, had earned enough votes to prevail in the Electoral College until the outcome of the tight contest in Florida could be determined. Thousands of voters in southern Florida, most of whom would have voted for Gore, had incorrectly marked their confusingly constructed ballots. Without these votes, Gore trailed Bush by a handful of votes. Bush claimed victory, but Gore demanded a recount, the complicated mechanics and implementation of which remained in dispute. After the Florida Supreme Court, controlled by Democrats, issued a ruling that would have favored Gore, the conservative majority of the United States Supreme Court, departing from its usual states' rights emphasis, imposed a federal mandate on Florida, awarding the election to Bush.

George W. Bush had run as a moderate conservative and received fewer votes than his Democratic opponent. However, once in office he revealed a conservative will far more right-leaning and resolute than even Reagan's. Bush and other conservatives, restored to power and with control of both houses of Congress, seemed determined to complete the unfinished business of the "Reagan Revolution." Bush's domestic agenda called for tax cuts for the wealthy far beyond those implemented by Reagan, embraced massive deficits as an acceptable economic alternative, endorsed much of the "faith-based" agenda of the religious right, and advocated an even more draconian reduction of federal social programs.

Bush populated his administration with veterans of the Reagan and George H.W. Bush regimes. With the Cold War over, neoconservatives from the Committee on the Present Danger had now regrouped into the Project for a New American Century (PNAC). The PNAC called for "a Reaganite policy of military strength and moral clarity" in American dealings with the world. Its members dominated Bush's foreign policy team.

The advanced technology applied to conventional weaponry since the Reagan years had given the United States an extraordinary level of military superiority over all nations in the post-Cold War world. The neoconservatives in the George W. Bush administration advocated that the United States use this military edge to secure an uncontested American empire, reintroducing the old conservative doctrine of pre-emptive strikes as a staple of national defense policy. The terrorist attacks of September 11, 2001, enabled the Bush Administration to not only rally the nation to support retaliatory strikes, but to exercise its enhanced political leverage to advance its foreign and domestic conservative agenda.

In his sunset years, his mind stilled by the ravages of Alzheimer's disease, Reagan remained unaware of the extent to which his foreign and domestic policies had prevailed during the early years of the twenty-first century. He remained in seclusion in his home in Bel-Air, his devoted wife Nancy emerging as caregiver, protector, and assiduous keeper of the flame that preserved Reagan's place in history. Mrs. Reagan embraced most of her husband's legacy, but at times disappointed members of the conservative coalition he had forged. In 2003 when Republican congressional representatives proposed replacing the image of liberal icon Franklin D. Roosevelt on the dime with that of President Reagan, Nancy Reagan voiced not only her own opposition, but noted that her husband also would never have approved. She became one of the most prominent leaders in the call for federal funding for stem-cell research, an anathema to most leaders of the religious right, who linked the issue to the abortion fight. In 2001, she wrote a letter urging President George W. Bush to support stem-cell research, arguing that it might lead to breakthroughs in treating Alzheimer's disease and save other families from the tragedy that had struck the Reagans.

On June 5, 2004, Ronald Reagan, after a decade of decline, finally succumbed to the ravages of old age and Alzheimer's. His passing initiated a week of public mourning emblematic of his impact on the nation and characterized by the ceremonial trappings that Reagan had so loved. The occasion also offered a reminder of the carefully scripted nature of Reagan's public persona. Orchestrated much like a Hollywood spectacle, the ceremonies combined the military elements of traditional state funerals and the desires of the Reagans to shape his memory.

The mourning period reawakened Americans to the romance of Reagan's life. The Movie Channel presented a 24-hour marathon of Ronald Reagan movies. Millions of Americans watched seemingly nonstop footage of the ceremonies and retrospectives on network and cable broadcasts. Tens of thousands visited Reagan's closed casket at the Reagan Presidential Library in Simi, California, before his body was flown to Washington, D.C., where it lay in state in the Capitol Rotunda. Upwards of 100,000 people, some waiting in line for as long as seven hours, passed through the viewing area. Government leaders and former leaders from all over the world joined the four surviving former United States presidents among the dignitaries attending the memorial service at the National Cathedral. Reagan friends and family then flew with his body back to California to fulfill one last request. With the sun setting over the Pacific Ocean as a backdrop, Reagan was buried at a spectacular hilltop site that he had selected on the grounds of his presidential library.

His death revived the partisan debates over his legacy, albeit in a muted form. Conservatives uniformly hailed him as the savior of the nation and forefather of their modern ascendancy. Liberals reminded people of his failures and shortcomings, but grudgingly conceded his enormous impact on the nation's history. The glow remained one year later. In spring 2005 the Discovery Channel televised a series in which viewers could select the "Greatest American" in the nation's history. Participants selected Reagan as the top choice, immediately ahead of Abraham Lincoln, Martin Luther King, George Washington, and Benjamin Franklin.

Conservative theorist D'Souza argues that "Reagan's greatness derives from the fact that he was a visionary—a conceptualizer who was able to see the world differently from the way it was." Reagan had, as his political opposite Senator Edward Kennedy allowed, "stood for a set of ideas . . . he meant them, and he wrote them not only into public law, but into the national consciousness." At the time of Reagan's death, the United States and the world adhered more closely to his vision than at any time during his active adult life. The Soviet Union had disappeared, its communist ideology largely discredited. United States foreign policy operated in a unilateral universe, a dominant military power unchecked by powerful foes, treaty obligations, international law, or entangling alliances, a world where ideology shaped reality rather than the logical opposite. The extremes between not only rich and poor, but rich and middle class, had grown ever wider. Conservatism had replaced liberalism at the core of American political discourse. The social contract of mutual dependence and governmental oversight forged during the New Deal had been rewritten to reflect a less compassionate brand of unrestrained economic acquisition and individualism. Even immensely popular programs like Social Security and Medicare, long on Reagan's wish list for elimination, seemed endangered in the foreseeable future.

Ronald Reagan, like the hero of *That Printer of Udell's*, the book that had inspired him as a youth, had marched steadily into ever larger "fields of wider usefulness." His improbable life spanned, and at times encapsulated, the broad historical breadth of twentieth-century America. From his modest beginnings in the Midwest, he had advanced to radio broadcasting, then a respectable Hollywood career. As an actor he occupied only a second rank of stardom, but he eventually transcended all of his more celebrated film companions in his fame and influence. He became a union leader, television pioneer, business spokesperson, political advocate, and governor of California. He ascended to the presidency of the United States and led the nation through one of the most momentous periods of its modern history. To Americans, living in a world that he had played an extraordinary role in creating, neither Ronald Reagan nor his contested legacy will ever be forgotten.

Study and Discussion Questions

Introduction

1. In what ways does Ronald Reagan's life personify the United States in the twentieth century?

2. Identify the problems faced by historians and biographers in assessing Ronald Reagan's legacy.

3. What is Reagan's "most remarkable self-deception"?

Chapter 1: A Midwestern Boyhood

1. How did Reagan's family experiences embody American cultural conflicts during the 1920s?

2. What role did his father's alcoholism play in his childhood?

3. What role did religion play in Reagan's upbringing?

4. What does Reagan's experiences as a lifeguard tell us about his character?

Chapter 2: Surviving the Great Depression

1. How did the Great Depression affect Reagan's family life and education?

2. What were the most significant elements of Reagan's college experiences? What do they tell us about his character?

3. How did Reagan's experiences as a pioneer radio broad-caster shape the skills he would use in later life as an actor and politician?

4. Why did Reagan leave a lucrative radio career for the risks of Hollywood?

Chapter 3: The Making of a Hollywood Star

1. How was the movie industry organized in the 1930s? What was the role of the Production Code Administration?

2. What were Ronald Reagan's strengths and weaknesses as an actor?

3. What were Reagan's political inclinations during these years?

4. How did World War II affect Reagan's film career?

5. In which capacities did Reagan serve his country during World War II?

Chapter 4: Fighting the Cold War

1. What were the reasons for the breakup of Reagan's marriage to Jane Wyman?

2. Why did Reagan begin to move from the political left to the political right during this era?

3. How were Cold War tensions reflected in Hollywood during the postwar years?

4. What were the issues in the 1945–46 CSU Studio conflicts?

5. Assess Reagan's performance as President of the Screen Actors Guild.

6. What role did Reagan play in the creation and perpetuation of the blacklist?

Chapter 5: The Shift to Conservatism

1. What are the influences that convinced Reagan to become a conservative during the 1950s?

2. Why did Reagan's movie career falter in the postwar era?

3. Do Reagan's actions while president of the Screen Actors Guild on behalf of MCA, the talent agency that represented him, constitute a serious conflict of interest?

4. How did Reagan's experience as host of GE Theater and representative of General Electric influence his political and personal development?

5. What are the themes and rhetorical elements that Reagan developed in his speeches during the 1950s?

6. Describe family life in the Reagan household.

7. By the early 1960s did Reagan seem to be a success or a failure?

Chapter 6: Entering Politics

1. What is the significance of Reagan's speech on behalf of Barry Goldwater during the 1964 campaign?

2. Identify the key tenets of conservative ideology as it emerged in the 1960s.

3. What were the key events in California and the nation between the 1964 presidential election and the 1966 gubernatorial campaign?

4. How did the issues of race relations and student protest manifest themselves in the 1966 campaign?

5. What were Reagan's strengths and weaknesses as a campaigner?

6. How did the Reagan campaign signal a transformation of the political landscape?

Chapter 7: From Governor to President

1. How effective was Ronald Reagan as governor of California?

2. How did Governor Reagan advance the conservative agenda on the issues of welfare, taxation, and law and order?

3. What were the major challenges confronting the nation during the Carter Administration from 1977–1981?

4. Describe the elements that came together during these years to form the conservative coalition.

5. Which themes did Reagan develop during his radio speeches in the late 1970s?

6. Were the results of the 1980 election more the product of a triumph of Reagan's beliefs or a rejection of Jimmy Carter?

Chapter 8: "Stay the Course": The Reagan Presidency: 1981–1982

1. What are the paradoxes of Reagan's leadership style and administration?

2. How did Reagan and his advisors see the Soviet Union and its role in the world? What actions did they take as a reflection of this viewpoint?

3. Was the Reagan military buildup justified?

4. What was Reagonomics? What were the assumptions behind Reagan's economic policies?

5. How did the attempt on his life influence the Reagan presidency?

6. How did the Reagan Administration approach the subject of arms control?

7. From the vantage point of 1982, did the Reagan presidency seem a success or a failure?

Chapter 9: The Road to Reelection: The Reagan Presidency: 1983–1984

1. What were the origins and elements of the Strategic Defense Initiative?

2. When Reagan praised "freedom fighters" throughout the world, who did he include? How did he define freedom?

3. How did the shooting down of a Korean airliner and events in Lebanon and Grenada shape people's perceptions of the Reagan Administration?

4. Describe the evolution of Reagan's thinking on arms control during these years.

5. What were factors contributing to Reagan's landslide re-election victory in 1984?

Chapter 10: The Reagan Doctrine: The Reagan Presidency: 1985–1986

1. What was the Reagan Doctrine?

2. How did the rise of Gorbachev in the Soviet Union change U.S.–Soviet relations? How did the Reagan Administration view Gorbachev?

3. What were the primary motivations for Reagan's policies in the Middle East? How successfully did his administration respond to terrorism?

4. What were the accomplishments and results of the Geneva Summit?

5. What actually happened at the summit in Reykjavik? Was it a success or a failure for Reagan?

Chapter 11: Scandals and Summits: The Reagan Presidency: 1987–1988

1. What was the Iran-contra Scandal? What role did Reagan himself play in these events?

2. How did the Iran-contra Scandal and Reagan's handling of it affect his image? In which ways did it reflect the general values and practices of his administration?

3. What were the effects of Reagan's deregulation policies? What caused the savings and loan scandals?

4. What were the results of the summit meetings in Washington and Moscow? To what extent had relations between the U.S. and the Soviet Union changed?

Chapter 12: Legacy

1. Did Reagan's policies "hasten the collapse of the Soviet Union" and bring an end to the Cold War?

2. What were the results of Reagan's policies in Afghanistan, Eastern Europe, and Central America?

3. What were the successes and shortcomings of Reagonomics?

4. In which ways did Reagan advance the conservative agenda?

5. How did the Reagan Administration reshape the federal courts?

6. What are the similarities between the Reagan presidency and that of George W. Bush?

7. Was Ronald Reagan one of the great American presidents?

A Note on the Sources

Any study of Ronald Reagan must begin with the works of Lou Cannon. Cannon, a journalist who covered Reagan both as governor of California and president of the United States, has written several books on this subject, including *Ronnie and Jessie: A Political Odyssey* (Garden City, New York, 1969); *Reagan* (New York, 1982); *President Reagan: The Role of a Lifetime* (New York, 1991); and the recently published *Governor Reagan: His Rise to Power* (New York, 2003).

Reagan himself wrote two biographies, one at the beginning and one at the end of his political career: Ronald Reagan and Richard C. Hubler, *Where's the Rest of Me? Ronald Reagan Tells His Own Story* (New York, 1965) and Ronald Reagan, *An American Life* (New York, 1990). In addition, several compilations of Reagan's speeches and writings have appeared. These include Ronald Reagan, *Speaking My Mind* (New York, 1989); Kiron R. Skinner, Annelise Anderson, and Martin Anderson, eds., *Reagan in His Own Hand* (New York, 2001); and Kiron R. Skinner, Annelise Anderson, and Martin Anderson, eds., *Reagan: A Life in Letters* (New York, 2003). Several members of Reagan's immediate family have written memoirs: Nancy Reagan with William Novak, *My Turn, the Memoirs of Nancy Reagan* (New York, 1989); Maureen Reagan, *First Father, First Daughter* (Boston, 1989); Michael Reagan with Joe Hyams, *On the Outside Looking In* ((New York, 1988); and Patti Davis with Maureen Strange Foster, *Home Front* (Crown, 1986).

Full biographies of Reagan include Edmund Morris, *Dutch: A Memoir of Ronald Reagan* (New York, 1999); Garry Wills, *Reagan's America* (New York, 1989); William E. Pemberton, *Exit with Honor: The Life and Presidency of Ronald Reagan*

(Armonk, NY: 1998); and Peter Schweizer, *Reagan's War: The Epic Story of His Forty-Year Struggle and Final Triumph Over Communism* (New York, 2002). For Reagan's childhood and pre-political years, see Anne Edwards, *Early Reagan: The Rise to Power* (New York, 1987) and Bill Boyarsky, *The Rise of Ronald Reagan* (New York, 1968). On various aspects of Reagan's years in Hollywood, see Stephen Vaughn, *Ronald Reagan in Hollywood: Movies and Politics* (Cambridge, 1994); Michael Rogin, *Ronald Reagan, the Movie: And Other Episodes of Political Demonology* (Berkeley, 1987); Dan E. Moldea, *Dark Victory: Ronald Reagan, MCA, and the Mob* (New York, 1986); and Gerald Horne, *Class Struggle in Hollywood: Moguls, Mobsters, Stars, Reds & Trade Unionists* (Austin, 2001). Outside of the seminal works of Lou Cannon, Reagan's years as governor of California have received surprisingly little attention. Matthew Dallek, *The Right Moment: Ronald Reagan's First Victory and the Decisive Turning Point in American Politics* (New York, 2000) describes the election of 1966. W.J. Rorabaugh, *Berkeley at War: The 1960s* (New York, 1989) offers a perspective of student and political protest.

Several recent books address conservatism in the 1960s and 1970s. These include Stephen F. Hayward, *The Age of Reagan: The Fall of the Old Liberal Order* (New York, 2001); Lisa McGirr, *Suburban Warriors: The Origins of the New American Right* (Princeton, 2001); Michael Schaller and George Risling, *The Republican Ascendancy: American Politics, 1968-2001* (Wheeling, IL, 2001); Jonathan M. Schoenwald, *A Time for Choosing: The Rise of Modern American Conservatism* (New York, 2001); and Kurt Schuparra, *Triumph of the Right: The Rise of the California Conservative Movement* (Armonk, NY, 1998). Michael Kazin, *The Populist Persuasion: An American History* (New York, 1995) also provides critical insights. For divergent views of the 1970s, see Peter Carroll, *It Seemed Like Nothing Happened: The Tragedy and Promise of America in the 1970s* (New York, 1982) and David Frum, *How We Got Here: The 70's, The Decade That Brought You Modern Life for Better or Worse* (New York, 2000). Peter Schrag, *Paradise Lost: California's Experience, America's Future* (Berkeley, 1999) covers California's Proposition 13 and its consequences.

The literature on Reagan's presidency is extensive. Virtually all of his top advisers and many lesser lights in the Reagan Administration wrote memoirs or reflections upon leaving government service. The most important include Martin Anderson, *Revolution: The Reagan Legacy* (New York, 1988); Michael K. Deaver with Mickey Herskowitz, *Behind the Scenes* (New York, 1987); Donald T. Regan, *For the Record: From Wall Street to Washington* (New York, 1988); David A. Stockman, *The Triumph of Politics: How the Reagan Revolution Failed* (New York, 1986); George P. Schulz, *Turmoil and Triumph: My Years As Secretary of State* (New York, 1993); and Caspar Weinberger, *Fighting for Peace: Seven Critical Years in the Pentagon* (New York, 1990). Dinesh D'Souza, *Ronald Reagan: How an Ordinary Man Became an Extraordinary Leader* (New York, 1997) and Peggy Noonan, *When Character Was King: A Story of Ronald Reagan* (New York, 2001) offer appreciative and informative retrospectives.

Key overviews of the Reagan presidency include: Haynes Johnson, *Sleepwalking Through History: America in the Reagan Years* (New York, 1991); Paul Boyer, editor, *Reagan As President* (Chicago, 1990); Theodore Draper, *A Very Thin Line: The Iran-Contra Affairs* (New York, 1991); Michael Schaller, *Reckoning with Reagan: America and Its President in the 1980s* (Oxford, 1992); and W. Brownlee and Hugh Graham Davis, eds., *The Reagan Presidency: Pragmatic Conservatism and Its Legacies* (Lawrence, KS, 2003). Two books by Kevin Phillips, *The Politics of Rich and Poor: Wealth and the American Electorate in the Reagan Aftermath* (New York, 1990) and *Wealth and Democracy: A Political History of the American Rich* (New York, 2002) examine the impact of Reagan's economic policies on wealth distribution. An assortment of Reagan gaffes and misstatements can be found in Mark Green and Gail MacColl, *Reagan's Reign of Error* (New York, 1987).

The following books were helpful in understanding the Reagan foreign affairs legacy: Raymond L. Garthoff, *The Great Transition: American-Soviet Relations and the End of the Cold War* (Washington, DC, 1994); Peter Schweizer, *Victory: The Reagan Administration's Secret Strategy That Hastened the Collapse of the Soviet Union* (New York, 1994); Dan Obendorfer, *The*

Turn: From the Cold War to A New Era, 1983–1990 (New York, 1991); Beth Fischer, *The Reagan Reversal: Foreign Policy and the End of the Cold War* (Columbia, MO, 1997); Bob Woodward, *Veil: The Secret Wars of the CIA* (New York, 1987); and Frances Fitzgerald, *Way Out There in The Blue: Reagan, Star Wars, and the End of the Cold War* (New York, 2000). See also John Prados, "Notes on the CIA's Secret War in Afghanistan," *Journal of American History* (September 2002), 466–71; and Celeste A. Wallendar, "Western Policy and the Demise of the Soviet Union," *Journal of Cold War Studies* (Fall, 2003), 137–77. Reagan Era National Security Decision Directives may be found at the Federation of American Scientists Intelligence Resource Program website: http://www.fas.org/irp/offdocs/nsdd/index.html

Index

Abbas, Abul, 201
Able Archer 83, 185–187
"About Mother", 7
Achille Lauro, 201
Advertising Club, 30
Afghanistan
    mujahedin support by U.S.,
        178–179, 192, 207, 226,
        230, 242
    and Al Qaeda, 242
    Soviet invasion, 138, 150, 196,
        207
    Soviet withdrawal, 224, 230,
        238
    Stinger sale/buy-back, 179,
        207, 242
    Taliban, 242
Agnew, Spiro, 131
AIDS, 226
Air traffic controllers strike,
    158–159
Albert, Eddie, 46
Albert, Margo, 46
Albert, Stew, 127
Aleksei II, Russian Orthodox pa-
    triarch, 231
Allyson, June, 46
Alpha Epsilon Sigma, 19
Altschuler, Sid, 24
Alzheimer's disease, 233–234
Americans for Democratic Ac-
    tion, 73
American Veterans Committee
    (AVC), 58–61, 66, 68
Anderson, John, 142
Anderson, Martin, 145
Andropov, Yuri, 182, 194

Angels Wash Their Faces, 41
Anti-Ballistic Missile (ABM)
    pact, 149, 174, 198–200,
        209, 225
Arab-Israeli War (1973), 133
Aria da Capo (Edna St. Vincent
    Millay), 20
Arms control. *See* Nuclear arms
    control
Assassination attempt, 156–157
Audience Research Institute, 45
Avalon Casino, 32

B-1 bombers, 160
B-2 Stealth bomber, 151, 160
Bacall, Lauren, 72
Baker, James A., 145, 194
Bancroft, Brass (film character),
    40–43, 69, 175
Bank failures, 165, 220–221
Banking deregulation, 166–167,
    220–222
Barnett, Ross, 97
Bedtime for Bonzo, 81
Begin, Menachim, 165
Behavior Sciences Corporation
    (BASICO), 112, 114
Bellamann, Henry, 49
Benny, Jack, 87
Berlin, Irving, 54
Berlin night club bombing, 205
Berlin Wall
    end of, 238
    Reagan speech at, 226
Bin Laden, Osama, 242
Birth of a Nation, 10
Blacklist, 73–74, 77–78

Black Power, 110, 117, 123
Boesky, Ivan, 220
Bogart, Humphrey, 61, 72
Boland Amendments, 169,
    193–194
Boll weevils, 157
Bolte, Charles, 59
Bonanza, 95
Booster Club, 20
Bootleggers' Knob, 6
Bork, Robert, 228, 249–250
Boys' Hi-Y, 9
Breen, Joseph I., 37–38, 45, 49
Brezhnev Doctrine, 184–185,
    192, 239
Broderick, Helen, 48
Brother Rat, 40, 42
Brother Rat and a Baby, 42
Brown, Jerry, 131
Brown, Pat, 106–107, 111,
    115–117, 121, 123, 129
Bryan, William Jennings, 100
Brzezinski, Zbigniew, 178–179
Buchenwald, 54–55
Budget deficits, 154–155, 158,
    165–166, 188, 243–244,
    248, 252
Burford, Anne Gorsuch, 153,
    168, 181
Burghardt, W. Franklin, 22
Burnham, James, 102–104
"Bus Burke, Lifeguard" (Rea-
    gan), 12
Bush, George H. W., 141, 149,
    153, 180, 231–232,
    235–236, 241–242,
    244–246, 248–249
Bush, George W., 251–255

Cagney, Jimmy, 31, 55
California Committee for Gold-
    water, 99
California governorship. *See*
    Reagan, Ronald, governor-
    ship
California Welfare Reform Act
    (1971), 129–130

Cannon, Lou, 114, 120, 142,
    165, 190, 215, 235
Carmichael, Stokely, 117
Carter, Jimmy, 133–135, 138,
    141–142, 149–151,
    160–161, 167–168,
    178–179, 195, 245, 248
Casablanca, 51
Casey, William, 150–152,
    162–163, 178, 186–188,
    192, 197, 203, 214, 222
Castro, Fidel, 183
Catalina Island (California),
    31–32
Cattle Queen of Montana, 87
Ceausescu, Nicolae, 238
Central America. *See also* El Sal-
    vador; Nicaragua
  Reagan policies, 161, 168–169,
    177–178, 183–184, 204–205
Chavez, Cesar, 110
Chernenko, Konstantin,
    194–195, 198
Chernobyl, 206, 224
Chiang Kai-shek, 59
Chicago, 5, 13, 25, 29, 32, 67
Chief executive officers (CEOs)
    income, 246
Christian Anti-Communist Cru-
    sade, 97
Christopher, George, 113–114
"City On a Hill" metaphor, 7,
    90, 140–141, 148, 254
Civil Rights Act (1964), 105,
    109, 134, 231
Civil Rights Movement, 105, 109
Civil Rights Restoration Act, 231
Civil Works Authority (CWA),
    27, 31
Clark, William, 125
Clean Water Act, 225
Cleaver, Ben, 7
Cleaver, Eldridge, 125
Cleaver, Margaret, 9, 13, 19, 24,
    29–30
Clinton, Bill, 243, 245, 249, 251
Code of the Secret Service, 40

Cold War. *See also* Communism; Soviet Union
  end of, 224, 235, 236–239, 237–238, 242
  Reagan impact on, 237–242
Comiskey Park, 29
Committee on Present Danger (CPD), 149, 239, 253
Communism. *See also* Soviet Union
  American, rise of, 46–47, 61–62
  end of, 235, 237–238
  Hollywood defensive organization, 77–78
  House Select Committee on Un-American Activities (HUAC), 71–73, 78–79
Conference of Studio Unions (CSU), 62–69, 73
Conscience of a Conservative, The (Goldwater), 102
Conservatives
  economic conservatives, 101, 103
  ideological inconsistencies, 104–106
  political ideals of, 101–105
  Reagan legacy, 247–248, 255–256
  religious right, 135, 135–136, 139, 153, 175, 226, 248, 250–251, 250–252
  traditional conservatives, 101
Continental Illinois Bank, 221
Contract with America, 250–251
Contras. *See* Nicaragua
Creative Society, 113
Crosby, Bing, 55
Crowe, William J., 224
Cuba, 150–151, 183–184, 205
Cummings, Robert, 49
Czechoslovakia, 238

Dales, Jack, 48, 77, 93
Dallek, Matthew, 116
Dark Victory, 41
Dart, Justin, 46, 111
Davenport (Iowa), 25–27, 30, 40

Davis, Bette, 41
Davis, Loyal, 83, 90, 123
Davis, Nancy. *See* Reagan, Nancy
Davis, Patti (daughter)
  birth of, 84
  on Reagan's as parents, 92–93
Day After, The, 185
Day the Earth Stood Still, The, 202
Dead End Kids, 41
Death Valley Days, 97
Deaver, Michael, 128, 146, 194, 217–218
Decca Records, 85
Defense spending, 151–152, 155, 159–160, 168
  Strategic Defense Initiative (SDI), 172–177
Deficit spending, 138, 155, 188, 243–244
Department of Defense corruption, 217
Deregulation, 152–153, 166–167, 180–181
  banks, 166–167, 220–222
Des Moines Dispatch, 28, 32
Desperate Journey, 51–52
Dewey, Thomas, 74
Dickinson, Angie, 97
Disciples of Christ Church, 1–2, 4, 12, 15–16, 30
  Eureka College, 12–30
Dixon (Illinois), 2, 6–13, 16, 19–22, 24–26, 39, 48
Dixon Family Theater, 9
Dixon High School, 8–16, 19, 26
Dixon Home for the Feeble-Minded, 19
Dixonian, 9
Dixon State Hosptial, 7
Dmytryk, Edward, 78
Doe, Sidney K., 178
Donovan's Brain, 86
Drake College, 30
Drake Relays, 28
D'Souza, Dinesh, 184–185, 255
Dunckel, Earl B., 90

Eastern Europe, 152, 163–164, 182, 188–189, 224–226, 232, 237–241
East Side, West Side, 83
Economic Bill of Rights, 226
Economic Recovery Tax Act, 157
Economy, Reaganomics, 154–158, 161–162, 165–166, 188, 243
Edwards, Anne, 41
Eisenhower, Dwight, 90, 235
El Rancho Hotel, 87
El Salvador, 150, 161, 168–169, 177–178
"Encroaching Control," 92
Enemy Within, The, 43
Environmental policy, 114, 141, 153, 167, 167–168, 181, 251
Environmental Protection Agency (EPA), 153
Equal Rights Amendment, 135
Eureka College, 12–30
Eurkeka Plan, 23
"Evil empire," 171–172, 175, 231, 238

Fairness doctrine, 153
Fair Store (Chicago), 5
Falwell, Jerry, 136
Family Support Act, 231
Family values, 120
Fashion Boot Shop, 6, 9–10, 16, 19
Faubus, Orville, 97
Faulkner, William, 61
Federal Communication Commission (FCC), 153
Federal Home Loan Bank Board, 220–221
First Christian Church (Dixon, Illinois), 2
First Motion Picture Unit (FMPU), 52–55
Fitzgerald, Frances, 176, 241
Flynn, Errol, 45, 48, 51, 58, 68, 76, 228
Ford, Gerald, 131–133, 141

Forest Lawn cemetery, 43
For God and Country, 53
Fort Dodge, 30
Fort Roach, 52–54
Fowler, Mark S., 153
Foy, Brian, 37–38, 41
Free Speech Movement, 108
Friar's Club, 81
Friends of Ronald Reagan, 111–112, 119
Fulton, Illinois, 3–4

Gable, Clark, 55
Galesburg, Illinois, 5
Gann, Paul, 137
Garfield, John, 72
Garn-St. Germain Act, 167, 220–221
Garthoff, Raymond L, 184, 211, 240–241, 265
Gates, Robert, 230
Gelb, Leslie, 146
Gemayel, Bashir, 165
General Mills, 28, 32
Geneva summit, 198–202, 200–202, 205, 207, 239
G. E. Theater, 87–97
"Gethsemane" (Reagan), 9
Ghorbanifer, Manucher, 197, 201, 204, 207
Ghost Mountain, 76
Ginsberg, Douglas, 228
"Gipper," 44–45
Gipp, George, 21, 29, 44–45
Girl from Jones Beach, The, 75
Girls on Probation, 40
Giuliani, Rudolph, 218
Glasnost, 224–226, 241
Goldwater, Barry, 99–110, 113, 187
Gorbachev, Mikhail
  and arms control, 195–196, 198, 200–202, 205–206, 208–209, 223, 228–230, 238–241
  perestroika/glasnost, 224–226, 241

at Reagan funeral, 254
at Statue of Liberty, 232
Gore, Al, 251–252
Graham, Daniel, 174
Grant, Cary, 38
Graybill, Ed, 11
Graybill, Ruth, 11
Gray, Ed, 221
Great Communicator, 148, 232
Great Depression, 15, 17, 22–27,
    35–36, 101, 162, 165, 227
Greenspan, Alan, 146, 180
Greider, William, 161
Grenada, 183–185, 188
Grimm, Charlie, 32
Guatemala, 178

Haig, Alexander, 149, 151, 161,
    173
Haiti, 178
Hakim, Albert, 193, 204
Hall, Fawn, 325
Harrod, Samuel, 16–18
Hasenfus, Eugene, 214
Hasty Heart, The, 75–76
Havel, Vaclev, 238
De Havilland, Olivia, 45
HAWK missles, 201, 203–204, 208
Hayakawa, S.I., 127
Hayden, Sterling, 79
Heclo, Hugh, 140, 219
Hellcats of the Navy, 92
Hell's Kitchen, 41
Hemingway, Ernest, 97
Hepburn, Katharine, 68
Hersch, Seymour, 182
Hillcrest Country Club, 47
Hinckley, John, 156
Hitchcock, Alfred, 175
Hodges, Joy, 31–32
Holden, Kenneth, 112
Hollywood, studio system,
    36–37, 57
Hollywood-Beverly Christian
    Church, 40
Hollywood Committee for the
    First Amendment, 72

Hollywood Democratic Commit-
    tee, 58
Hollywood Hotel, 39, 43
Hollywood Independent Citizens
    Committee of the Arts, Sci-
    ences, and Professions (HIC-
    CASP), 58–61, 66, 68
Hollywood Ten, 73, 78
Hope, Bob, 48, 94
Hostage taking, 138, 196,
    200–201, 203, 207–208
House Select Committee on
    Un-American Activities
    (HUAC), 71–73, 78–79
Housing and Urban Development
    corruption, 181, 217, 236
Humphrey, Hubert, 74
Husing, Ted, 25
Hussein, Saddam, 179–180, 241

Illinois Emergency Relief Com-
    mission (IERC), 24, 27
Inflation
  Carter administration, 133
  Reagan administration, 156,
    166, 188
Intercontinental Ballistic Missiles
    (ICBM), 151
Interest rates, 154, 161, 166–167,
    188, 220, 243
Intermediate-range Nuclear Force
    (INF) Treaty, 195, 198,
    205–206, 209, 225,
    228–229, 231, 242
Intermediate-range nuclear force
    (INF) weapons, 160, 172,
    186, 195
International Alliance of Theatri-
    cal Stage Employees and
    Motion Picture Operators
    (IATSE) labor dispute
    (1945–1946), 62–66
International Squadron, 48, 51
Iowa, 198
Iowa Fair Grounds, 29
Iran, American hostages, 138,
    179

Iran-contra weapons deal, 192–194, 197–198, 203–204, 213–216, 222–223, 225, 236–237
Iran-Iraq War, 179–180, 215, 241
Iraq
 and Hussein, 179–180, 215, 241
 Iran-Iraq War, 179–180, 215, 241

Jacobsen, David, 213
Jarvis, Howard, 137
J. C. Pitney's General Store, 4–6
Jessel, George, 81
Jim Crow, 104–105
John Birch Society, 97, 113
John Loves Mary, 75
Johnny Belinda, 70, 75
John Paul II, Pope, 163
Johnson, Haynes, 216, 265
Johnson, Lyndon B., 99, 101, 106, 109
Judicial appointments, 249–250
Judicial Selection Committee (JSC), 154
Juke Girl, 51
Junior Secret Service Club, 41
Junk bonds, 219–220
J. W. Broadhead's Dry Goods, 3–4

Keating, Charles, 221
Keller, Bill, 148
Kennedy, Anthony M., 250
Kennedy, Edward, 255
Kennedy, John B., 44
Kennedy, John F., 95, 107
Kerr, Clark, 124
Keynesian economics, 138, 188
"Killed in Action: A Short Story" (Reagan), 21
Killers, The, 97
Kindleberger, Charles, 245
Kings Row, 49–50, 52
Kirkpatrick, Jeane, 177–179
Kissinger, Henry, 132
Knowland, William, 111

Knute Rockne–All American, 21, 29, 44–45, 47
Korean Air Line (KAL), 182
Kraft Suspense Theater, 97
Krauthammer, Charles, 191
Ku Klux Klan, 3, 10, 105
Kuwait, 241

Labor union membership decline, 247
Lakeside Country Club, 47
Land and Live in the Desert, 53
Last Frontier, 87
Last Outpost, The, 82
Lavelle, Rita, 181
Lawson, John Howard, 60, 73
Leach, Archie, 38
League of Decency, 37
Lebanon, 164–165, 182–187, 196–198, 203, 208, 223
Lest We Forget, 54
Liberals, political ideals of, 101–102
Liberia, 178
Libya, 159, 205
"Life" (Reagan), 9
Lincoln Federal Savings and Loan, 221
Lithuania, 238
Loeb, James, 73
"Long Way 'Round," 88
"Losing Our Freedom on the Installment Plan," 92
Lost Weekend, The, 57
Love Is On the Air, 38
Lowell Park (Dixon), 11–13, 20, 23–25
Luckett, Edie, 83
Lupino, Ida, 66

MacArthur, Peter, 26–28
MacFarlane, Robert, 176, 193–210, 213, 222–223, 226
Mayer, Louis B., 73
McIntyre, Francis Cardinal, 123
McKinzie, Ralph, 16, 22
McNamee, Graham, 25

"Meditations of a Lifeguard"
(Reagan), 12
Medusa Cement Plant, 12
Meese, Edwin, 125, 145, 153,
194, 215–216, 218
Misery index, 141, 243
Mondale, Walter, 189–190
Monmouth (Illinois), 5
Montgomery, Robert, 48, 61, 66,
68, 72, 93
Moral Majority, 136
"Moral Victory: A Football
Story" (Reagan), 21
Moretti, Bob, 129
Morris, Edmund, 21–22, 42,
119–120, 234
Motion Picture Industrial Council
(MPIC), Reagan as chairman,
77–78
Motion Picture Producers and
Distributors of America
(MPPDA), 37
Mountain States Legal Founda-
tion, 153
Mount St. Helens, 141–142
Mujahedin, support by U.S.,
178–179, 192, 207, 226,
230, 242
Mulroney, Brian, 254
Murder in the Air, 43, 69, 175
Murphy, George, 54, 61, 72,
128, 203
Music Corporation of America
(MCA), 50, 84–85, 87,
93–96, 111.
See also Screen Actors Guild
(SAG)
Mutually Assured Destruction
(MAD), 139, 173–174, 177
MX missiles, 160, 168, 240

Nader, Ralph, 252
National Labor Relations Board
(NLRB), 35, 63
National Review, 105
National Security Defense
Directive (NSDD)-32, 163

National Security Defense
Directive (NSDD)-66, 171
National Security Defense
Directive (NSDD)-75, 171
National Security Defense
Directive (NSDD)-114, 180
National Security Defense
Directive (NSDD)-166, 192
Neal, Patricia, 75
Negro National Assembly, 114
New Deal, 15, 27, 30–31, 35–36,
47, 90, 94, 101, 134, 220,
256
Newman, Paul, 175
Next Voice You Hear, The, 83
Nicaragua, 150–151, 161,
168–169, 177–178, 187,
230
Iran-contra, 192–194, 197–198,
204–205, 213–216, 222–223,
225, 236–237
Night Unto Night, 61, 66, 67, 70
Nitze, Paul, 209
Nixon, Richard, 95, 111, 126,
130–134, 149
Nofzinger, Lyn, 106, 120, 125,
217, 228
Noonan, Peggy, 145, 265
Noriega, Manuel, 178, 241
North American Accord, 140
North, Oliver, 193, 203–205,
207–208, 213–216,
222–223, 226–227, 236
"November 11, 1918" (Reagan),
21
Nuclear arms control
ABM pact, 149, 174
Geneva summit, 198–202,
205, 207, 239
INF Treaty, 195, 198,
205–206, 209, 225,
228–229, 231, 242
Reykjavik summit, 208–211,
223, 239
SALT I and II, 149, 160, 207
START, 160, 164, 186, 238,
242

Nuclear arms control, continued
   Washington summit, 228–229
   zero-zero option, 160, 186,
      205, 209, 211
Nuclear Freeze Movement, 168,
   177

O'Brien, David M., 250
O'Brien, Pat, 44
O'Connor, Sandra Day, 250, 254
Olivier, Laurence, 51
O'Neill, Tip, 158
Opera House (Tampico), 5
Operation Desert Storm, 241
Operation Staunch, 196–198

Palestine Liberation Organization
   (PLO), 164–165, 201
Palmer Chiropractic College, 27
Palmer, Colonel Bartlett Joshua
   (B.J.), 27–28
Panama, 178, 241
Panama Canal, 132, 134, 205
Paramount Studios, 57, 82, 93
Parker, William, 109
Parkinson, Gaylord, 113
Parsons, Louella, 39, 42–43, 46,
   48, 75
Payne, John, 92
Pearl Harbor attack, 51
Pegasus, The, 19
Penn Square Bank, 165–166
Pentagon attack (2001), 242
Perestroika/glasnost, 224–226, 241
Perle, Richard, 160, 200
Perot, Ross, 249, 251
Pershing Missiles, 198
Persian Gulf War, 241
Philippines, 178
Phillips, Kevin, 246
Pierce, Leslie, 17
Plog, Stanley, 112
Poindexter, John, 210, 213–216,
   222, 226, 236
Poland, Solidarity, 162–163, 169,
   226, 238
Polaris submarines, 151

Powell, Dick, 39, 46
Production Code (1930), 37
Production Code Administration
   (PCA), 37–38, 45, 49
Professional Air Traffic Controllers
   Organization (PATCO),
   158–159
Prohibition, 3, 4, 6, 10, 11
Project for A New American
   Century (PNAC), 253
Proposition One, 130, 137
Proposition 13, 137
Proposition 14, 107–108

Al-Qaddafi, Muammar, 159, 205
Al Qaeda, 242

Rattan, Jim, 22
Reagan Doctrine, 191–193, 194,
   241
Reagan, Jack (father)
   alcoholism of, 3, 5–10, 47
   death of, 47
   as Democrat, 24, 47
   drama-related activities of, 5
   extramarital affair of, 22
   family background, 3–4
   Hollywood as residence, 40, 47
   illness of, 31
   political/civic activities, 6, 24
   work of, 5–8, 10, 19, 22–23,
      31, 40
Reagan, Maureen (daughter), 52,
   71, 75
   birth of, 46
   and governorship campaign,
      113
Reagan, Michael (son)
   adoption of, 55
   lives with Reagan's, 92
   on Reagan/Wyman as parents,
      71
Reagan, Nancy (wife)
   and astrological advisors, 119,
      147
   breast cancer, 227
   deep connection to Reagan, 92

films of, 83
meeting/marriage to Reagan,
    83–84
as parent, 92
Patti, birth of, 84
on Reagan personality, 119
Reagan presidency, role in, 147
Ron, Jr., birth of, 92
TV roles, 88
Reagan, Neil (brother)
    birth of, 4
    college years, 20
    Hollywood as residence, 46
    jobs of, 12, 30, 40, 97
    nickname of (Moon), 8
    politics of, 46–47
    temperament of, 2, 7
Reagan, Nelle (mother)
    drama-related activities of, 3,
        5, 7
    family background of, 3
    Hollywood as residence, 40,
        47
    and Reagan children, 71
    religious involvement, 6–7, 40
Reagan, Patti. See Davis, Patti
    (daughter)
Reagan Presidential Library,
    254–255
Reagan Revolution, 153, 165,
    232, 247, 250–252
Reagan, Ron, Jr., birth of, 92
Reagan, Ronald
    and actors' union. See Screen
        Actors Guild (SAG)
    agency representation, 32,
        50–51, 58
    Alzheimer's disease, 233–234
    audience/attention, need for,
        12, 18, 20, 30
    birth of, 4
    childhood/teenage years, 1–11
    children of, 46, 55, 84, 92
    college years, 15–33
    death/funeral of, 254
    defense policy/spending,
        172–177

Democratic Congress actions,
    167–168
drama activities as youth, 7, 9,
    19–21
economic policy (Reaganomics),
    154–158, 165–166
economy during, 154–155
environmental policy, 167
family background, 1–6
film career, end of, 81–83, 92
film critics on, 39–41, 48, 50,
    76
film popularity of, 44–45
films (1930s), 38–55
films (1940s), 44–45, 48–79
films (1950s), 81–82, 86, 92
films, military training films,
    53–55
flying, fear of, 90
and *G.E. Theater*, 87–90,
    93–94, 96
as "Gipper", 44–45
and Great Depression, 15,
    22–24, 27, 35
health issues, 222, 233
horse ranch, 86, 111
Las Vegas work, 87
as lifeguard, 11–13, 23–24
marriages/family. See Reagan,
    Nancy; Wyman, Jane
military service, 32–33, 51–55
and Motion Picture Industrial
    Council (MPIC), 77–78
nearsightedness, 8, 29, 32, 52
nickname of (Dutch), 8, 13, 26
as parent, 70–71, 92–93, 120
political/civic activities, 10
political ideals/career. See Rea-
    gan, Ronald, presidency;
    Reagan, Ronald, governor-
    ship; Reagan, Ronald, politi-
    cal development; Reagan,
    Ronald, presidency
on racial discrimination,
    21–22, 47, 106–107
religious involvement of, 2–3,
    7, 40, 120

Reagan, Ronald, continued
  rhetorical style, 74, 89–92,
    119–121, 146, 148
  screen test/first contract, 32–33
  self-centeredness, 21
  Social Security plan, 157–158
  sports activities of, 8–9,
    11–13, 19–21
  as sportscaster, 24–33
  as sports columnist, 21, 32
  Strategic Defense Initiative
    (SDI), 172–177
  tax reform, 166
  temperament/personality traits,
    13–14, 21, 29, 46, 117,
    119–120, 147
  TV roles, 88, 97
  and World War II, 43
  writings of (youth), 9, 21
Reagan, Ronald, governorship
  abortion issue, 122–123
  appointments, 125–126
  and Black Panthers, 124–125
  budget deficit/tax increase,
    121–122, 126
  campaign handlers, activities
    of, 113–115
  campaign rhetoric, 112, 114,
    116
  campus revolts, 126–127
  conservative backers of,
    110–113
  first term, 119–129
  governorship campaign,
    112–115
  governorship victory, 117
  re-election (1970), 127–128
  second term, 128–131
  and state university system,
    122, 124
  TV campaign, 114
  welfare reform, 128–130
  workfare program, 130, 249
Reagan, Ronald, political devel-
    opment
  American Veterans Committee
    (AVC), 58–61, 66, 68

  and Communist Party, 46–47,
    59, 63, 65, 77–78
  conservatism, shift to, 90–91,
    97–98
  as Democrat, 10, 26, 30–31,
    47, 58, 68, 74, 90, 95
  FBI file on Reagan, 59
  as FBI Red-baiter, 69, 73
  Goldwater campaign, 99–101
  Hollywood Independent Citi-
    zens Committee of the Arts,
    Sciences, and Professions
    (HICCASP), 58–60
  and House Select Committee
    on Un-American Activities
    (HUAC), 71–73, 77–78
  and IATSE-CSU strike (1946),
    62–66
  political development, 18,
    21–22, 46–47
  political discussion, enjoyment
    of, 54
  taxation, Reagan attacks on
    system, 86
Reagan, Ronald, presidency
  Achille Lauro attack, 201
  Afghanistan *mujahedin*, sup-
    port of, 178–179, 192, 207,
    226, 230, 242
  on AIDS, 226
  air traffic controllers' strike,
    158–159
  anti-terrorism law, 208
  arms control. *See* Nuclear arms
    control
  assassination attempt, 156–157
  banking deregulation,
    166–167, 220–222
  Berlin Wall speech, 226
  budget deficits, 154–155, 158,
    165–166, 188, 243–244,
    248, 252
  Central America policies, 161,
    168–169, 177–178,
    187–188, 204–205
  and Cold War, end of,
    237–238

defense policy/spending,
151–152, 155, 159–160,
168, 171–172, 183–184
Democratic Congress actions,
231
deregulation, 152–153,
166–167, 180–181
economic policy
(Reaganomics), 161–162,
188
economy during, 161–162,
165, 188, 227–228, 243–247
environmental policy, 153, 181
federal government downsiz-
ing, 152–153, 217, 219
federal judge appointments,
153–154
as Great Communicator, 148,
232
Grenada intervention,
183–185, 188
as Hollywood production,
145–146
hostage taking, 196
Iran-contra weapons deal,
192–194, 197–198, 203–204,
207–208, 213–216, 226–227,
236–237
Iran-Iraq War, 179–180
Korean Air Line (KAL) downing, 182
leadership style, 147, 159
Lebanon violence, 164–165,
182–183, 187
legacy of, 235–256
Libya/Gulf of Sidra attacks, 159
Moscow visit, 231
Nancy Reagan, role in, 147
paradox of, 145–148,
235–236
Poland Solidarity, 162–163
political/ideological achieve-
ment of, 247–249
presidential campaign
(1976–1980), 131–143
presidential campaign (1984),
188–190

presidential victory (1980),
142–143
presidential victory (1984), 190
Reagan Doctrine, 191–192, 241
Reagan Revolution, 165–166,
232, 250–252
scandals/corruption, 217–221,
226, 236–237
Social Security plan, 180
Soviet Union, early policy toward, 149–150, 160,
163–164, 171–172,
178–179, 182, 184–187. See
also Gorbachev, Mikhail
Strategic Defense Initiative
(SDI), 198–200, 209–210,
225, 238–239
Supreme Court justice appoint-
ments, 250
tax reform, 157–158, 162,
211–212, 244
as Teflon President, 236–238
and welfare/social programs,
157–158, 166
Reagan, William (uncle), 4
Rear Gunner, 53, 55
*Recognition of the Japanese Zero
Fighter*, 53
Red Wing Shoe Company, 22–23
Regan, Donald, 146, 194, 197,
211, 215
Rehnqiust, William, 250
Religious right, 135–136, 139,
153, 175, 226, 248, 250–252
"Return of Jerry Dale, Senior,
The" (Reagan), 21
Revere, Anne, 71, 78–79
Revue Productions, 84–85, 87, 97
Reykjavik summit, 208–211,
223, 239
Roberts, Bill, 112–113
Robinson, Edward G., 68
Rockefeller, Nelson, 132
"Rock Redux: A Tale of the Su-
pernatural" (Reagan), 21
Roe v. Wade, 135
Romania, 238

Ronald Reagan Legacy Project, 255

Roosevelt, Franklin D., 15, 26, 30, 36, 47, 100, 118, 177, 236, 248

Roosevelt, James, 58, 60

Rousselot, John, 97

Rubel, A. Y., 111

Rumford Fair Housing Act (1963), 106–107, 126

Rumsfeld, Donald, 180

"Sad Dollar and the Glad Dollar, The", 7

Sakharov, Andrei, 224–225

Salvatori, Henry, 99, 111

Sandinistas, 161, 169, 213, 230

San Francisco State College, 127

Santa Fe Trail, 45, 77

Saudi Arabia, 179, 193

Savas, Emanuel S., 181

Scalia, Antonin, 250

Schaller, Michael, 246, 248

Schlesinger, Arthur, Jr., 95

"School Spirit" (Reagan), 9

Schrag, Peter, 136–137

Schrieber, Taft, 111

Schultz, George, 173, 177, 186, 193, 197, 200, 203, 209, 214, 225

Schwarz, Frederick, 97

Schweizer, Peter, 237

Screen Actors Guild (SAG)
  anti-trust violations of, 95–96
  as conservative organization, 61
  first contract of (1937), 35–36
  and House Select Committee on Un-American Activities (HUAC), 71–73, 78–79
  and IATSE-CSU strike (1946), 62–66
  MCA residuals dispute, 84–85, 94, 96
  and MCA TV deal, 84–85, 87, 94
  Reagan as president, 68–69, 81, 84–85, 94
  Reagan resigns presidency, 86, 94
  Reagan's first position in, 47–48, 61

Secord, Richard, 193, 204, 226

Secret Service of the Air, 40

Securities and Exchange Commission, 153, 219

September 11 terrorist attacks, 242, 253

Sergeant Murphy, 38–39

Shad, John, 153

Shah of Iran, 138

Sheridan, Ann, 48, 50

Smashing the Money Ring, 41

Smith, Al, 10–11

Smith, Robert, 127

Social program cuts. *See* Welfare reform

Social Security, 122, 132, 154–155, 157–158, 180, 244, 248, 256

Solidarity, 162–163, 169, 226, 238

Sondergaard, Gale, 78–79

Sorrell, Herb, 62–64, 66, 69

South Africa, 178, 193

Soviet Union
  Afghanistan invasion, 138, 150, 196, 207
  Afghanistan withdrawal, 224, 230, 238
  and arms control. *See* Nuclear arms control
  arms race, 139–140
  communism, end of, 235, 237–238
  as evil empire, 171–172, 175, 231, 238
  Gorbachev era. *See* Gorbachev, Mikhail
  perestroika/glasnost, 224–226, 241
  U.S. policy (pre-Gorbachev), 149–150, 160, 163–164, 171–172, 182, 184–187

Speakes, Larry, 210

Spencer, Stu, 112–113

"Stadium, The" (Reagan), 21
Stagflation, 133
Stallion Road, 61
Stapp, Henry, 108
Star Wars. *See* Strategic Defense Initiative (SDI)
Stealth aircraft, 151, 160
Stein, Jules, 111
Stinger anti-aircraft missiles, 179, 207, 242
Stockman, David, 154–155, 157–158, 160, 162
Stock market, October 19 drop, 227
Storm Warning, 76
Strategic Arms Limitation Treaties (SALT I and II), 149, 160, 207
Strategic Arms Reduction talks (START), 160, 164, 186, 238, 242
Strategic Defense Initiative (SDI), 171–177, 191, 195, 198–202, 209–210, 224–225, 229, 239–241
Submarine D-1, 39
Summers, Lawrence, 246
Superfund, 168, 181
Supply-side economics, 138, 141, 155, 162, 166, 243–244, 246

Taft-Hartley Act, 71, 74
Talbot, Strobe, 210
Taliban, 242
Tampico, Illinois, 4–6, 13
Task Force on Regulatory Relief, 180
Tau Kappa Epsilon (Teke), 17, 19–20, 23
Taxation
  Reagan attacks on system, 86
  tax reform, 157–158, 162, 166, 211–212, 244, 246
Tax Equity and Fiscal Responsibility Act, 166
Tax Reform Act (1986), 211–212
Tax revolt, 136–138

Teke (Tau Kappa Epsilon), 17, 19–20, 23
Teller, Edward, 174–175, 199
Temple, Shirley, 70
Tennessee's Partner, 86, 92
Tennessee Valley Authority (TVA), 94
Terrorism
  Achille Lauro, 201
  anti-terrorism law, 208
  Berlin night club bombing, 205
  hostage taking, 138, 196, 200–201, 203, 207–208
Thatcher, Margaret, 183, 254
That Hagen Girl, 70, 75, 76
That Printer of Udell's: A Story of the Midwest (Bell), 1–2, 256
Thayer, Pat, 217
Third World Liberation Front, 127
This Is the Army, 54–55
"This Younger Generation" (Reagan), 9
Thomas, Clarence, 217
"Time for Choosing, A", 100
Todd, Richard, 76
Torn Curtain, 175–176
Tower, John, 222–223
TOW missiles, 197, 204, 208
Trickle-down economics, 162, 246
Trident submarines, 151, 160
Truman, Harry, 68, 74
Trumbo, Dalton, 60, 73
Tuttle, Holmes, 99, 111
Twentieth Century Fox, 111

Uncle Sam Awakens, 43
Unemployment rate, 133, 141–142, 161, 165, 243, 245
United America Day, 59
United Nations, 177, 183, 189, 233
Universal Studios, 76, 81–85
University of California Berkeley student riots, 108–109, 115–117, 123–127
Unruh, Jesse, 122

Vaughn, Stephen, 37
Vessey, John W., 173
Vietnam syndrome, 138, 150,
    161, 179
Vietnam War, 109, 115, 117,
    132–133, 184, 235
Voice of the Turtle, 70
Volcker, Paul, 161, 166, 188
Voting Rights Act (1965), 109,
    230

Wagon Train, 97
Waldorf Declaration (1947),
    73–74
Walesa, Lech, 254
Wallace, George, 106
Wallace, Henry, 74
Wallis, Hal, 37, 44, 49
Walsh, Lawrence, 216, 227, 237
Walt Disney studios, 62, 119
Ward, George, 32
Warner Brothers, 32, 36–45,
    48–61, 64–70, 75–77, 81–83
Warner, Harry, 36–37
Warner, Jack, 36, 51–52, 70,
    75–76
Wasserman, Lew, 50–51, 55,
    75–76, 84–85, 93, 96
Watergate, 131, 133, 223
Watt, James, 153, 167, 181
Watts riots, 109–110, 115, 117
Wayne, John, 45, 58
Weapons deals. *See* Iran-contra
    weapons deal
Wedtech Corporation, 218
Wee Kirk o' the Heather church,
    43
Weinberger, Caspar, 125, 150,
    155, 159, 168, 173, 186,
    197–198, 224–225, 229, 236
Weir, Benjamin, 201
Welfare reform
    Clinton era, 249
    during governorship, 128–130
    during presidency, 158, 166
"What's At Stake", 92
WHO radio station, 27, 31–33

Wilder, Billy, 57
Will, George, 119
William Meiklejohn Agency, 32,
    50, 97
Wills, Garry, 29, 43, 55, 138
Wilson, Bert, 16
Wilson, Nelle. *See* Reagan, Nelle
    (mother)
Wings for This Man, 53
Winning Team, The, 82
Winthrop, John, 254
Wirthlin, Richard, 148
WOC (World of Chiropractic
    radio station), 27
Woodward, Bob, 152
Workfare, 130, 231, 249
Works Progress Administration
    (WPA), 31
World Court, 149
World Trade Center attack (2001),
    242, 253
World War II, Reagan military
    service, 32–33, 51–55
Wright, Harold Bell, 1–2, 256
Wrigley Field, 29
Wyman, Jane
    agency representation, 50–51
    divorces Reagan, 75
    family life with Reagan, 46,
        52, 55, 70–71
    films of, 42, 57–58, 70–71, 76
    Maureen, birth of, 46
    meeting/marriage to Reagan,
        42–43
    Michael, adoption of, 55
    as mother, 70–71
    and SAG, 48
    third child, loss of, 70
    wartime activities, 55

Yearling, The, 57–58, 70
Yorty, Sam, 115
You and I, 9

Zanuck, Richard, 111
Zero-zero option, 160, 186, 205,
    209, 211